Penguin Books

THE PENGUIN GUIDE TO A

CW00362562

The Penguin Guide to
AMSTERDAM

Edited by VINCENT WESTZAAN

Translated from the Dutch by PAUL VINCENT

Penguin Books

PENGUIN BOOKS

Published by the Penguin Group
27 Wrights Lane, London W8 5TZ, England
Viking Penguin Inc., 40 West 23rd Street, New York, New York 10010, USA
Penguin Books Australia Ltd, Ringwood, Victoria, Australia
Penguin Books Canada Ltd, 2801 John Street, Markham, Ontario, Canada L3R 1B4
Penguin Books (NZ) Ltd, 182–190 Wairau Road, Auckland 10, New Zealand

Penguin Books Ltd, Registered Offices: Harmondsworth, Middlesex, England

First published 1990
10 9 8 7 6 5 4 3 2 1

The Penguin Guide to Amsterdam was conceived, edited
and produced by B I S Book Industry Services,
Nieuwe Spiegelstraat 36, 1017 D G Amsterdam

Filmset in Monotype Bembo by
R.A.D. & S.A.D., Amsterdam

Made and printed in Great Britain by
Richard Clay (The Chaucer Press) Ltd, Bungay, Suffolk

Contents

PREFACE

The *Penguin Guide to Amsterdam* is a special kind of guidebook for a special kind of city, which continues to enjoy a huge influx of foreign visitors each year. I note with satisfaction that Amsterdam is not only a favourite destination for tourists; its importance as a business centre is also steadily growing.

One of the things that draws so many people to Amsterdam is the physical beauty of the city. Much of heritage has been preserved, and there are few places whose architecture is so evocative of the atmosphere of the Golden Age; few cities have a history recorded so graphically or in such fascinating detail; by renowned Dutch painters, but also by memorial stones on house fronts and by street names.

Amsterdam street life has for centuries given visitors an impression of great diversity and still does, particularly because of the many kinds of people who pursue very different lifestyles in their city, imparting a special flavour to the districts where they live, and so adding to Amsterdam's attractions.

This Guide contains more than just factual information about the city. It tells one about the people who live there, about life in Amsterdam. Various journalists and writers give a personal view of the neighbourhood where they live, of cafés, architecture, shopping, museums, in short the things that make the city so well worth a visit. In addition the necessary practical information is provided.

In my opinion the authors have succeeded admirably in their aim of giving a description of the town which is not only accurate and informative, but entertaining, and you could not wish for a better guide.

I wish you a pleasant stay in Amsterdam, and hope that you will share my enthusiasm for the city.

E. van Thijn, mayor of Amsterdam

Introduction: Welcome to Amsterdam

Amsterdam greets a million and a half foreign visitors a year, making it one of the most popular tourist centres in Europe. It is a relatively small capital city, with less than 800,000 inhabitants, which may be its greatest asset: it is manageable in size, peaceful, and at the same time has an immense amount to offer. Amsterdam has the easy-going look of a provincial town but the attractions of a metropolis: the largest historical city centre in Europe, more than forty museums, an enormous variety of music, ballet, dance, films and theatre, restaurants featuring the cuisine of some forty different countries, ranging from dirt cheap to decidedly pricey, and a lively but fairly mild assortment of round-the-clock and affordable entertainment.

In proportion to its total area Amsterdam has a largish centre, which is nevertheless easy to get around on foot. It contains most of the main attractions. The districts outside the centre are almost always referred to by the appropriate point of the compass. In 1977 the city council gave the outlying districts numbered and lettered codes, but virtually no one can remember them, so that people still talk about Amsterdam-North, across the river IJ and without much to offer the tourist; Amsterdam-South, which has a new, fairly anonymous section and an older one containing both poorer working-class areas and the exclusive Concertgebouw quarter; Amsterdam-East, the section of the city on the east bank of the Amstel bounded by the Sarphatistraat; and Amsterdam-West, also covering a large area, from the former squatters' bastion of the 'statesmen's quarter' to the western edge of the Vondelpark.

The city centre is roughly contained by the Stadhouderskade and its northern continuation the Nassaukade, and the rivers Amstel and IJ. Within this crescent-shaped area is the famous ring of canals, the four principal ones being the Singel, the Herengracht, the Keizersgracht and the Prinsengracht, which, as one can see from a map, run parallel to each other. They are linked by narrow streets, in almost all of which there are congenial cafés, restaurants and shops. What makes the city centre even more attractive is that it is actually lived in, which means that there is a lively atmosphere in the evenings as well as during the day.

There are three areas whose names you will encounter frequently: the so-called 'Pijp', around the Albert Cuyp market, the Jordaan, situated west of the canal ring, and the red-light district or 'Wallen', with the

Oudezijds Voorburgwal and Oudezijds Achterburgwal as its principal thoroughfares.

TRANSPORT

Almost all the tourist sights are either in the centre or on the edge of it, so that everything can be reached on foot. To give some idea of the distances involved: from the Utrechtsestraat to the Brouwersgracht along the Keizersgracht – not the shortest route between the two – is about three-quarters of an hour's walk, while the walk from the Nieuwmarkt to the Leidseplein via the Munt Square takes about half an hour.

Amsterdam has good public transport – on which you will find full information on p. 265 – but this will not always provide a means of getting about the city centre; the canals and small side-streets are (fortunately) unsuitable for trams or buses. This means that the best alternative to walking is cycling, which is by far the quickest way of getting about Amsterdam. It might need a little practice, and you will have to get used to traffic conventions: red lights, for example, appear to have only a warning function nowadays. Watch out for bike-riding natives: they are a law unto themselves, and can suddenly loom up silently out of nowhere.

A car will be nothing but trouble to you in Amsterdam. A seventeenth-century town centre is of course by definition unsuitable for vehicles and there is no question of an unimpeded flow of traffic along the narrow quays or in the side streets. There are lots of one-way systems and pedestrian precincts, and parking is a terrible business. Besides which foreign cars are a favourite target for thieves.

WHEN TO VISIT THE CITY

The Dutch are great complainers, and their favourite subject is the weather – not without some justification, let it be said, as the climate of the Low Countries is damp and unreliable. Generally speaking, late spring, preferably May or early June, is an excellent time to visit the city. The weather is usually a bit more settled by then, and the hordes of tourists have not yet taken over. Earlier in the year the city is very hectic only during holidays such as Easter and Whitsun.

The busy season continues into the middle of August. At the end of July, when the inhabitants of the city go away on holiday, it sometimes feels as if there are nothing but foreigners in Amsterdam. In places off the main tourist track – there are plenty of them, and they are often very worth while – it is wonderfully quiet at that time. By the end of August the high season is over. During September the weather is still often fine, making this another excellent time to pay a visit to the city.

Autumn is characterized by a great amount of rain and a biting wind. In winter, in February particularly, it can get very cold. But when it is dry and the sky is blue, the canals are frozen over and full of skaters, and if there happens to be snow as well, the city has a fairy-tale look. You have to be very lucky to see this kind of idyllic picture. There are tourists all year round, but except during high season from June to the end of August, the city is never overrun with them.

USING THE GUIDE

This guide is very simply organized. No symbols have been used, but at the end of the book you will find an extensive index. The only section about which something needs to be said is Chapter 13, in which we divided the centre up into a number of more or less self-contained units. In addition, two interesting districts just outside the centre were included. Next we asked a number of writers to provide a personal sketch of the area they live in. We have given each description a district number, which has nothing to do with the divisions used, for example, by the city council, and the same numbers are used in the other chapters. So that if, say, a restaurant is marked as being in District 7, that means that it is in the Jordaan. Each district description in Chapter 13 has a corresponding map showing the location of the principal restaurants, cafés, museums, etc.

THE DARK SIDE OF AMSTERDAM

Though there are many nice things one can say about the city, there is of course another side to it. Amsterdam has a bad reputation in some quarters. Some sections of the media and some politicians, at home and abroad, seem determined to play up the less attractive aspects of the city and to depict it as a muggers and junkies paradise, a cesspit of vice, where the police stand nonchalantly by and do nothing. This image is to a large extent the result of the tolerant attitude taken by the authorities towards drugs.

Drugs policy

In contrast to that of most other countries, Dutch legislation draws a sharp distinction between soft and hard drugs. Possession of up to 30 grams of hash or marijuana is treated not as a crime but as a misdemeanour, which means in practice that in most cases offenders are not prosecuted. Coffee shops selling soft drugs do not fall foul of the law provided they obey a number of conditions: they must not advertise their products in any way whatsoever, not create a public nuisance, not sell to anyone under the age of eighteen and not allow any use or sale of hard drugs on their premises. Any infringement of the last rule leads to the immediate closing-down of the establishment. Measures like these have resulted in the virtual decriminalization of soft drugs, and the circuit where they are used and traded is quite distinct from that of hard drugs.

The use and possession of hard drugs is still a criminal offence under Dutch law, but in fact the Amsterdam police have largely given up the fight against hard drugs: relief organizations and the judicial authorities have come to the conclusion that it is impossible to root out the evil entirely and have limited themselves to containing the problem as far as they can.

One method of containment used is the prescription of methadone, which is not made conditional on coming off drugs. Methadone, a substance which suppresses withdrawal symptoms in heroin addicts, is available from the so-called 'methadone bus' – a city bus with its windows screened off, which follows a fixed daily route – and from district centres. Only Dutch citizens are eligible. Originally it was hoped that the prescription of methadone would lead addicts to give up heroin, but the hope proved in vain. Nowadays it serves as a kind of safety net, an insurance against hard times. If a junkie manages to score, then the methadone is an extra and often winds up on the black market. If he does not, then at least he is not reduced to boiling up dirty cotton-wool swabs, injecting the leftovers from used syringes or other highly dangerous and demeaning alternatives.

Another method of keeping the heroin problem within bounds is to limit its sale as far as possible to a single district. For a number of historical reasons that dubious honour has fallen to the red-light district. Anyone found within its limits with a gram of hard drugs on them is not usually arrested. Local dealers who do not create a public nuisance are low on the wanted list. The centre of the trade is the Zeedijk, on the edge of the red-light district, which has become the most infamous street in the country. Junkies hustle for their drug money and until recently the street was a succession of boarded-up properties and seedy cafés where the principal source of income was hard drugs. The Amsterdam police have been trying for years, somewhat inconsistently, to clean up the street by means of a series of ordinances. The most recent tack being taken is to make the street attractive to investors in the belief that a clean, respectable street will automatically keep out the junkies. This aim has been only partially successful, and the dislodged dealers and their customers have spread over the whole of the red-light district.

From turning a blind eye to the possession of a small quantity of heroin to legalization of the substance is still quite a big step, but more and more relief agencies and policy-makers are beginning to think along those lines. About three years ago Amsterdam planned to experiment with making heroin freely available, but the initiative was blocked by the veto of the Dutch government. In 1988 the Scientific Council for Government Policy (WRR) published a report whose conclusion was that the hard drug problem is ineradicable and that a tough approach only plays into the hands of the organized crime associated with it. The report recommended that henceforward dealing in and using hard drugs should be decriminalized.

Dutch drugs policy and the discussion on legalization are still a source of great irritation abroad. Neighbouring Germany in particular exercises considerable political pressure on the Dutch government, and even saw fit to lure one soft drugs dealer, who in the Netherlands was allowed to carry on his business unmolested, to the Federal Republic, where he was given a prison sentence he would never have received in Holland. If foreign governments are afraid that drugs will spread all over Europe from the Netherlands, the Dutch authorities are trying to limit the influx of foreigners in search of drugs. Foreign addicts should be prepared for tougher treatment from the police, and kinds of help which until recently were available to everybody are now no longer available to addicts from abroad.

The critics of Holland's softly-softly approach have not been able to prove their point with statistics: comparable figures relating to drug use in the various European countries are not available. After a good deal of pressure a report will appear in 1990 under the auspices of the Pompidou group in which drug use in a number of large European countries will be compared, using standard criteria.

In the Netherlands, statistics on the number of hard drug users have only recently been made public, although actual figures are still used with caution. Among researchers and institutions one hears the repeated view that the number of addicts in Holland decreases the more exacting one's research methods become; preliminary estimates tend generally to be on the high side. According to the Netherlands Institute for Alcohol and Drug Abuse (NIAD) Amsterdam has 6,500 addicts, of which a third, on evidence supplied by the Amsterdam public health authorities, are foreigners. NIAD puts the total number of addicts in the Netherlands at 20,000. By way of comparison, Boston, a city of approximately the same size as Amsterdam, also has an estimated 20,000 addicts. One important finding of research carried out by the Scientific Research and Documentation Centre (WODC) is that the average age of junkies is going up; it is now between thirty and thirty-five, and from this the conclusion is drawn that the influx of younger users is small.

In 1992, with the creation of a single European market, borders will be thrown open and for that reason there is increasing interest in Dutch drugs policy. Although the general opinion is that many measures go too far, the Dutch police and the relief organizations note a greater degree of understanding and the adoption of certain elements of Dutch policy in other countries.

Crime and the tourist

It is a tricky business trying to compare Amsterdam's crime figures with those of other large European and American towns. The method of recording crime differs from country to country, as do the processing of the facts reported and the willingness of victims to report crime. To be able to state without reservation that Amsterdam is relatively dangerous or safe, solid scientific research would be required. Figures available to the WODC might lead to the cautious conclusion that the chance of getting robbed in Amsterdam is relatively greater than in London. Crimes against the person – assault, murder and manslaughter – are relatively less frequent than in the British capital. The chance of falling prey to this kind of crime in an American city is much greater.

Crimes against property score very high in Amsterdam by virtue of the high incidence of thefts from cars and pickpocketing: in 1987, according to Amsterdam police statistics, there were 11,374 cases of pickpocketing and 40,818 cars were broken into. Pickpocketing is a problem that the Amsterdam police are having great difficulty in getting under control. After the number of incidents had continued to rise for some time, according to the Amsterdam police, the number of reported incidents levelled off in 1989. The main culprits in this kind of crime are, say the police, North African and South American gangs. They are trained in their home countries, sent round the European tourist centres, and subsequently send their loot back home. Thefts from cars have decreased since 1987: in 1988 the police recorded 34,931 cases, and in last year a further 10 per cent fall was expected. This kind of crime is usually perpetrated by drug addicts; the chance of the visitor to Amsterdam having any other kind of undesirable contact with them is very small.

These then are the two kinds of crime with which tourists are most commonly confronted. As far as thefts from cars are concerned it can be said that many visitors show a great degree of naïvety, leaving luggage, cameras and even jewellery on open display in their cars. Pickpockets are found principally on the main tourist routes: the Dam, Damrak, Rokin, Rembrandtplein, on the routes to the Albert Cuyp market and in the market itself. Watch out for the apparently helpful bystander who brushes a mark off your jacket, or the straps of your shoulder bag being cut, or someone jostling you when getting on a tram. Be on your guard in places where there are lots of people milling about. A very obvious but often ignored precaution is to leave valuable documents and possessions in the hotel safe. Tourists often take unnecessarily large quantities of valuable items out with them.

Finally a few brief words about the red-light district: it is the most crime-ridden patch in the whole of the Netherlands and you must keep on your toes; the criminal will soon spot that you aren't a local. During the day there is no risk to speak of, but at night it is better not to visit the Wallen alone.

Amsterdam is not an unsafe city. If you divide the annual number of visitors by the sum total of cases of pickpocketing and car thefts, you will find that the apparent chance of your being exposed to crime is about 3.5 per cent. Despite the fact that there is an outside chance of your being involved in some other kind of crime, the real likelihood is much lower, because some of the two million Dutch visitors and Amsterdammers themselves also get robbed.

In certain areas drug use takes place openly in the street, so that the city can sometimes seem more menacing than it really is. The public relations officer of the Amsterdam police calls it a 'visibility problem'. One promising development is that the crime rate as recorded by the police is falling at the moment. In 1987 there was a levelling-off, in 1988 there was a fall of 6 per cent and at the time of going to press the figures point to a further decrease. The motto is a simple one then: tourists are a favourite prey of crooks the world over, but the visitor to Amsterdam who takes the obvious precautions will in all probability return home without any unpleasant experiences.

1 · A History of Amsterdam

THE BEGINNINGS

Working from the oldest authentic town plan of Amsterdam, made by Cornelis Anthonisz towards the middle of the sixteenth century, it is no easy task to reconstruct the earliest settlement of some three hundred years earlier. The oldest traces of the city have been found along both banks of the river Amstel, in the Warmoesstraat and the Nieuwendijk. Archaeological evidence of this earliest period – excavated fragments of wood, stone, slate, iron, glass, cork, leather, silk, earthenware, etc. – must have been brought in from elsewhere, pointing to an involvement even at this stage in long-distance trade.

The area would have been uninhabitable had not dykes been immediately built along the Amstel and the IJ to protect the settlers from flooding and tidal currents. A dam was built across the river at an early date, separating the Amstel from the IJ, an inlet of the Zuiderzee. It is from this dam on the Amstel that the city takes its name: Amstelledamme. We should picture such a dam as a built-over outlet sluice, also acting as a lock, through which small craft could pass.

Alongside the dam was the market square, on old maps designated as 'die Plaetse', or the Square, the spot now known as the Dam. The actual site of the dam must have been about where the National Monument now stands. To the north of the dam was a harbour reach (rak), which was given the obvious name of Damrak; further inland, to the south of it, was the Rak-in, now the Rokin.

The first mention we find made of the town is in the 'toll privilege' of 1275 in which the count of Holland, Floris V, granted those living on the dam on the Amstel free passage on all waterways within his domain. Some thirty years later Amsterdam acquired its charter and the town began to fortify itself. This was done simply by digging a canal-moat around the built-up area and piling the earth on the inside into ramparts reinforced with wooden palisades. A number of street names – Zeedijk, Nieuwendijk, Haarlemmerdijk – recall this remote period, and it will not escape the observant visitor that these streets are a little higher than their surroundings. Take a look from the Sonesta Hotel.

Even at that time the Dam was the centre of town. It was here, in the fifteenth century, that the Gothic town hall, of which a painting can be seen in the Rijksmuseum, was built. (Like its predecessors and like so many wooden buildings at the time, it later burned to the ground.) On the east side of town, where there was a sandbar just below the surface of the peaty soil, the Oude Kerk (Old Church) was built in 1306. Recent research has shown that until the sevententh century the most prosperous craftsmen lived in this part of town, the so-called 'Oude Kerk Side'. When in 1408 another church, the Nieuwe Kerk, was built on the west side, the two halves of town became known as the Oude and Nieuwe Zijde, names which are preserved to this day in the street names Nieuwezijds and Oudezijds Voorburgwal.

In the first quarter of the fifteenth century the digging of new canals – the Geldersekade and the Kloveniersburgwal on the east side, the Singel on the west – created the city as recorded by Cornelis Anthonisz, in 1538 in a painting (to be seen in the Amsterdam Historical Museum in the Kalverstraat) and in 1544 in a woodcut, which has become widely known in reproduction.

As well as trade, handicrafts and the carrying of cargo, religion also added to the general liveliness of the town. In 1345 an event took place which has gone down in history as the legend of the 'Miracle of Amsterdam'. The story goes that in a sick person's house in the Kalverstraat a consecrated host fell into the fire and the following morning was found intact among the ashes. To commemorate this miracle a chapel was erected on the west side of the Rokin and from here a procession through the streets was held every March; Amsterdam became a place of pilgrimage and acquired its first tourist attraction.

There were sometimes eminent visitors among the pilgrims – Maximilian of Habsburg, for example, the 'last medieval knight', who was to bear the title of Holy Roman Emperor. Maximilian was constantly in financial difficulties, and took part in the pilgrimage not only to be cured of an illness, but at the same time to ask the Amsterdam city council for money and ships. Both missions were successful and in 1489 the grateful ruler granted Amsterdam the right to include the imperial crown in its coat-of-arms, the same crown which sits atop the tower of the Westerkerk. After the Second World War Queen Wilhelmina completed the city's coat-of-arms with the motto 'Heroic, Resolute, Compassionate'.

The Heiligeweg (Holy Way) and the annual 'silent procession' by Catholic Amsterdammers preserve the memory of the 'miracle'.

The first foundations of prosperity

The early development of the city owed much to cargo-carrying and the associated trade. To begin with this was mainly transit trade between the IJssel towns and Hamburg to Holland and Flanders, but quite soon Amsterdam skippers were themselves sailing to the lands bordering the Baltic and loading up with cargoes of grain, wood, fur, tar and iron. From Hamburg they imported beer, in those days the principal popular drink, because of the unreliabilty of the drinking water. In addition there were stockfish and whale-oil from Norway, wool and coal from England, salt and wine from France and Portugal, cloth from Flanders. As far as necessary these products were resold, and home produce such as herring, dairy products and Leiden cloth were exported along with them. Expert seamanship and the advantage that its ships seldom had to carry ballast enabled Amsterdam to compete on favourable terms with other ports, giving it dominance in sea-borne trade in the course of the sixteenth century.

Religion

To return to the matter of religion: the Reformation did not leave Amsterdam untouched. One of the memorable episodes in the succession of religious upheavals in the sixteenth century was the emergence of the Anabaptists, who at one point occupied the old town hall, not only to reinforce their religious demands but also with the intention of bringing about a social revolution. The Anabaptists set out to prove that Christian equality need not be just pie in the sky, but could actually be put into practice.

The Habsburg government of the time, which saw its policy of unifying the Low Countries (corresponding approximately in area to the present Benelux) threatened by this social and religious radicalism, reacted by prosecuting with the utmost severity all who could be branded as heretics and held responsible for the unrest. Many adherents of the new creed, including members of the prosperous merchant class, fled to various Baltic and North Sea ports, from where they were able to continue their commercial activities.

For the first decade of the Eighty Years' War (1568–1648), the revolt of the Northern Netherlands against the central authority of the Spanish Habsburgs, the city dithered over choosing sides. In 1578 Amsterdam finally joined the resistance led by the Prince of Orange, and a new group of (Calvinist) town councillors took over the reins of government. Roman Catholic priests, nuns and monks and all those wishing to remain loyal to Spanish authority were expelled from the city, or 'ditched' as the saying went. No less than sixteen convents and five monasteries were razed to the ground or put to different use.

The Gebed Zonder End (Endless Prayer), a narrow alley near the Grimburgwal, runs right through the former monastic quarter, and the Sint Luciënsteeg also retains memories of a monastery whose shape can still be traced in the former Municipal Orphanage, now the Amsterdam Historical Museum. In 1632 the chapel of the convent of the Sisters of St Agnes, on the Oudezijds Voorburgwal, was converted to house the Athenaeum, the nucleus of what in 1876 became the city's university.

Other monastic houses were given a new function: the grounds of the former convent of the Sisters of St Clare on the Heiligeweg became the Rasphuis (Rasping House), a house of correction for male criminals which sometimes housed political prisoners (its gate still stands), while a female equivalent, the Spinhuis (Spinning House), was built on the Oudezijds Achterburgwal. The Begijnhof (Béguinage), founded as early as 1346, was preserved. The present houses in it date mostly from the sixteenth century, but one, No. 34, with a wooden front, is late fifteenth century.

The first Calvinist church in the city, the Zuiderkerk in the Zandstraat, was built by the architect Hendrick de Keyser, and the first service was held there in 1611. Subsequently De Keyser began work on the Westerkerk, designed in North Netherlands Renaissance style and completed in 1631.

THE CITY FLOURISHES: THE GOLDEN AGE

In 1579 the seven northern provinces of the Low Countries formed a union, officially called the Republic of the United Netherlands, though often mockingly known as the United Republics of the Netherlands, since it was in fact a fairly loose confederation. This 'Dutch Republic' had a permanent princely court at The Hague, where the States-General, the assembly of representatives of the provincial States, also met. The city of Amsterdam was soon to play a dominant role in the Republic.

The influx of foreigners

A number of developments on the European political stage helped boost Amsterdam's economy.

The Spaniards ridded Amsterdam of a serious rival when Antwerp fell into their hands on their advance through the Southern Netherlands (1585). The Republic immediately sealed the mouth of the Schelde, thus depriving western Europe's principal commercial centre of its access to the sea. Merchants and scholars from the Southern Netherlands headed in large numbers for the city on the Amstel, bringing with them their expertise, commercial experience, capital and entrepreneurial drive.

The capture of Lisbon by the Spanish in 1580 – there had been a lively trade between that city and Amsterdam – led to an influx of Sephardic Jews from Portugal, who brought with them both their commercial ties with the Mediterranean and their capital, which was, for example, invested in diamond-cutting. Soon numbers of Ashkenazim, Jews fleeing from Germany and Poland, who were in the main less prosperous than their Portuguese co-religionists, also settled here. They specialized in street trading and added a spicy Yiddish accent to Amsterdam popular speech. Both groups had their own synagogues, which still adorn the eastern part of the city centre.

A century after the exodus from Antwerp, French Huguenots found sanctuary in Amsterdam, having fled their country because of the revocation by the French king in 1685 of the Edict of Nantes, which had guaranteed them limited religious freedom. The Hospice Wallon on the corner of the Vijzelgracht and the Prinsengracht, which now houses the Consulate-General of France and the Institut Français des Pays Bas, is a reminder of their coming.

Armenians settled here as merchants and shippers in order to retain contacts with the Levant. Their church can still be found on the Krom Boomssloot.

In addition large numbers of Lutherans arrived from Germany, as did many Netherlanders from north of the river IJ and from Friesland. 'De Vries' ('the Frisian') is still the commonest surname in the city, occupying twenty columns in the telephone directory.

Around 1600 a Venetian envoy wrote in a letter to his superiors that the town had approximately 50,000 inhabitants. By 1625 that number had doubled, and by 1650 it had increased fourfold. The population was not to grow much further during the town's most flourishing period.

It is interesting to note the opinion of the seventeenth-century playwright and economist Antoine de Montchrestien. Having fled France after a duel and having lived for years in England and Holland, he had a sharp eye for the ins and outs of economic life in the three countries, and in 1615 wrote a book on the subject. In his view the emergence of Amsterdam, compared with Paris and London quite a small town, from a regional centre to the hub of a complex trade network embracing most of the known world, was truly miraculous.

Overseas expansion

The Baltic trade, the 'mother of commerce', remained an important cornerstone of prosperity and led to the establishment of links with Russia. In addition, contacts with Italy and the Levant were extended by voyages through the Straits of Gibraltar. In this way Russian goods reached the Mediterranean through the agency of Amsterdam and vice versa.

Whalers hunted successfully in northern waters, although attempts to find a north-east passage to the East Indies in order to elude the hostile pirates came to nothing. The Heemskerk and Barentsz expedition of 1596-7 did, however, become one of the most popular tales in Dutch history.

In 1595, commissioned by Amsterdam merchants, Cornelis de Houtman and Pieter Dirks Keyser set out to explore the southern sea route to the Indies. The expedition was successful, but of the 249 seamen who set out only eighty-nine returned two years later, and eight of those had to be carried ashore and died soon after. Nevertheless it was clear that there were enormous profits to be made in the Far East, and in order to prevent competition among themselves the merchants of Holland and Zeeland joined forces in the United East India Company, half of which was financed with Amsterdam capital. This soon gave them control of the Indian Ocean and the Pacific. The 'Oost-Indisch Huis' (East India House) on the corner of the Oude Hoogstraat and the Kloveniersburgwal was the administrative headquarters of the East India Company. In 1655 the Admiralty's Naval Store (now the Maritime Museum) was set up on Kattenburg.

In 1609 Henry Hudson, the English mariner who was then in Dutch service, annexed an area on the north-east seaboard of North America, the present New York State. The settlement of New Amsterdam established on Manhattan Island was lost to the English in 1664 and was rechristened New York.

The West India Company, founded in 1621, again with Amsterdam capital, was given a complete trade monopoly to the west of Africa. Long (far too long) after peace was made with Spain in 1648, after piracy ended and Brazil was finally lost in 1654, the West India Company continued its involvement with the slave trade. In Amsterdam the Company's directors met on the Herenmarkt, in the cellars below was stored the treasure from the Spanish silver fleet captured in 1628 by Admiral Piet Hein in a famous naval exploit. On the corner of the Prins Hendrikkade and 's-Gravenhekje some fine warehouses bear witness to the heyday of the West India Company.

The turnover figures of the Amsterdam Exchange Bank show 1648 as an economic peak year. This was the same year as that in which peace was concluded with Spain, and it saw the driving of the first of the nearly 14,000 piles which were to support the new Town Hall, the masterpiece of Jacob van Campen, completed in 1655. The previous Gothic building had burned down in 1652.

In contemporary travel accounts the same metaphors are repeatedly encountered: the town is one huge warehouse, while the hundreds of ships' masts thronging the harbour, together with the hundreds of thousands of piles on which the city was founded, created a forest not only above but below ground as well.

The seventeenth-century expansion of the city

By about 1600 the old town had become completely congested with the stream of new inhabitants, and expansion became an urgent priority. As early as 1585 a start was made on the extension of the town around the Montelbaan tower, and over the next three-quarters of a century three further phases were to follow. In 1593 new canals (some of which have since been filled in) were dug to join the new extension in the area around the Waterlooplein, in what used to be once Amsterdam's Jewish quarter.

The third extension, decided upon in 1610, which was so ambitious in scope that its execution was to take more than two centuries, involved the digging of the three most famous canals. They were in turn surrounded by a defensive moat – the present Singelgracht – thus giving the city its splendid crescent shape. The town authorities first ordered the digging of the Brouwersgracht in the north-west, and then, leading off from it, the Herengracht, Keizersgracht and Prinsengracht, as far as the Leidsegracht. If the three main canals were designed as a residential area for merchants and other prominent citizens, the need for an area to house the workforce was also realized. This was located beyond the Prinsengracht and was to become known as the Jordaan. In contrast to the meticulous planning which characterized the construction of the canal ring, the architects of the Jordaan did not bother to design a canal and street plan. The existing waterways and ditches were retained, with the result that the streets and canals are set at a strikingly oblique angle to the canal ring.

The fourth extension in 1658 brought the plan to its completion. The canals were extended to the Amstel and on the far side as far as the Plantage, then a pleasure garden, now the site of the Artis zoo.

The digging of all these canals was necessary for the houses to remain dry. The canals served to drain off the groundwater and at the same time, with the peaty soil excavated, the level of the building plots could be raised. This was called 'aanmodderen' ('muddling along'). It stood to reason that the canals should also be used for the transport of goods to and from the merchants' houses, and today they make attractive routes for tour boats.

The names of the ring of canals reveal the view of society held by those in authority at the time. As members of the commercial patrician class they considered themselves the Elite, and so called the first and grandest canal after themselves, the Herengracht, or Gentlemen's Canal. Also distinguished, but a little less so, was the Keizersgracht or Emperor's Canal. The name referred to the Holy Roman Emperor, to whom they technically owed allegiance, but who was a long way off and moreover often in debt, so that they were in practice masters of their own house. The last of the three principal canals, the Prinsengracht, alludes to the *stadholder's* Orange party. There was no love lost between the patrician 'regents' and the House of Orange.

If not literally then figuratively at least, seventeenth-century Amsterdam was founded on the piles driven in the sixteenth century. Dutch historians are wont to describe the seventeenth century as a 'Golden Age'. The prosperous merchant city after all was also the home of numerous scholars and poets, artists and thinkers. Painters from all over the land – Rembrandt, Nicolaas Maes, Ferdinand Bol, Jacob van Ruysdael, Pieter de Hooch, Hercules Seghers and many others – set up their studios there. The poet Joost van den Vondel, the philosopher Spinoza and the naturalist Jan Swammerdam were contemporaries, and René Descartes was also a long-time resident.

It was a great era for the book trade, and the town was the cradle of the newspaper industry. It also led the world in map-making – in the Kalverstraat especially there was a concentration of map-engravers, map-printers and map-sellers.

However, the seventeenth century was not all glamour. The historian Jacques Presser believes this list should be supplemented with hunger, sickness, unemployment, exploitation. In short, he feels that poverty in the midst of splendour should not be overlooked and that there could even be certain causal connections between the two. The beggars, paupers and invalids of the period are immortalized in Rembrandt's prints.

THE DECLINE OF THE CITY

The city owed its remarkable position as an entrepôt for almost the whole of world trade to a particular set of circumstances which was to prove transitory. In the eighteenth century the international balance began to shift. England in particular, with its move to industrialization, was coming into its own. Around 1650 the volume of Dutch trade was five times that of England; a hundred years later the scales had tilted in favour of the British.

In Amsterdam the emphasis changed from trade in goods to trade in securities. From being an entrepôt for international trade Amsterdam became one of Europe's great financial centres. Around 1750 Amsterdam provided between a fourth and a fifth of the total income of the Dutch Republic. Along with this change came the growing discontent among the middle classes with the monopolization of power by the regents, a small group of interrelated families who pursued their own political ends and often clashed with the House of Orange, which represented national unity.

In the middle of the eighteenth century the social and political unrest erupted. Influenced by the ideas of the Enlightenment, a popular movement opposed to regent rule gained ground. The middle classes, or at least a part of them, comprising shopkeepers, lesser merchants, manufacturers, doctors and lawyers, appealed to the stadholder, who as the head of the Orange party was the only person who could stand up to the regents. Another patriotically motivated group had a more revolutionary programme, envisaging a democratic constitution. They were totally opposed to the Orange party, but fled the country when in the last quarter of the eighteenth century Prussia came to the aid of the House of Orange. In 1795, on the night of 18–19 January, they returned and along with a French revolutionary army of *sansculottes* occupied the city. They put up a maypole, the symbol of the French Revolution, on the Dam. The old Republic and with it old Amsterdam, a republic within a republic in the words of the historian Jan Romein, was no more, and the people could look forward to better times.

The Napoleonic period (1795–1813) was not to bring them. On the contrary Amsterdam, although officially the third city of the French empire, fell into decline, and it was to be another fifty years before things improved. It is true that after 1815 in the new Kingdom of the Netherlands, which until 1830 included Belgium, Amsterdam became the official capital, but that meant little more than that the king was inaugurated in the Nieuwe Kerk on the Dam. This ceremony, again in the words of Professor Romein, did not mean that Amsterdam regained its sovereignty or that the old prosperity returned.

ECONOMIC RECOVERY

If prosperity was to return to Amsterdam it had to be built on a new foundation – and that foundation was eventually found. The revival in the last third of the nineteenth century was based principally on three factors, to quote Romein yet again:

- the modernization of Dutch industry, in the areas of shipbuilding, metals, clothing, building, food, alcohol and tobacco, diamond-cutting and graphics;
- the opening-up (from 1870 onwards) of the East Indies to private capital, which made Amsterdam the centre of trade in colonial goods;
- the industrialization of the German empire, a capital-rich hinterland

from which not only the port of Rotterdam but also that of Amsterdam profited, especially after the opening of the North Sea Canal (1876), the improvement of links with the Rhine and the city's connection with the German rail network.

Amsterdam's revival was also given new impetus by the inspirational figure of Dr Samuel Sarphati, a medical practitioner and philanthropist who made a great contribution to the expansion of the city and was responsible for a number of major building projects. Sarphati had modern ideas on house-building, popular education and refuse collection.

In 1889 the Central Station was opened to traffic. The building of the station along the IJ finally closed off Amsterdam from the open sea and changed it from a sea-port to a land-based city with nevertheless improved access to the sea. Although there were many objections to the station island, which blocked the view over the water, the central location of the station enhanced the status of the Damrak–Dam–Rokin axis, which became the hub of the bustling city centre.

The economic revival went hand in hand with the new cultural renaissance marked by among other things the foundation of the municipal university in 1876, the opening of the Rijksmuseum in 1885 and the Carré circus theatre (1887), the inauguration of the Concertgebouw in 1888, the launch of a new Municipal Theatre on the Leidseplein (1894), the opening of the Stedelijk Museum for contemporary art (1895), and the opening of the Tropical Institute (1926). In 1903 Berlage's great creation, the Exchange on the Damrak, was completed.

From 1870 the number of inhabitants again rose sharply. In 1880 there were 300,000, in 1900 more than half a million, in 1940 800,000.

Housing

The physical face of Amsterdam also changed radically after the turn of the century. The need for space to expand was met by the annexing of outlying municipalities, increasing the city's area from less than 18 to nearly 70 square miles. Through the Housing Act of 1901 the government exercised tighter control over the quality of new housing and environmental planning. The heyday of Amsterdam building activity in the 1920s and 1930s was made possible partly by a powerful Social Democrat town council. The council introduced a new leasehold system that attracted international attention by itself commissioning building.

Between the Amstel and the Olympic Stadium Berlage masterminded the impressive development of Amsterdam-South, built largely in the style of a group of architects who became known as the 'Amsterdam School' and produced socially committed, Romantic architecture in brick. The same years saw the emergence of the picturesque garden villages of Betondorp, Nieuwendam and Oostzaan built on the outskirts of the city.

In 1934 the General Extension Plan, adequate for the year 2000, was drawn up, taking a new pragmatic approach and introducing a sharp division between living, working, recreational and traffic functions. By 1960 the plan had been largely put into effect, including the creation of the Amsterdamse Bos in the south, more than 2,000 acres of woodland with no less than 45 km of bicycle paths and a rowing course over two kilometres long.

Subsequently a new suburb, the Bijlmer, was built in the south-east of the city, which since 1978 has been linked to the centre by a metropolitan railway.

The capital has suffered a number of severe setbacks in the course of this century. The Depression of the 1930s caused an unprecedented degree of unemployment, far more harrowing than the recessions of the 1970s and 1980s, which have been mitigated somewhat by the cushioning effect of the welfare state.

The severest blow of all, however, was the deportation and murder during the occupation of 1939–45 of tens of thousands of the city's inhabitants, including virtually the whole Jewish population. Although powerless to resist the Nazi terror, Amsterdammers expressed their rage in the February Strike of 25 and 26 February 1941. The statue of the Docker on the Jonas Daniël Meijerplein commemorates this act of popular resistance.

In the last year of the war, the winter of 1944–5, the population was hit by a severe food shortage as a result of reprisals taken by the occupying forces in response to the national railway strike of September 1944. The western Netherlands found themselves entirely without food, fuel or electricity. At least 2,000 people died during this 'Hunger Winter'.

The city emerged from the war very much the worse for wear, but set energetically about rebuilding.

THE POST-WAR PERIOD

After Indonesia became independent in 1949, the pessimism of political reactionaries in the Netherlands, summed up in the phrase 'the Indies lost, disaster the cost', proved largely unfounded. Amsterdam did indeed lose its role as a market for tropical goods, but the city's economy was quickly put on a new footing.

Much effort went into improving communications: Amsterdam has at all costs to remain a port, with motorways and rail connections guarantee-

ing easy accessibility. The opening of the IJ tunnel and the the Mobil
Oil refinery in 1968 marked the end of a period of economic expansion,
partly because further growth of the petro-chemical industry in the harbour area was halted by the protests of the people of Amsterdam, who
had learned how to publicize their cause through campaigns and pressure
groups.

In 1964 Amsterdam reached a peak of 868,000 inhabitants, which subsequently dropped to 673,000 as a result of movement away and suburban-
ization, but has since again climbed to 700,000 and to over a million for
greater Amsterdam. In the last few decades certain profound changes
have taken place within the city:

- the city's economy has become based increasingly on high-quality service industries: stockbroking and banking, a large range of artistic
  attractions, tourism and entertainment, specialized education and
  media specialists;
- there has been a radical process of urban renewal, monument conservation and rehabilitation of the old housing stock;
- large groups of immigrants from the Mediterranean, the Caribbean
  and elsewhere – principally Turks, Moroccans and Surinamers – have
  settled in the city, making up a total of 16 per cent of the population.

These developments have helped reinvigorate Amsterdam, which from
Schiphol to the IJ is growing into a multi-faceted, multi-cultural society.

2 · Amsterdam Today

The writer Simon Carmiggelt was the archetypal Amsterdammer, a native of The Hague who, as soon as he had reached the age of discrimination, settled on the banks of the Amstel. He immortalized Amsterdam in many thousands of unerringly accurate pages. Occasionally, with a healthy urban reluctance, he would take a holiday, usually somewhere in the country, only to inform his readers upon his safe return that the warbling of the speckled oystercatcher could best be compared to the ringing of a telephone.

One day he found the answer to the holiday problem. Together with his wife he boarded the tram and booked a room in the Americain, an imposing *fin-de-siècle* hotel on the Leidseplein. *That* was what you called a holiday! Away from it all, yet at home, strangers in familiar surroundings, able to see all those familiar streets, alleyways, squares and avenues in a new, unexpected light:

'There you all sit in the square and there are jugglers and musicians and clowns, just like in the Middle Ages, and everyone's having a good time and suddenly lots of people come running out of the Leidsestraat and you think to yourself: "I expect there's a scrap going on somewhere. . . " Which turns out to be right, because the police are in hot pursuit. It can't disrupt the aimiable atmosphere on the Leidseplein. You glance sideways and think: "Christ, they must be raiding some place or other." And that's the kind of absurdity that gives Amsterdam its special charm.'

With slightly over 700,000 inhabitants Amsterdam is the world's smallest metropolis. Its importance derives from the combination of its compact size and metropolitan pretensions. You can find your way around with your eyes closed, the chairman of the council's Public Works Committee lives round the corner, there are ducks bobbing about on the canals (which rate three stars in the Guide Michelin) and the mayor is just plain Ed. The ring of canals, unlike London's City, is a real city centre, where people both live and work, and which as a result loses none of its vitality after 6 p.m.

It is difficult to remain unmoved by the dazzling beauty of, say, the sundrenched Lijnbaansgracht or the Groenburgwal in the snow. Even Amsterdam's red-light district is picturesque. Within walking distance of the other entertainment centres, its stepped gables look benignly down on the casual passer-by and its illuminated windows cast a warm, ruddy, inviting glow over their surroundings.

How does one define the concept of a metropolis? I'll have a try: in a metropolis you can both live and work, you have a multinational choice of food and drink, you're offered an immense cultural range of diversions, and the country's principal dailies and weeklies are produced there. Amsterdam meets these criteria more than adequately. It is true that there is something of a housing shortage and the dreaded curse of unemployment has struck here too, especially among non-natives (24.3 per cent). But for their more fortunate – white, reasonably prosperous, personable and pleasure-seeking – fellow-citizens Amsterdam is an earthly paradise.

Thanks to the internationalization of the capital's population, its gamut of restaurants is the most sophisticated in the world. One can choose at will from Argentinian, Bolivian, Chinese, Cypriot, Danish, Egyptian, English, French, Greek, Hungarian, Indian, Indonesian, Italian, Japanese, Jewish, Korean, Malay, Mexican, Moroccan, Norwegian, Portuguese, Russian, Spanish, Surinamese, Tunisian, Turkish, and Yugoslav cuisine. With some difficulty one can even find the odd *Dutch* eating establishment, though these are best avoided. Virtually the whole daily and weekly press is located in Amsterdam, from the *Parool* (once socialist, now independent) to the *Volkskrant* (once Catholic, now independent), from the *Groene Amsterdammer* to – notwithstanding its name – the *Haagse Post*.

The better bookshops, unlike those in other parts of the world, are amply stocked with the latest foreign items. Films are mercifully not dubbed. In the Concertgebouw you can hear Mahler (nowhere is Mahler better played than in the Concertgebouw) and in De IJsbreker you can hear Xenakis (nowhere is Xenakis better played than in De IJsbreker). There is scarcely a street corner in Amsterdam without its own alternative, less alternative or non-alternative theatre. *Everything* is on offer: Dutch theatre, foreign theatre, alternative gay groups, post-modern feminist mime, lunch-time theatre, pocket theatre, and conservative popular theatre. Which makes it a terrible shame, as the Dutch can't act, or at least not very well.

Oddly enough, two institutions which in principle belong in a metropolis are based outside Amsterdam. These are, firstly, the radio and T.V. studios – back in the early days the wife of the inventor of Dutch radio was loth to expose her maid to the temptations of the big city, which is why that mass medium eventually descended on rural Hilversum. Secondly there is the government, which resides in The Hague, a provincial backwater to the north of the bulb-fields. There is a practical reason for this. If it were based in Amsterdam the seat of government would be under permanent siege, regardless of whether parliament were debating legislation on the fish-processing industry or the raising or lowering of the speed-limit, which in Amsterdam happens to be 50 kph and provides what is more or less the only common ground between Amsterdam and the country's other urban agglomerations.

Because Amsterdammers are on principle *anti*. In the course of earning my living I have attended many hundreds of meetings, so that I know that whether it's the annual meeting of the Humanist Alliance, or the pre-election conference of the Christian Democrat party, or the national mating day of the Society for Sexual Reform, the Amsterdam contingent is always the dissenting element, representing the rational, progressive viewpoint, which is subsequently overwhelmingly defeated by the votes of the hinterland.

The Amsterdammer is an adherent of the doctrine of permanent revolution. Forbid him to indulge in the fairly brutal late nineteenth-century popular pastime of 'eel-heading', whose object was to tear the head off a live eel tied to a post, or route the underground network through his run-down neighbourhood, and he'll pack his tupperware lunch-box with smelly cheese sandwiches and take to the barricades.

Seen in perspective, with hindsight, such expressions of popular intransigence may be seen as questionable in some respects. But there is one manifestation of popular resistance whose significance will always remain beyond dispute: that is the day on which the workers of Amsterdam downed tools *en masse* to express their sympathy with the plight of the persecuted Jews, the so-called February Strike of 25–26 February 1941, just over six months after the Nazis had taken control of the goverment. People frequently sneer at the supposed fact that workers can be mobilized only on issues of cash and percentages. In this case, however, for two glorious wintry days, everything was shut down because of something that had nothing to do with cash or percentages, and everything to do with compassion and morality. It had never happened anywhere in the world, and to this day it is unique in the annals of social history. It is true that the February Strike happened almost half a century ago, nine months before this writer was born. And yet for me that event is reason enough to spend the whole of my life in Amsterdam, despite all the petrol fumes, dogshit, big-city speculators, pirate broadcasters, muggers, noise pollution, car thieves and incompetent city corporations.

Amsterdam's inhabitants are made up of a native population, plus talented provincials who know that natural gifts, regardless of whether one is a poet or a computer-hacker, can flourish only in the big city. 'Amsterdam remains the refuge of all those striving to free themselves from the stifling atmosphere of small communities, and that too forms part of the city's strength and vitality,' writes the Amsterdam specialist Geert Mak. Unfortunately Amsterdam exerts an equally powerful pull on all kinds of criminal riff-raff, the contemporary fungus which nowadays affects *every* metropolis. 'It's something of a miracle,' says the writer Marijke Höweler with a degree of overstatement, 'if you manage to make it from the Central Station to Dam Square without getting a knife between your shoulder-blades. But generally that's what happens, and you find they've hung your emptied handbag from it.'

Another unpleasant aspect of the city is the unmistakable *pollution*, caused principally by that Hydra-headed legion of dachshunds, bouviers, pekinese, alsatians, bull-terriers and golden retrievers which is set loose upon the unsuspecting population. In fact I know only two Amsterdammers who are inclined to make light of this enormous problem: one is the head of the municipal refuse collection service, the other is the local writer Harry Mulisch.

Mulisch made a subtle distinction between pollution and messiness. 'Dog turds I regard as messiness. From an ecological point of view that's fine: it helps the trees grow. No, I think plastic cups are much worse. That's real urban pollution, real garbage.' Come to that, Mulisch welcomes a certain degree of *disorder*, as part and parcel of an adult community. 'Our official propaganda, put out by KLM, etc., always used to concentrate on the windmills and tulip bulbs; that has now been shattered by the shocking state of affairs in Amsterdam: drugs, heroin, crime. That's how we're portrayed in the world press, which is good politics, because now everyone says: "Oh, it's not just a country of backward clog-wearers and tulips, it's a *real* country." I'm strongly in favour of the degeneration of Amsterdam, as regards the image of Dutch culture and literature throughout the world. I said as much to the mayor, but he couldn't see my point.'

Another connoisseur of Amsterdam, the journalist W.L. Brugsma, is inclined to place even the high crime rate in a global, relativizing, Euro-sociological light. '*So what?*' he says. 'The chance of getting beaten up is twice as great in Paris as in Amsterdam, and in Paris the chances are that it will be by the police. The chance of getting mown down or blown sky high by terrorists in an airport in Frankfurt or Rome is far higher. Over there the *carabinieri* use automatic weapons, at Schiphol they use their heads: the El-Al counter is tucked away discreetly in a side room.'

Schiphol is the city's airport. It provides work for 25,000 men and women, which makes it the region's largest employer apart from the city council. Without Schiphol, Amsterdam would *really* be a second-rate community from an economic point of view. Of course there is some industry, albeit much less than one would expect for a city with such pretensions. And Amsterdam has long since lost out to its rival Rotterdam in the struggle for dominance as a port. Oddly enough, this fact can only add to the honour and glory of the country's first great city.

Let's once again define the characteristics of a great city, this time with the help of the views of the historian Donald Olson, an addict of asphalt and concrete, as voiced in conversation with the urban sociologist Lodewijk Brunt.

The city, he maintains, no longer has the same function it once had, for example at the time of the Industrial Revolution. At that time most cities or urban agglomerations had a primarily economic significance. They were the centres of production and functioned as the powerhouses of the national economy. In the meantime, however, technology has made such massive strides that physical concentration of large numbers of people – in offices or at the conveyor belt – is more or less superfluous. This means that the large, modern city will have to offer its inhabitants not primarily work, but *fun*. 'It looks,' says Olson, 'as if towns are again beginning to serve their pre-industrial function and are geared more towards expressive than towards practical ends, as symbols of prestige, centres of consumption, places to devote oneself to luxury entertainment, to spend the money one has earned elsewhere. The new metropolitan "paradigm" will be more like decadent ancient Rome than Dickens's Coketown.'

And more like ancient, decorative, messy Amsterdam than its traditional rival, the modern, businesslike, economically expanding Rotterdam. I flick through my Amsterdam library and light upon an illustrative anecdote by a young Amsterdam reporter. At eleven o'clock in the evening he was stopped by a Rotterdam taxi-driver. He had a trio of chaps from The Hague in his cab who had been on a business trip to Rotterdam and subsequently wanted to 'live it up'. So they had asked the first Rotterdam taxi-driver they came across for advice, and he had replied with hesitation: 'If you want to live it up, gentlemen, then of course you'll have to go to *Amsterdam*.'

This is the paradigm of the new urbanity, reflected in the relative position of Rotterdam, pride of the Maas, and Amsterdam, the country's capital: Rotterdam is where the money is earned that is subsequently squandered in Amsterdam.

Leafing further through my Amsterdam library, I come across an essay by the late publicist Henri Knap, who when he was alive edited the city section of the most important Amsterdam daily and so – one would assume – knew what he was talking about. Or maybe not? 'Big cities are actually monsters,' wrote Knap, 'tumorous growths in countries full of fields and woods, symptoms of cultural sickness.'

This is a point of view which is as odd as it is *apolitical*, for every right-minded person knows where the tumours actually fester: in the leafy countryside, with its rustic clumps of trees and idyllic panoramas. Texas and 'the Texas of West Germany', Bavaria, along with 'the Bavaria of the Netherlands', Limburg, are the true breeding-grounds of backward arch-conservatism, *not* concrete jungles reeking democratically of petrol fumes like Amsterdam, London or Budapest.

'City air liberates,' observes the urban sociologist Lodewijk Brunt – and if that is true of any city in the world, then it is the city state of Amsterdam, that many-headed, multi-coloured, libertarian haven, glared at with suspicion both at home and abroad.

The glarers are Argus-eyed, disapproving – and *green with envy*.

3 · Eating Out

The Netherlands does not have the reputation of being a gastronomic Mecca. A few years ago visiting foodies were advised to bring a hamper with them.

Fortunately things have changed a bit in recent years. Not in the field of Dutch cooking, let it be said. Although essentially a simple country cuisine, it has many tasty dishes. This is not entirely unconnected with the fact that for centuries the Dutch controlled a large part of world trade in foodstuffs and condiments. The seventeenth century – known in Holland as the Golden Age – owed its opulence to the fortunes earned from the virtual trading monopolies in salted fish, spices, spirits and coffee. Anyone walking through Amsterdam can still find traces of this. Amsterdam is really a great cosmopolitan village. There is no country with more foreign ties than the Netherlands and in the streets of Amsterdam you can find, besides the traditional Dutch eating establishments, the traces of some forty-five other gastronomic cultures.

EATING HABITS

At home the urban Dutchman no longer eats as traditionally as his country-based compatriot still does. This traditional meal cycle consisted of a substantial breakfast of bread, spread with a sweet topping (jam, honey, hundreds-and-thousands) and hearty items such as sausage and cheese, supplemented with or even replaced by porridge. This was accompanied by coffee, tea, milk or buttermilk.

The midday meal was the hot meal, as it is virtually everywhere in pre-industrial and non-urbanized households. That midday meal almost invariably comprised three courses: soup or a simple hors d'oeuvre, a main course made up in turn of three elements – potatoes, vegetables and meat (always listed in that order) – and a dessert.

The main course might also consist, especially in winter, of a single dish or hot-pot. It is striking that the names of the many varieties of hot-pot often first mention the vegetable used, and even with a three-part main course it is the vegetable that tends to take pride of place. The Dutch are vegetable-eaters and that is often also noticeable in restaurants. Potatoes do not count as vegetables (the Dutch word *groente* corresponds more to 'greens' than to 'vegetables') and the salad is a separate entity.

The traditional midday meal is nowadays of course eaten mostly in the evening. The old-fashioned Dutchman requires his evening meal to be on the table at six o'clock sharp. Given the present very light lunch or *koffietafel*, which is not much more than an extended breakfast, that is not surprising. There are now many restaurants which specialize in copious lunches for businessmen, thus appearing to reinstate an old-fashioned country custom, but generally speaking city-dwellers have forgotten the hot lunch. What is happening is that the hot evening meal is gradually being eaten a little later. The food is no longer invariably served at 6, but at 7, 8 or even 9 o'clock. Oddly enough there are still restaurants, clinging obstinately to tradition, which close at eight.

SNACKS BETWEEN MEALS

Given the light breakfast (lighter than its English or American counterpart), the light lunch and the now somewhat later evening meal, there are naturally odd moments during the day when sudden pangs of hunger have to be appeased. The Dutch – and especially Amsterdammers – have a large number of ways of dealing with this problem.

To start with there are the many kinds of shops selling snacks or food which can be consumed as snacks:

Patisseries (*banketbakkerijen*) of course sell all kinds of pastries, but in addition often have an extensive range of hearty hot snacks: *saucijzebroodjes* (puff-pastry filled with meat, but sometimes also with a chicken or vegetarian filling), croquettes (see below), mini-pizzas and cheese- and/or onion-flavoured rolls.

Butchers' shops (*slagerijen*) often sell croquettes, hot mincemeat balls and all kinds of filled rolls which are often cheaper than in the specialized roll shops.

Greengrocers (*groenteboeren*) of course have fresh fruit, and apples and oranges are often sold individually, at least in the centre.

Fishmongers (*vishandels*) always have snacks for sale. You will find *lekkerbekjes*, usually fried fillet of whiting or plaice. Fish can also be had from herring stalls, but fishmongers often have a much bigger selection: herring of course, both raw and marinated, rollmops, fried fish, fishcakes, prawn croquettes, everything served on a roll or without as one prefers. There may also be salmon or eel or smoked halibut or smoked herring or mackerel or baked mussels. Even oysters may be found at some fish shops, although Amsterdammers, who a century ago ate oysters everywhere in the street, have to re-acquire the habit.

Herring stalls (*haringkarren*) nowadays sell almost as large a variety as fishmongers, except for fresh fish, and can often heat your fish in a microwave. Herring is of course eaten raw, and Amsterdammers eat them not by their tails but cut into pieces with a cocktail stick off a piece of paper or a cardboard plate. Try them *without* chopped onions. The latter used to serve to mask the rancid taste, but herring is no longer rancid. Instead of onion ask for pepper: that brings out the flavour.

Besides these shops, which sell snacks on the side, a lot of shops specializing in snacks have sprung up:

Chip stalls (*frietkramen*) sell chips, croquettes and many other snacks which are often fried in batter. A typical snack is the croquette: it contains beef or pork and, if mentioned separately, veal, always in a sauce with a béchamel base. Besides that they sell mincemeat balls called *frikadellen*. No one knows what goes into them, but they are like sausages fried in batter. Other snacks are the *nassibal*, a deep-fried ball of spicy rice, and the *bamibal*, with spiced noodles – both derived from Indonesian cuisine.

Snack bars and **automats** usually sell the same range, often supplemented by salads, half chickens and drinks. They are distinguished from the shops and chip stalls by usually staying open long after the official closing time.

Espresso bars, besides coffee, usually sell light snacks, filled rolls, toasted sandwiches and of course pastries all day long.

Roll shops (*broodjeszaken*) are a Dutch speciality. Often they originated from a butcher's shop which started selling rolls as a side-line. There are two kinds: those where you order what you want and take it away, which usually have a very small seating area for you to eat what you have bought on the premises, and those which are more geared to consumption on the spot. You can always take away.

Cafeterias are a bit like the latter kind of roll shop, geared more to on-the-spot consumption, with their selection often expanded with *uitsmijters* (large open sandwiches of meat or cheese and fried eggs), soup and so on. In fact, cafeterias are small restaurants.

Hamburger joints in Amsterdam serve virtually the same fare as all over the world, which needs no further explanation.

To conclude, a final list of possible ways of appeasing hunger between meals.

Domestic catering services (*traiteurs*) are a phenomenon of the last few years. They are usually take-aways for complete meals, but there is usually snack-type fare available.

Take-away Chinese are often Dutch-style Chinese restaurants from which complete meals can be taken away.

Pizza delivery companies deliver your telephone orders by moped – usually only in the centre.

Pastry stalls, selling *oliebollen* (a kind of doughnut), nougat and other sweet pastries, which used to be found only at fairs around the turn of the year, are now seen everywhere in town all year round.

And then there are the small independent **street-sellers** dispensing New York-style hot dogs or empanadas or brownies or saté from mobile salespoints. Because such small businesses usually have no way of keeping their food cool, you are of course running more of a risk.

Anyone wanting to shop after 6 p.m. can find a **night shop** in any district in Amsterdam. Often there is a snack bar or *traiteur* attached to it and some night shops have specialized in luxury food.

It is obvious that a tourist in Amsterdam can eat very well without ever setting foot in a restaurant.

RESTAURANTS

Like all big cities Amsterdam has a number of expensive restaurants serving *haute cuisine*, a number selling a poor imitation for (almost) the same price, a number of less pretentious middle-priced establishments with a more or less regional-style French cuisine, a number of restaurants catering especially for tourists serving Dutch meals (Dutch people eating out are keen to eat anything but Dutch food) and a large number of exotic restaurants (representing perhaps forty-five nationalities in all) of vastly differing quality: some serve an honest cuisine, others are quite simply tourist traps where the quality does not make one eager to pay them a second visit.

Most of the tourist traps are located around the busy entertainment centres like the Leidseplein. Avoid those restaurants if you are fond of good food. The restaurants in this guide are places that Amsterdammers themselves like eating in and going back to. Our choice could easily be expanded – there are more reasonably good restaurants than we mention.

Unfortunately the Dutch do not have a real restaurant tradition. Eating out is more something for special occasions and the atmosphere is consequently often more important than the quality of the food. The restaurants listed below keep a good balance between atmosphere and food quality, but whenever we had to choose we went for the food, not for the wallpaper, the carpets or the glassware.

Most of the larger hotels have their own restaurants, some better than others and often variable in quality. Because the frequent changes of management and policy lead to varied results, they have not been extensively listed here. There are also many cafés serving excellent meals (a number of possibilities are listed on p.61 onwards), often at very reasonable prices, but here too the quality is very variable.

Most restaurants nowadays have either a special menu for vegetarians or a number of vegetarian dishes on the main menu. And otherwise the chef is usually prepared to accommodate vegetarian customers. Sometimes cooks, given adequate notice, can fit other types of diet into a menu. All prices on the menu (which by law must be displayed outside the restaurant!) are inclusive of VAT and service, although the wages of the serving staff often presuppose an additional tip. Usually 10 per cent of the bill is given, but it is sensible to stick to a maximum amount per guest, say 10 guilders. Reservations are usually necessary only for the more expensive restaurants.

Below you will find fifteen restaurants described at some length, offering different sorts of cuisine and in different price-brackets. Telephone numbers, addresses, etc. are given at the end of the chapter, where sixty other recommended restaurants are also listed. Restaurants marked with an asterisk are those given a fuller description. After the addresses you will find an indication of the district as given in Chapter 13 and the maps in that chapter.

We have not given the exact prices charged for meals; these change too frequently to be of much use for long in a travel guide. Instead we have divided the restaurants into categories:

Price-range A indicates a simple, modestly-priced restaurant, where the most expensive dishes cost between 15 and 25 guilders.

Price-range B indicates a medium-priced restaurant, where the average cost of a main course is approximately 35 guilders.

Price-range C refers to de luxe establishments where the average main-course price is around 50 guilders.

American
An American Place is a fairly unpretentious American restaurant. Huge and excellent hamburgers, good steaks, Cajun dishes, American wines and other drinks and very friendly serving staff, who, in true American style, always greet you with a glass of iced water. For Americans who really cannot tear themselves away from home cooking or want to show their hosts how they do things at home, this is the place. Short, American wine list and a French house wine.
Price-range A/B

Argentine
Tango is a small Argentine grill-restaurant, in the middle of the red-light

district. It is not only the food but particularly the quiet atmosphere that makes this restaurant more attractive than the more touristy grill-restaurants, which are usually part of a chain. Tango is a real family restaurant with – of course – tango music playing in the background. We never leave the place without rounding off our meal with *budin de pan*, the Argentine version of bread-pudding. Short wine list.
Price-range A

Chinese
Treasure is one of the restaurants owned by Ho Man Kin. This is his most luxurious establishment and you can tell from the décor alone that Ho is an artist. The calligraphy on the wall is his own. His artistry is also apparent in the kitchen, although he has recruited good, specialist cooks, with a mastery of the different regional cuisines. Accordingly you can ask for a complete regional menu. Peking duck is also available, but must be ordered in advance.
Price-range B/C

Moy-Kong is the sort of Chinese restaurant where you can always see Chinese families sitting down to eat. Although at first sight it may strike the outsider as a run-of-the-mill restaurant, it is a place where you can get a wide choice of excellent authentic Chinese dishes for surprisingly little money. The surroundings are not chic, but one comes here to eat well and for no other reason.
Price-range A/B

Dutch
De Roode Leeuw is a large, rather old-fashioned hotel-restaurant on the Damrak, which was once a popular place to stay, especially for people from the provinces. For some time, under new management, it has been trying its hardest to show the best side of Dutch cooking, and so it serves a Dutch menu with a choice of three courses, which give one a good impression. This is of course aimed primarily at tourists, but you don't get the feeling here of having stumbled into a tourist trap. Short, good wine list.
Price-range B

French regional
Dineau is a spacious restaurant in the Jordaan, where Dino, the chef and owner, occasionally reveals his Egyptian origins. His dishes are aromatic and light and the atmosphere of the place can be described in the same terms. The walls are covered with paintings by Herman Brood, a Dutch pop-star. A short, good-quality wine list.
Price-range B

L'Ambiance is the least Amsterdam-like of Amsterdam restaurants. It is in the north-east of the city, near the former slaughterhouses, in detached doll's-house-like premises. In the beautiful, spacious and simply laid-out dining room, you can relax over the food cooked by the lady owner in her small kitchen. She speaks mainly the French of her native region, the Côte d'Azur, which is also the origin of her very homely cuisine. She serves a five-course menu with fixed elements and changing main courses, depending what is available in the markets. Frenchmen may imagine themselves at home, everyone else will feel as though they are on the Riviera. A short, simple but palatable wine list.
Price-range B

Haute cuisine and luxury restaurants

Halvemaan is owned by John Halvemaan, a chef whose approach is very eclectic and combines influences from all over the world in a cuisine which is not only international, but also very inventive and harmonious. The décor of this splendid restaurant, set in the middle of a park on a lake, is very sober. A restaurant for adventurous gourmets. Short, but well-thought-out wine list.
Price-range B/C

De Trechter is a small, classically laid-out restaurant with a short, classic menu. Jan de Wit, the chef and owner, uses unexpected aromas to give his impeccably prepared dishes the *cachet* befitting his reputation as a top chef. Extensive wine list.
Price-range C

Christophe has acquired many fans in a short space of time thanks to the refined dishes from which his French origins are apparent. His southern French way of dealing with fish is refreshing. The décor of the restaurant is ultra-modern and sober – as is the service – but very stylish. A light, delicate cuisine for those who like a Mediterranean touch. Short, good wine list.
Price-range B/C

De Kersentuin is the chic restaurant of a small hotel next to the Hilton. The chef, Jon Sistermans, has been proving for years that he is now one of the Netherlands' best and most inventive cooks with dishes in which he experiments with daring combinations. The atmosphere of the restaurant has been determined in part by the former manager, the flamboyant Joop Braakhekke, who once in a while has been known to tinkle the keys of the piano. The cuisine is French-orientated, as is the extensive wine list.
Price-range C

Indonesian

Lonny's is a small Indonesian restaurant where the food has not been adapted too much to Dutch taste, as often happens, with the result that everything becomes blurred and tastes the same. In this small, busy restaurant you get an approximation of what the food must be like in Indonesia. Next to the restaurant Lonny has a *toko*, a shop from which you can take many of the dishes away and eat them at home (you can also eat them on the premises as a snack) and where you can buy the ingredients if you cook yourself.
Price-range B

Semarang is possibly the best but also the smallest Indonesian restaurant in Amsterdam. In fact it's in a garage in a suburb. Indonesian cuisine is a true family cuisine and so it is logical that in Semarang it should be a family that serves you your food. You feel as though you are a personal guest, and that's how you should behave, not as a tourist.
Price-range A

Italian

Da Canova is the restaurant of Primo Canova, a real live Italian, and his wife, a real live Dutchwoman. He works in the kitchen, she serves, and they do it with a striking attention to detail and quality. The cuisine is Italian domestic; not a pizza parlour or a pasta place, but somewhere to take a whole evening over a complete meal. Primo's hand-made pastas are incomparable. His vegetable dishes are worth a visit in themselves and the way he serves salad is an example to others. A short, naturally thoroughly Italian wine list.
Price-range B

Moroccan

Marakech is the only Moroccan restaurant in Amsterdam, though not the only North African one. We always enjoy coming back here because of the low prices and the consistent quality of the marvellous tajins, couscous and bastilla. The roast lamb cutlets are also delectable and we never leave without eating a couple of pieces of the excellent Arab pastries with coffee. A few well-chosen North African wines.
Price-range A

ADDRESSES OF RECOMMENDED RESTAURANTS

An asterisk after the name indicates that the restaurant is described in more detail above

American

An American Place★, Utrechtsedwarsstraat 141 (District 4), tel. 20 73 93, price-range A/B, no lunches, dinner 5–11.30 p.m., closed Tuesdays and Wednesdays

Cajun, Ceintuurbaan 260 (District 8), tel. 662 43 68, price-range B, no lunches, dinner 5–11 p.m., open all week

Argentine, Uruguayan

Alberto's Carreta, Spui 8 (District 1), tel. 26 80 24, price-range A/B, lunch 12–6 p.m., dinner 6 p.m.–midnight, open all week

Tango★, Warmoesstraat 49 (District 1), tel. 27 24 67, price-range A/B, no lunches, dinner 5 p.m.–midnight, open all week

Brazilian

Do Brasil, Lange Leidsedwarsstraat 84 (District 4), tel. 22 63 32, price-range A/B, lunch 12–4 p.m. (except Tuesdays), dinner 4p.m.–midnight (Fridays and Saturdays till 1 a.m.), open all week

Chinese

There are 140 Chinese restaurants in Amsterdam, with a large number in every district. A few very good ones are:

Moy-Kong★, Zeedijk 87 (District 1), tel. 24 19 06, price-range A/B, lunch 1–6 p.m., dinner 6–11 p.m., closed Mondays

Sichuan Food, Reguliersdwarsstraat 35 (District 4), tel. 26 93 27, price-range B, no lunches, dinner 5–11.30 p.m., closed Wednesdays

Tong Fa, Joh. Huizingalaan 192, tel. 15 26 55, price-range B, lunch 12–6 p.m. (except Sundays), dinner 4–10 p.m., closed Saturdays

Treasure★, Nieuwezijds Voorburgwal 115 (District 6), tel. 23 40 61, price-range B/C, lunch 12–3 p.m., dinner 5–10.30 p.m., open all week

Dutch

Claes Claesz., Egelantiersstraat 24–26 (District 7), tel. 23 53 06, price-range B, no lunches, dinner 6–10 p.m., closed Mondays, Tuesdays and Wednesdays

Piet de Leeuw, Noorderstraat 11 (District 4), tel. 23 71 81, price-range A/B, lunch 11.30 a.m.–5 p.m. (except Saturdays and Sundays), dinner 5–11.30 p.m., open all week

De Roode Leeuw★, Damrak 93–94 (District 1), tel.24 03 96, price-range A/B, lunch 12–6 p.m., dinner 6–10 p.m., open all week

d'Vijff Vlieghen, Spuistraat 294–302 (District 5), tel. 24 83 69, price-range B/C, no lunches, dinner 5–10.30 p.m., open all week

Witteveen, Ceintuurbaan 256–258 (District 8), tel. 662 43 68, price-range B, no lunches, dinner 5–11 p.m., open all week

Filipino

At Mango Bay, Westerstraat 91 (District 7), tel. 38 10 39, price-range A/B, no lunches, dinner 6–10 p.m., closed Thursdays

Fish restaurants

Lucius, Spuistraat 247 (District 5), tel. 24 18 31, price-range B, no lunch, dinner 5.30–11 p.m., open all week

De Gouden Leeuw (Dutch), Prinsengracht 274 (District 7), tel. 23 94 20, price-range A/B, no lunches, dinner 5–10 p.m., closed Mondays

French regional and Bourgeois cuisine

L'Ambiance★, Cruquiusweg 27, tel. 92 06 54, price-range B, lunch 12–4 p.m. (except Saturdays and Sundays), dinner 6–10 p.m., open all week

Bordewijk, Noordermarkt 8 (District 7), tel. 24 38 99, price-range B, no lunches, dinner 6.30–10.30 p.m., closed Mondays

Sjef Schets, Leidsestraat 20 (District 4), tel. 22 80 85, price-range B, lunch 11 a.m.–3 p.m. (except Saturdays), dinner 5.30–10 p.m., closed Sundays

Brasserie 404, Singel 404 (District 5), tel. 23 35 22, price-range B, no lunches, dinner 6–11 p.m., closed Sundays

Dineau★, Laurierstraat 63–65 (District 7), tel. 25 25 22, price-range B, no lunches, dinner 6.30–11 p.m., closed Mondays

L'Entrecôte, P.C. Hooftstraat 70 (District 2), tel. 73 77 76, price-range B, no lunches, dinner 5.30–11 p.m., closed Sundays and Mondays

De Geparkeerde Mossel, Nieuwezijds Voorburgwal 306 (District 5), tel. 24 94 25, price-range B, no lunches, dinner 6–10 p.m., closed Sundays

De Gouden Reael, Zandhoek 14, tel. 23 38 33, price-range B, lunch 12–2 p.m. (except Saturdays and Sundays), dinner 6–10 p.m. (Saturdays from 5 p.m.), open all week

Paris-Brest, Prinsengracht 375 (District 5), tel. 27 05 07, price-range A/B, lunch 12–2.30 p.m. (except Saturdays and Sundays), dinner 6 p.m.–midnight, open all week

Tout Court, Runstraat 13 (District 5), tel. 25 86 37, price-range B, no lunches, dinner 6–11.30 p.m., closed Sundays and Mondays

Greek

Rhodos, Binnen Dommersstraat 13 (District 7), tel. 22 81 34, price-range A, no lunches, dinner 5–11.30 p.m., open all week

Haute cuisine and luxury restaurants

Beddingtons, Roelof Hartstraat 6–8 (District 2), tel. 76 52 01 (Zuid), price-range C, lunch 12–2 p.m. (except Sundays and Mondays), dinner 6–10.30 p.m., closed Sundays

Christophe★, Leliegracht 46 (District 6), tel. 25 08 07, price-range B/C, no lunches, dinner 7–11 p.m., closed Sundays

Excelsior, Nieuwe Doelenstraat 2–8 (District 1), tel. 23 48 36, price-range C, lunch 12–2 p.m. (except Saturdays), dinner 7–10.30 p.m., open all week

Halvemaan★, Van Leijenberghlaan 20, tel. 06-022 44 77, price-range B/C, lunch 12–2 p.m. (except Saturdays), dinner 7–10.30 p.m., closed Sundays

De Kersentuin★, Dijsselhofplantsoen 7, tel. 664 21 21, price-range C, lunch 12–2.30 p.m. (except Saturdays), dinner 6–10.30 p.m., closed Sundays

Les Quatre Canetons, Prinsengracht 1111 (District 4), tel. 24 63 07, price-range C, lunch 12–2.30 (except Saturdays), dinner 6–10.30 p.m., closed Sundays

La Rive, Prof. Tulpplein 1, tel. 22 60 60, price-range C, lunch 12–2.30 p.m. (except Saturdays and Sundays), dinner 6–10.30 p.m., open all week

De Trechter★, Hobbemakade 63 (District 2), tel. 71 12 63, price-range B/C, lunch 12–2.30 p.m. (except Saturdays), dinner 6–10.30 p.m. closed Sundays and Mondays

Indian

Annapurna, Torensteeg 4–6 (District 6), tel. 22 03 03, price-range B, no lunches, dinner 5.30–11 p.m., open all week

Koh-I-Noor, Westermarkt 29 (District 5), tel. 23 31 33, price-range B, no lunches, dinner 5–11.30 p.m., open all week

The Tandoor, Leidseplein 19 (District 4), tel. 23 44 15, price-range B, no lunches, dinner 5.30–11.30 p.m., open all week

Indonesian

Indonesian cuisine is so established in the Netherlands that it is almost regarded as typically Dutch. Although connoisseurs maintain that the best restaurants are in The Hague, you can also eat excellent Indonesian food in Amsterdam, at among other places the following:

Djago, Scheldestraat 99, tel. 664 20 13, price-range B, lunch 12–4 p.m. (except Sundays), dinner 4–9 p.m., closed Saturdays

Kantjil en de Tijger, Spuistraat 291 (District 5), tel. 20 09 94, price-range A, lunch 11 a.m.–6 p.m., dinner 6–11 p.m., brasserie till 1 a.m., closed Mondays

Lonny's★, Rozengracht 48 (District 7), tel. 23 89 50, price-range B, no lunches, dinner 6–11 p.m. (in winter 5–10 p.m.), open all week
Poentjak Pas, Nassaukade 366, tel. 18 09 06, price-range A/B, no lunches, dinner 4–11 p.m., closed Mondays
Semarang★, Grote Geusplein 15, tel. 13 49 11, price-range A/B, no lunches, dinner 4–10 p.m., closed Mondays
Sukasari, Damstraat 26 (District 1), tel. 24 00 92, price range A/B, lunch 12–6 p.m., dinner 6–9 p.m., closed Sundays
Tempo Doeloe, Utrechtsestraat 75 (District 4), tel. 25 67 18, price-range B, no lunches, dinner 6–11.30 p.m., open all week

Italian (excluding pizzerias)
Da Canova★, Warmoesstraat 9 (District 1), tel. 26 67 25, price-range B, no lunches, dinner 6–10 p.m., closed Sundays and Mondays
Mirafiori, Hobbemastraat 2 (District 2), tel. 662 30 13, price-range B, lunch 12–3 p.m., dinner 5–11 p.m.
Tartufo, Singel 449 (District 4), tel. 27 71 75, price-range B, lunch 12–2.30 (except Saturdays and Sundays), dinner 6–11 p.m., open all week
La Torre di Pisa, Reguliersgracht 95 (District 4), tel. 25 05 12, price-range A/B, no lunches, dinner 5–9.30 p.m., closed Mondays
Tre Stelle, Amstelveenseweg 172, tel. 662 07 23, price-range B, no lunch, dinner 5–11 p.m., open all week

Japanese
Kaiko-Sushi, Jekerstraat 114, tel. 662 56 41, price-range B, lunch 12–2.15 (except Saturdays), dinner 6–9.45 p.m., closed Sundays
Kyo, Jan Luykenstraat 2a (District 2), tel. 71 69 16, price-range C, no lunches, dinner 6–10 p.m., closed Sundays
Umeno, Agamemnonstraat 27, tel. 76 60 89, price-range B/C, lunch 12–2 p.m. (except Saturdays and Sundays), dinner 6 p.m.–midnight, closed Wednesdays
Yamazato, Ferdinand Bolstraat 333 (District 8), tel. 78 71 11, price-range C, lunch 12–2.30 p.m., dinner 6–10 p.m., open all week
Yoichi, Weteringschans 128 (District 4), tel. 22 68 29, price-range B, no lunches, dinner 6–11 p.m., closed Wednesdays

Jewish
Betty Braasem, Rijnstraat 75, tel. 44 58 96, price-range A/B, lunch 10 a.m.–6 p.m., dinner 6–9 p.m., closed Mondays

Mexican
Pacifico, Warmoesstraat 31 (District 1), tel. 24 29 11, price-range A/B, no lunches, dinner 5.30–10.30 p.m., open all week

Rose's Cantina, Reguliersdwarsstraat 38 (District 4), tel. 25 97 97, price-range A/B, no lunches, dinner 3–11 p.m., open all week

North African

Hamilcar, Overtoom 306, tel. 83 79 81, price-range A, no lunches, dinner 5–11 p.m., closed Mondays

Marakech*, Nieuwezijds Voorburgwal 134 (District 6), tel. 23 50 03, price-range A, no lunches, dinner 5–10.30 p.m., closed Wednesdays

Sousse, Lijnbaansgracht 274 (District 4), tel. 23 10 76, price-range A/B, lunch 12–3 p.m., dinner 5 p.m.–midnight, open all week

Portuguese

Girassol, Weesperzijde 135 (District 8), tel. 92 34 71, price-range A, no lunches, dinner 6–10 p.m., closed Tuesdays

Spanish

Centra, Lange Niezel 29 (District 1) tel. 22 30 50, price range A, lunch 11 a.m.–6 p.m., dinner 6–11 p.m., open all week

Rias Altas, Westermarkt 25 (District 5), tel. 24 25 10, price-range A/B, no lunches, dinner 3–11 p.m., open all week

Surinamese

Surinamese cuisine is an amalgam of Creole, Indonesian, Hindustani, Chinese and even Dutch cooking. Throughout the city you can find mostly very simple Surinamese restaurants, especially in the 'Pijp' district, where there are a number of very good ones.

La Cherna, Utrechtsestraat 124 (District 4), tel. 27 27 82, price-range A, lunch 11.30 a.m.–6 p.m., dinner 6–10.30 p.m., closed Saturdays

Swiss and Fondue

Café Bern, Nieuwmarkt 9 (District 1), tel. 22 00 34, price-range A, no lunches, dinner 6–10.30 p.m., open all week

Thai

Dynasty, Reguliersdwarsstraat 30 (District 4), tel. 26 84 00, price-range C, no lunches, dinner 5.30–10 p.m., closed Tuesdays

De Kooning van Siam, Oudezijds Voorburgwal 42 (District 1), tel. 23 72 93, price-range B, no lunches, dinner 6–11 p.m., closed Tuesdays

Lana Thai, Warmoesstraat 10 (District 1), tel. 24 21 79, price-range B/C, no lunch, dinner 5–10.30 p.m., open all week

Tom Yam, Staalstraat 22 (District 1), tel. 22 95 33, price-range B/C, no lunches, dinner 5.30–11 p.m., open all week

Turkish

Türkiye, Nieuwezijds Voorburgwal 169, tel. 22 99 19, price-range A/B, no lunches, dinner 4 p.m.–midnight, open all week

Vegetarian

De Bast, Huidenstraat 19 (District 5), tel. 23 04 50, price-range A, lunch 11.30 a.m.−5 p.m.(except Sundays), dinner 5−8.30 p.m., open all week

The Salad Garden, Weteringschans 75 (District 4), tel. 23 40 17, price-range A, breakfast and lunch 8 a.m.−6 p.m., dinner 6−10 p.m., open all week

4 · Cafés and Night-life

Although Amsterdam is a small city by comparison with other European capitals, it offers a round-the-clock range of possibilities for refreshing the inner man or woman. During the day, for example, one can relax in a number of *design-cafés* (white cafés). After *borreltijd*, the early-evening drinks hour around seven o'clock, things slacken off in most cafés, which a number of establishments compensate for by serving cheap meals: they don't earn much from the food, but at least it keeps them nice and full. At about 11 p.m. the first cinemas and theatres start emptying and the above-mentioned design-cafés and the brown and neo-brown pubs gradually fill up. After closing time – during the week 1 a.m., Fridays and Saturdays 2 a.m. – there are two possibilities: the so-called 8–2 cafés, which on Fridays and Saturdays stay open till 3 a.m., and of course the discothèques. The last of these stay open till 4 or 5 a.m. And finally, for those who just can't get enough, there are the night pubs. These establishments, which do not officially exist, as they are not licensed to stay open so late, do not close their doors until the last customer has staggered out, and by that time the first cafés are opening up again.

The number of ways of spending a night on the town in Amsterdam has continued to increase in recent years. At the end of the 1960s the city had only one sort of café: the brown café, a substitute living room for students, mothers and workers. In the cosy interior, cured brown by the smoke, your problem was everyone's problem and the landlord was a stern but just guardian-figure. Such cafés still exist, but since the exodus of the original inhabitants of the inner city in the 1970s and the revival of the centre in the 1980s a whole range of cafés and discothèques has emerged, where preferences and trends fluctuate rapidly.

This development first got under way in the Reguliersdwarsstraat. At the end of the 1970s it was a pretty dead area, until an out-of-work psychiatrist created Oblomow. This café represented everything that the brown pub was not: there was lots of room and light, the interior consisted largely of natural stone and the turnover among the impersonal staff was as rapid as the changes in the taste of the sophisticated clientele. From then on the new design-cafés followed one another in quick succession. 'Design' has now become a buzzword, but as such is prone to inflation. Even the waste-pipes have become the subject of creative reflection, as a columnist in one of the city's dailies scoffed.

Nevertheless, for young designers especially, the white café is a way of bringing their architectural ideas to the attention of a wide public. Some café-architects have had half an eye on the grand café, as created by the architect Adolf Loos in turn-of-the-century Vienna. So that a nice parallel can be drawn between the celebrated Viennese Café Museum (also called Nihilismus) and Amsterdam's Luxembourg: both are stylish and classical.

Often the white cafés are supported by other breweries than Heineken and Amstel, two beer giants who have meanwhile merged and who until recently had a near-monopoly in Amsterdam. Despite the sometimes enormous sums with which the breweries support café proprietors, the path to a successful business is long and beset with obstacles. There are plenty of examples of prestigious cafés which were popular for a short while with a sophisticated public, until across the street a competitor opened up a place that was just a little newer, just a little more exclusive. Overnight the honeymoon is over and the precious interior is converted into a run-of-the-mill pizza joint. The reader should therefore be warned: cafés mentioned as popular in this guide may suddenly become completely 'out' or even vanish off the face of the earth.

The opposite extreme to the white café, the brown pub, can be divided into three types: the dimly lit space with rugs on the tables and silent old men thoughtfully sipping at their glasses; the lively working-class pub where native Amsterdammers set the tone and regularly launch into a rousing sing-song (not always in tune, but very atmospheric); and the neo-brown pub, which originated in the seventies. The latter category is largely inhabited by a mixed public of students, people working in the more or less creative professions and artists, successful and otherwise. Native Amsterdammers are in the minority here. The neo-brown pub has neither the standoffishness of the white café or the nosiness of the true brown pub.

Apart from the differences in format and interior, there are further differences that can be noted between the brown and white pubs. The revival of the white apron among the staff of the latter establishments, for example, which in a number of cases compensates for a lack of professional know-how. A large proportion of the present staff in neo-brown and white cafés is made up of semi-professionals, people earning a bit on the side. The carefully drawn glass of beer is the hallmark of the classic landlord in the real brown pubs, probably a species in danger of extinction.

ENTERTAINMENT CENTRES

The inner city has between 600 and 700 pubs and can be divided into five entertainment centres: Leidseplein, Jordaan, Rembrandtplein, the Reguliersdwarsstraat and the red-light district.

The **Leidseplein** (District 4) is Amsterdam's traditional entertainment centre. Alongside the hordes of tourists one can see many Amsterdammers sporting deep tans, who to judge from the way they carry themselves have annual subscriptions to a fitness club. In the pubs and discos, the predominant ethos is one of pulling and getting pulled. On and around the large terraces there are swarms of buskers, fire-eaters and other performers.

The **Jordaan** (District 7) – the area *par excellence* where the brown café flourishes – has a wealth of small, attractive pubs with a much more stable feel than their white counterparts. Here there are lively popular cafés, as well as neo-brown pubs where the new inhabitants of the city centre – students, careerists and artists – meet.

The **Rembrandtplein** (District 4) was fairly dead for a while, but was given a thorough facelift some years ago. There are now two enormous discos, pavement terraces and an obscure appendage in the form of the Thorbeckeplein, where topless bars eke out an existence. Besides the tourists it is mainly a provincial public that comes here, to be entertained in the cafés with Dutch accordion music. In the direct vicinity of the square there are a few gay pubs.

Oblomow can still be found in the **Reguliersdwarsstraat** (District 4) but has not been part of the trendy circuit for years. It is sometimes jokingly called the 'bathroom' or the 'swimming pool' on account of the generous use of tiles and natural stone in its interior. Besides a straight disco, some cafés and restaurants, there is a concentration of coffee shops, cafés and discos which are a hunting-ground for gays. The Reguliersdwarsstraat is a thoroughfare with chic pretensions, and the same can be said of a large proportion of the visitors to this entertainment centre.

The **red-light district** (District 1; also known as the 'Wallen', or Quays) is traditionally the area for those with more extravagant desires. The area still does not disappoint visitors and is quite a bit safer than it is often made out to be, as there are always lots of people in the street. There are transvestites, striptease joints, sex-shows and leather boys, but also brown cafés where the hubbub outside is muffled by the moquette table-covers.

Besides these entertainment centres there are a few other parts of the city centre where the concentration of cafés may be smaller, but where strollers can find something to their liking. For example, on the **Marte-laarsgracht** (District 6) are a number of cafés where many foreigners, especially Englishmen, gather. The watering-holes here, though, do make a rather down-at-heel impression. On one long section of the **Prinsengracht** (Districts 5 and 6), from the Leidsestraat to the Brou-wersgracht, there are lots of neo-brown pubs, not only on the canal itself but in the many little side-streets.

DRINK

The draught (lager) beer found in the cafés is by no means always the Heineken that Americans particularly tend to know. Amstel, Brand, Grolsch, Dommelsch and Oranjeboom are some of the brands available on draught. Distinguishing the difference in taste between these brands is probably within the reach only of the *real* expert. The price of draught beer fluctuates around 2 guilders 25. Near the places where tourists congregate, like the Leidseplein or the Damrak, you pay a little more.

However, most cafés no longer confine themselves, as they used to do, to Dutch lager. Belgian beers like Vieux Temps, De Koninck, Palm, Dentergems and Hoegaarden are often sold on draught. The first three kinds are somewhat darker and richer-flavoured than ordinary beer; the last two are so-called 'white beers', which have a fresh taste and are often drunk with a slice of lemon.

In addition, a great deal of Belgian bottled beer is drunk, for example: Duvel, Triple and Dubbel, all three of which are quite heavy and strong; Geuse, Liefmans and Kriek, which are all fairly sweet. In Amsterdam a small number of cafés carry beers from the small local brewery 'Het IJ': Natte, Zatte, Struis and Columbus. It would take us too far to discuss their merits in detail, but they certainly taste good.

Bottled beers are usually served in special glasses: every type of beer has its own glass, which brings out the flavour of the beer best. Duvel, for instance, should be drunk from a glass with a wide mouth, Hoegaarden from a sort of tankard and De Koninck from a schooner. Connoisseurs are very particular about the temperature at which beer is served. Duvel, for example, ought not to be drunk straight from the fridge, but should be served at between 6° and 7° centigrade.

The alcohol percentage is often considerably higher than that of ordinary draught beer, and anyone not bearing this in mind is likely to find to his astonishment that he has drunk himself under the table more quickly than he would have liked.

Café wine is not always of good quality. In eighty per cent of cases it leads to gloomy reflections the following day. Distilled drinks like *jenever*

(Dutch gin) are popular and on average cost about the same as draught lager. Young gin has many nicknames in pubs, such as *pikketanissie*, *keiltje*, *borrel* or *hassiebassie*. Old gin is known as *oude klare*. Dutch gin is also drunk with ice. Typically Dutch drinks are *schelvispekel* (a herbal schnapps tasting of cinnamon – not always available), *berenburg* (bitter) and *bessenjenever* (sweet, and drunk mostly with ice).

Below you will find a list of cafés which are worthy of mention for one reason or another. They have been divided up on the basis of the various functions that cafés can serve, that is: those that are fun during the day, those with pavement terraces, cafés one can visit if one is outside the centre, and so on. The district numbers given after the names correspond to the districts described in Chapter 13 and shown in the map at the end of the book.

The chapter concludes with the addresses and other details of the cafés listed, (some cafés crop up in more than one place in this chapter).

DAYTIME CAFÉS

During the lunch hour, cafés with a good lunch menu and pavement terrace facilities are preferable. Examples of this are *Luxembourg* (District 5), *Het Land van Walem* (District 5), *Morlang* (District 5), *Rum Runners* (District 7), *Waterloo* (District 1), *Tisfris* (District 1) and *Americain* (District 4).

Until recently Americain was one of Amsterdam's few grand cafés with real class. In the fifties writers and intellectuals used to meet each other at the reading table. For years Americain was in the doldrums – the service was proverbially slow – but not long ago it was smartened up and is worth a visit for the sake of the Art Deco interior alone.

Het Land van Walem is a white café, but by now is so venerable that the interior is slowly but surely deteriorating. It is still a popular café during the daytime, however. Its neighbour, *Morlang*, which is also white, serves a reasonable lunch too and is a little less crowded. Both cafés are good examples of white cafés with unprofessional staff: the waiting times can give the customer grey hairs. At the end of the afternoon the cafés around the Spui are the traditional resort of the working population.

Hoppe (District 5) is renowned. In fine weather the café is obscured by a screen of well-dressed people in their thirties and forties standing on the pavement outside this small pub. Across the alleyway is *De Zwart* (District 5), where you will find the same sort of people, but here you can sit down. Hoppe's left-hand neighbour is the trendier *Luxembourg* (District 5), where lots of advertising types in striped shirts try to lower their adrenaline levels after a hectic day. Luxembourg is a café where you can decently take business colleagues, in the evenings too. In the Spuistraat, on the way to the Central Station, is *De Koningshut* (District 5). This is more the meeting place for non-creative executives. Outside this area, at the end of the congenial Utrechtsestraat, *Oosterling* (District 4) is a nice place for an early-evening drink: a beautiful, typical brown café, with expert bartenders, and regulars who are a mixture of bank employees and locals.

PAVEMENT TERRACES

As the climate is not really suitable, many small cafés do not have permanent terraces, but when the sun does show its face they put their tables and chairs out on the pavement or attach them to the *Amsterdammertjes* – those small, irritating metal posts designed to prevent pavement parking. This has produced an anarchic proliferation of terraces. The required terrace licence not having been obtained, the neighbours complain about the noise in the street that goes on till all hours, and the mayor dispatches the Amsterdam police to weed out the offenders. The spectacle of a nervous café-owner whisking tables and customers inside the moment a patrol car turns into the street is seen regularly.

Besides these nice illegal terraces there are plenty of other ways of sitting outside. The greatest concentration of terraces is on the Rembrandtplein and the Leidseplein. They are not the best places to sit out: both squares are too busy and touristy.

Rum Runners (District 7) has a beautiful terrace with a view of the tower of the Westerkerk. From *Waterloo* (District 1), next to the Town Hall, you look out over the Amstel. On the Spui, *Luxembourg* (District 5) has a nice terrace, and you can also sit at *De Zwart*.

One place you are unlikely to stumble across for yourself is the idyllic terrace of the *Vondelpaviljoen* in the Vondelpark (District 4). You can get to it by entering the park from the Leidseplein and bearing right at the first opportunity. The colossal building, dating from 1878, will quickly loom up on your right, with a staircase leading up to the comfortable terrace. Below is the café of the Filmmuseum, which is housed here. On fine summer days films are shown on the terrace. Amsterdammers *do* know the way to this terrace, so that it can get very crowded.

In the Jordaan the terrace scene is particularly good on the corner of the Prinsenstraat and the Prinsengracht: *De Vergulde Gaper* (District 6) and *De Twee Prinsen* (District 6) are both here. Close by, *De Prins* (District 7) is another possibility. Some canal-side cafés, such as *Van Puffelen* (District 5) and *P'96* and *'t Smalle* (both District 7), have solved the problem of narrow pavements by mooring a boat in the canal and putting tables and chairs on it. The view of the canals from these boats is fantastic.

Then there is *De IJsbreker* (District 8), a little way out of the centre (see below), but worth a mention for its beautiful view over the Amstel and the imposing neighbourhood it is situated in.

OUTSIDE THE CENTRE

Things don't stop when you leave the centre. Here are a few staging posts for those making their way around the city on foot.

South-east

After viewing the organic architecture of the NMB bank building (p. 125), try the *Flux de Bouche*. This is a white café, a chic café-restaurant designed on post-modernist lines – a compilation of styles from all periods and cultures.

East

This is not a very fashionable area, but *East of Eden* is a pleasant oasis. It is one of those pubs whose décor is tropical-cum-colonial in inspiration. Small hot snacks are served with early evening drinks. *Eik en Linde* (District 3; see p.188 for more details) is a classic, spacious café, frequented mostly by locals, but also by art-movie buffs, who drop in for a drink after visiting the adjacent Desmet cinema.

In an imposing area of Amsterdam on the Amstel is *De IJsbreker* (District 8), which is also a centre for new music (see also p. 141). The café has a colourful history as the first port of call for seamen and bargees, at a time when Amsterdam was smaller and the IJsbreker was in the middle of open country. That history, however, is not immediately apparent from the converted modern interior of the café. There is a terrace with a pleasant view of the Amstel; a good place to lunch out of doors.

Entrepotdok

This is an up-and-coming area, especially because of the restoration of some splendid warehouses. Here one can find *'t Entredok* (District 3).

South

Witteveen (District 8) and *Bodega Keyzer* (District 2) are two classic Dutch establishments which also cater for older visitors. *Wildschut* (District 2) has a large terrace where lots of people have work meetings during the daytime. The public is very varied in age and type. In the evenings the clientele generally tends to be somewhat younger. The very large café has a small bar which is open till 2.45 a.m. during the week and till 3.45 a.m. at weekends. *Welling* (District 2) is one of the city's curiosities. It's as if someone left the door of their living room wide open: small, with comfortable armchairs, the regulars are mostly older journalists.

Old-West
Tramlijn Begeerte has a mixed public in an area which for a while, because of the presence of a large number of properties occupied by squatters, had the reputation of being turbulent and disorderly. But the new and old inhabitants have achieved an excellent *modus vivendi*, as for example in this café. Near by a vision of the Virgin Mary was recently reported.

North
After a trip across the IJ on the ferry that leaves from behind the Central Station. On the far bank is *Break Point*. Not a spectacular café, but a pleasant waterside terrace.

SPECIALIZED CAFÉS

Scattered throughout the city are various cafés that have decided to specialize, from *literary cafés* like *De Engelbewaarder* (District 1) and *Henry Miller* (District 1) – what is literary about them is not clear at first glance – to a *chess café* like *Het Hok* (District 4) – that's clear enough: everyone plays chess. And from a *ping-pong café* to *squatters' cafés* like *Koevoet* (District 5). The last-mentioned café – also a disco – has a more easy-going atmosphere than the Koevoet, where if you are wearing a sports jacket you feel as uncomfortable as an unclean spirit at a seance.

The *theatrical café* has gone along with the designer boom. The older theatrical pubs are *De Smoeshaan* (District 4), with many actors and hangers-on: *Frascati* (District 1), a beautiful Italian café where one can also eat; and *Shaffy* (District 5), which is attached to a theatre for experimental and small-scale productions and where you will also find an alternative public. A new addition is *Waterloo* (District 1), which is large and rather annoyingly chic, but has a terrace at a marvellous point on the Amstel. *De Balie* (District 4), attached to the cultural and political centre of the same name, has a varied clientele. It is one of the few pleasant places on the Leidseplein. Café *Blincker* (District 1) is high tech, with lots of metal: actors and audience come after performances in the neighbouring Frascati theatre to chat about the evening's entertainment.

Student cafés
These are found in the area of the Binnengasthuis site, where a number

of faculties are situated. One type of student is easy to recognize: the *corpsbal*, or hearty. He dresses in a lambswool pullover over a shirt, wears immaculate jeans or grey trousers, sometimes a sports jacket or even a blazer, maybe with the tie of the student club he belongs to. The female equivalent generally wears a lambswool pullover with a scarf, a (trouser-) skirt and penny loafers. Originally the members of the student 'corps' came from the well-to-do classes. In the seventies there was a dramatic decline in membership, but recently they have had to introduce waiting lists. When hearties operate in groups, they are usually vociferous and hard to miss.

Kapitein Zeppos (District 1) is first and foremost a dive for law students; their faculty is round the corner. Zeppos is a nice café in a blind alley. There is a terrace and on Sunday afternoons there are musical jam-sessions; those who feel the urge can even get up and sing. *Café Crea* (District 1) belongs to the university and its customers are the quieter political-science and sociology students. Near by – on the other side of the Rokin – is the Voetboogstraat. Here, among other places, is *De Schutter* (District 4), a large, untidy first-floor café, full of youthful and eternal students. The food is cheap. Adjacent to it are a number of pubs, from where the occasional student yell can be heard in the street.

Beer cafés

The rise of Belgian beer has enriched the city with several cafés specializing in varieties of beer. *Gollem* (District 5) has an enormous choice of Belgian beer, but is slightly less rowdy than *De Beiaard* (District 6). In both pubs they are usually prepared to provide information about the dozens of varieties of beer.

Gay bars

Although the Netherlands' oldest gay dance hall, DOK, went bust in 1989, there is a varied choice of cafés for gays, especially in the area of the Rembrandtplein and the Reguliersdwarsstraat. *April* (District 4) in the Reguliersdwarsstraat is a clean-cut pub, full of young boys with short-cropped hair. Unlike many other cafés, it is busy from early evening onwards. Next door is the newly opened *Havana* (District 4), which is not really out to make a name as a gay café, but is on the site where until recently a celebrated gay disco operated. The architect has given a lot of thought to the décor and has cause to be especially pleased with the circular bar. The customers are not as young as in April and shortly after the opening women were spotted both at and behind the bar. *Traffic* (District 4) starts somewhat later, but also stays open an hour longer than April.

On the Amstel, behind the Rembrandtplein, is the *Amstel Taveerne* (District 4), a rather noisy place where they sing along to Dutch pop songs. By comparison, the nearby *Le Shako* (District 4) is an oasis of calm. In the Amstelstraat is *Gay Life* (District 4), where one can dance, and where men hang around who are dubbed 'office queens' by homosexuals. They wear jeans, but are a little too clean and tidy.

Women have less choice. There is one real women's café which does not admit men: *Saarein* (District 7) in the Jordaan. In addition there are a few pubs frequented by many female gays, for instance *Vivelavie* (District 4) and *Vandenberg* (District 7). Several attempts to set up a women's disco have come to nothing. The COC, the association for gay interests, does organize a special women's evening every Saturday.

Hash coffee shops

There is something odd about the attitude to soft drugs in Holland. Both hash and hard drugs are officially banned by law, but in practice the sale of soft drugs is tolerated. In Amsterdam there are about eighty coffee shops selling hash. On the one hand the authorities are tolerant, on the other they impose strict rules, obviously to prevent losing control of the sale of soft drugs.

Any form of bill-posting or advertising is taboo. That is the reason why the handy cannabis leaves, by which one used to be able to recognize a hash-selling coffee shop, had to be removed from the front. Now you have only your own nose to guide you. Coffee shops with 'assorted rolls' in great big letters on the window are usually 'straight' coffee houses. Price lists for soft drugs are not officially allowed, which is why the visitor is usually offered something like a comic containing the menu of grass and hash. There is almost never a liquor licence.

The best-known sales points for soft drugs are the branches of *The Bulldog*. Begun as a single café, the Bulldog has grown into a large-scale business with three branches, one of which – on the Oudezijds Voorburgwal (District 1) – is a cocktail bar, no less. Their most important branch is on the Leidseplein, housed in a former police station!

Cocktail bars

Cocktail bars are thin on the ground. *Harry's Cocktail Bar* (District 5) mixes nice drinks, but if you hit a bad evening the customers look a little blasé. Harry mixes everything himself, which means you occasionally have a long wait.

Rum Runners (District 6) does Caribbean cocktails, matching the style in which the café is designed: a large space, with ceiling fans and exotic birds. It all has a very tropical look. They also serve meals, regularly to the accompaniment of live Latin American music. Once upon a time this was the meeting place for trendy Amsterdam, but those golden days are long past.

EVENING AND NIGHT-TIME

Neo-brown cafés

As we have seen, after the early-evening drinks hour things tend to get quiet in the cafés. Some establishments which have solved the problem by serving meals are: *Schiller* (District 4), *De Prins* (District 7), *De Reiger* (District 7), *Van Puffelen* (District 5) and *Aas van Bokalen* (District 5). The fare offered varies in price and quality from student refectory to cheap restaurant. Even if you don't feel hungry, you can rest assured that those cafés will be livelier than others at the start of the evening.

Schiller is one of the pleasant surprises on the noisy Rembrandtplein. It is a popular café – around midnight it can get chock-a-block – with a rather dilapidated but splendid original Art Deco interior. The clientele is made up of representatives from the publishing world, journalists and intellectuals.

De Reiger is a pleasant, large, neo-brown café in the heart of the Jordaan. Here too it will probably be pretty crowded in the evenings. *De Reiger*, in common with *De Prins*, *De Tuin*(both District 7), *Van Puffelen* and *De Pels* (both District 5), has a large crowd of regulars. The clientele is hard to define: the average age varies between roughly twenty-five and fifty; there are lots of students, writers, musicians, all kinds of intellectuals, and some locals. The difference between students, artists, office-workers and unemployed is completely unimportant, which is very nice. It should also be mentioned that De Prins is a popular place to have breakfast, certainly on Sundays (till 4 p.m.!). At that time only classical or light music is played and loud talking is forbidden. In the red-light district *Bern* (District 1) is popular with artistic and art-loving customers who don't come to the area for the prostitutes. They also serve food. Opposite, on the other side of the Nieuwmarkt, is *Lokaal 't Loosje*. Here the commotion outside in the street is hardly noticeable, and if the conversation flags you can study the curious painted tiles at your leisure.

Brown cafés

Nol (District 7), for farmers and people from out of town, is the prototype of the Jordaan café. You may strike lucky and have a pleasant evening among a public consisting of real Jordaaners, supplemented with a few younger residents, but the occasional tourist bus tends to pull up, which gives the conviviality a rather forced tinge. *De Twee Zwaantjes*

(District 7) is also internationally famous, but more intimate than Nol. It seems that opera singers have begun their careers here, but you can't hit the jackpot every night. *'t Smackzeyl* (District 6) is an old pub that also serves Guinness, which is a big draw for English-speakers living in the area. *Kalkhoven* (District 6) is the prototype of an average brown pub; few remarkable features, but relaxed.

De Karpershoek (District 6) belongs on the list of curiosities, claiming as it does to be the oldest pub in the city (1629). Here too at the end of the working day many wage-slaves are to be seen taking a breather. Another phenomenon is the *proeflokaal*, or stand-up pub, of which *De Drie Fleschjes* (District 6) is a perfect example. There is large wall lined with vats from which the spirits are tapped. There is no furniture apart from a counter and the doors close at 8 o'clock.

White cafés

Luxembourg (District 5) is at present the most successful representative of the white café genre. Near by is *Café Markx* (District 4) in the Reguliersdwarsstraat. It opened in the spring of 1989 and still looks very chic. At the moment jazz-combos regularly endeavour to breathe some atmosphere into the place. *Het Land van Walem* (District 5) has already been mentioned under the daytime cafés (p. 51). The last three cafés are the places the yuppies go. 'Seeing and being seen', 'trendy', 'money' and 'chic' are the key words here.

Another trendily designed but slightly less perfectly executed café is *Het Paleis* (District 5), which is located at a beautiful spot on the Singel. It used to be a haunt of the fashionable set; at present the customers are mostly male. Just outside the red-light district, in a neighbourhood which was demolished some while ago – to the accompaniment of howls of protest – during the building of the city's underground, is *Tisfris* (District 1; see p.170). It is, or was, a nice café. It has degenerated rapidly in its short life, but it is still worth while. The customers are predominantly informally dressed young inhabitants of one of Amsterdam's better designed newly built projects.

In the area of the Leidseplein is *Café Cox* (District 4), a nicely decorated café where one can eat with a trendy clientele, as applies also to the nearby theatrical café *De Balie* (District 4), which has already been mentioned under specialized cafés (p. 54).

8–2 CAFÉS

After all the above cafés have closed – during the week at 1 a.m., on Fridays and Saturdays at 2 – those with a thirst do not have to resort immediately to the discos: the 8–2 cafés still offer sanctuary. In the Spui area you can go to *De Doffer* (District 5) or *Café Bruin* (District 4), in the Jordaan to *De Koophandel* (District 7), for many visitors the ante-room of the Mazzo disco (see p. 60). On the Prinsengracht, at the edge of the Jordaan, is *P'96* (District 7): the atmosphere is not always particularly cheerful, but the café is open very late. Nearby, in a side-street off the Prinsengracht, is *'t Kalfje* (District 6), of which the same can be said: the atmosphere is sometimes pretty depressing, but its doors stay open late.

From the Leidseplein *Weber*, *Onni's Verjaardag* and *De Gieter* (all three District 4) are possibilities. Near the Rembrandtplein you will find *De Favoriet* (District 4) and in the vicinity of the Dam *De Pieter* (District 1), off the Nes.

DISCOTHÈQUES

In Amsterdam people never talk of night-clubs. Amsterdam discothèques are not characterized by exclusivity or extravagance. Drinks are generally one guilder more than in the pub. It's best not to arrive before midnight, because there will be no one there apart from the staff.

A large number of discothèques have a formal system of membership. A 'members only' sign, however, need not mean that you can't get in; you can usually join for the evening. Occasionally it may happen that they won't let you in. They justify this with the 'members only' argument, but it's mostly because you're wearing the wrong kind of shoes, because it's too full inside or because the doorman is in a bad mood. If you're really keen to get in you can always try an hour later. Admission prices are between two and ten guilders.

The Leidseplein and its immediate surroundings is the area best served with discos. Most of them are interchangeable as regards atmosphere: hit-parade music and macho behaviour. *De Bios* (District 4) – a former cinema – is the biggest. The visitors make a flashy impression. There is a metal detector at the entrance. The Crown Prince of Holland is supposed to have passed through incognito – not necessarily a recommendation – but his armed bodyguard got caught out by the detector. Fairly expensive drinks, very plush.

In and around the Reguliersdwarsstraat there is a different kind of choice on offer. Still new and popular at the moment is *Exit* (District 4), a gay disco. Many of the people there have spent the first part of the evening in April. In the same street is *36 Op de schaal van Richter* (District 4). The interior appropriately suggests an earthquake. It was once exclusive, but the fall-off in interest obliged the management to admit non-celebrities. Expensive shirts, expensive dresses, but a good dance-floor and enough opportunity to talk uninterrupted out of earshot of the decibels.

Close to the Reguliersdwarsstraat, on the Singel, is the *Odeon* (District 5), which is both a pub and a disco. The Odeon is not recommended during the week, but on Fridays and Saturdays the upstairs floor – an old theatre – is open. The clientele is made up of young people in work and students; not very exciting, but not a bad atmosphere and at weekends – with music from the period 1955–75 – it gets very crowded.

The *Roxy* (District 4) belongs to quite a different circuit. When the disco – a scarcely modified cinema – opened in 1987, it appealed to a very sophisticated public with remarkably little brand loyalty. The expectation was consequently that it would be a flash in the pan. It has proved a stayer; it is still one of the most influential dance venues. The Roxy introduced Acid and House into Holland. Although that rage has since subsided, one can hear new house variants, especially on Fridays and Saturdays. Each evening, from Wednesday to Friday, has its own music and atmosphere: Friday is the regular underground dance evening, on Sundays the music and gear are more reminiscent of a night-club. Every month the Roxy's interior is adapted to a new theme, so that on one occasion visitors may imagine themselves in an Arabian Nights story and on the next in a science-fiction film. There are regular obscure but entertaining live acts.

Before the advent of Roxy, *Mazzo* (District 7) was the meeting place for the alternative scene. The disco was originally accessible only to those who were themselves in the audio-visual field, but now they let you in even if you haven't played a bit-part in a Dutch film. Despite the rise of the Roxy, Mazzo has remained reasonably true to itself. The disco is one of the centres of progressive and electronic dance music and now and then they feature live music. A large part of the lighting comes from slide projections on the walls and there are lots of black-clad dancers.

Escape (District 4), on the Rembrandtplein – also housed in a former cinema – is the biggest dance venue in town, but not everyone will feel at home among the sometimes very young public. It does have the best lighting and sound system of any disco. Lots of commercial and Top 40 dance music, though.

Be-bop (District 4), a little further along the Amstelstraat, is also large and youth-orientated and housed in premises where Japanese and Chinese gentlemen used to go through their martial arts paces on the silver screen.

The *Okshoofd* (District 6) is off the beaten track, but that fits in quite nicely with their image, because they don't take much notice of rapidly changing trends. It is probably the city's oldest disco. Lots of vintage disco music, but tastefully selected. Recommended for those who find the thump of Acid excruciatingly boring and don't mind ageing students.

More representatives of the studying classes can be found at *Dansen bij Jansen* (District 4). Set up by students, it isn't particularly progressive in its choice of music, but is certainly full to overflowing. The admissions policy is hard to fathom. They sometimes let in only students with a valid student card, at other times everyone is welcome, particularly women.

In the Warmoesstraat, diagonally opposite the Argos leather bar, is the *C'Ring* (District 1), or *Cockring*: a disco bearing the sign 'only for men'. They have a reputation for playing very individual and danceable music. Jam-packed.

Finally, for adventurous dance freaks, there are the warehouse parties that have been imported from London, great underground dance-ins that go on till the early hours of the morning. Announced only by leaflet, they are held at irregular times in constantly changing locations.

NIGHT PUBS

The discos close at around 4 or 5 in the morning. To hear the dawn chorus you have to go to a night pub. Officially there are no public houses apart from the discos licensed to stay open late. Nevertheless there are a few where – sometimes after knocking on the closed door – you will be let in. The problem is that after a while the police get wise to them and take the necessary steps. The atmosphere is a little obscure, which is not surprising at that hour. Pubs where you can try to drink the night away are: *Happy View* (District 4), *Twiggy's* (District 7) and *Tabasco* (District 7). The clientele is undefinable, because it is so mixed.

Another alternative are the morning pubs that open at around 6 a.m. for taxi-drivers and truckers. In these one can sometimes get an amusing amalgam of late revellers and customers who are just waking up.

ADDRESSES OF RECOMMENDED CAFÉS AND BARS

Aas van Bokalen, Keizersgracht 335 (District 5), tel. 23 09 17
Americain, Leidseplein 28 (District 4), tel. 23 48 13
Amstel Taveerne, Amstel 54 (District 4), tel. 23 42 54
April, Reguliersdwarsstraat 37 (District 4), tel. 25 95 72

De Balie, Kleine Gartmanplantsoen 10 (District 4), tel. 24 38 21

It, Amstelstraat 24 (District 4), tel. 25 01 11

De Beiaard, Herengracht 90 (District 6), tel. 25 04 22

Bern, Nieuwmarkt 9 (District 1), tel. 22 00 34

De Bios, Leidseplein 12 (District 4), tel. 27 65 44

Blincker, St Barberenstraat 7–9 (District 1), tel. 27 19 38

Bodega Keyzer, Van Baerlestraat 96 (District 2), tel. 662 07 78

Break Point, Spreeuwenpark 52, tel. 32 32 88

Bruin, Voetboogstraat 4 (District 4), tel. 26 23 34

The Bulldog, Oudezijds Voorburgwal 132 (District 1), tel. 27 02 95

Café Cox, Marnixstraat 427 (District 4), tel. 20 72 22

Crea Café, Grimburgwal 10 (District 1), tel. 525 45 49

C'Ring (Cockring) Warmoesstraat 96 (District1), tel. 23 96 04

Dansen bij Jansen, Handboogstraat 11 (District 4), tel. 22 88 22

De Doffer, Runstraat 12 (District 5), tel. 22 66 86

De Drie Fleschjes, Gravenstraat 18 (District 6), tel. 24 84 43

East of Eden, Linnaeusstraat 11a, tel. 665 07 43

Eik en Linde, Plantage Middenlaan 22 (District 3), tel. 22 57 16

De Engelbewaarder, Kloveniersburgwal 59 (District 1), tel. 25 37 72

't Entredok, Entrepotdok 64 (District 3), tel. 23 23 56

Escape, Rembrandtplein 11–15 (District 4), tel. 22 35 45

Exit, Reguliersdwarsstraat 42 (District 4), tel. 25 87 88

De Favoriet, Reguliersdwarsstraat 87 (District 4), tel. 26 61 84

Flux de Bouche, Bijlmerplein 522, tel. 97 37 60

Frascati, Nes 59 (District 1), tel. 24 13 24

Gay Life, Amstelstraat 32 (District 4), tel. 22 94 18

De Gieter, Korte Leidsedwarsstraat 174 (District 4), tel. 25 27 31

Gollem, Raamsteeg 4 (District 5), tel. 26 66 45

Happy View, Lange Leidsedwarsstraat 66 (District 4), tel. 27 72 58

Harry's Cocktail Bar, Spuistraat 285 (District 5), tel. 24 43 84

Havana, Reguliersdwarsstraat 17–19 (District 4), tel. 20 67 88

Het Hok, Lange Leidsedwarsstraat 134 (District 4), tel. 24 31 33

Hoppe, Spui 18–20 (District 5), tel. 23 78 49

't Kalfje, Prinsenstraat 5 (District 6), tel. 26 33 70

Kalkhoven, Prinsengracht 283 (District 6), tel. 24 86 49

Kapitein Zeppos, Gebed Zonder End 5 (District 1), tel. 24 20 57

De Karpershoek, Martelaarsgracht 2 (District 6), tel. 24 78 86

De Koningshut, Spuistraat 269 (District 5), tel. 26 42 76

De Koophandel, Bloemgracht 49 (District 7), tel. 29 97 41

Het Land van Walem, Keizersgracht 449 (District 5), tel. 25 35 44

Lokaal 't Loosje, Nieuwmarkt 32 (District 1), tel. 20 43 89

Luxembourg, Spui 22 (District 5), tel. 20 62 64

Markx, Reguliersdwarsstraat 12 (District 4) tel. 22 46 75
Mazzo, Rozengracht 114 (District 7), tel. 26 75 00
Miller, Binnen Bantammerstraat 27 (District 1), tel. 27 88 04
Morlang, Keizersgracht 451 (District 5), tel. 25 26 81
Nol, Westerstraat 109 (District 7), tel. 24 53 80
Oblomow, Reguliersdwarsstraat 40 (District 4), tel. 24 10 74
Odeon, Singel 460 (District 5), tel. 24 97 11
't Okshoofd, Herengracht 114 (District 6), tel. 24 18 76
Onni's Verjaardag, Marnixstraat 381 (District 4), tel. 25 44 82
Oosterling, Utrechtsestraat 140 (District 4), tel. 23 41 40
Het Paleis, Paleisstraat 16 (District 5), tel. 26 06 00
De Pels, Huidenstraat 25 (District 5), tel. 22 90 37
De Pieter, St Pieterspoortsteeg 29 (District 1), tel. 23 60 07
P'96, Prinsengracht 96 (District 7), tel. 22 18 64
De Prins, Prinsengracht 124 (District 7), tel. 24 93 82
Van Puffelen, Prinsengracht 377 (District 5), tel. 24 62 77
De Reiger, Nieuwe Leliestraat 34 (District 7), tel. 24 76 26
Richter, 36 op de schaal van, Reguliersdwarsstraat 36 (District 4), tel. 26 15 73
Roxy, Singel 465 (District 4), tel. 20 03 54
Rum Runners, Prinsengracht 277 (District 6), tel. 27 40 79
Saarein, Elandsstraat 119 (District 7), tel. 23 49 01
Schiller, Rembrandtplein 26 (District 4), tel. 24 98 46
De Schutter, Voetboogstraat 13–15 (District 5), tel. 22 46 08
Shaffy, Keizersgracht 324 (District 5), tel. 26 23 21
Le Shako, 's Gravelandseveer 2 (District 4), tel. 24 02 09
't Smackzeyl, Brouwersgracht 101 (District 6), tel. 22 65 20
't Smalle, Egelantiersgracht 12 (District 7), tel. 23 96 17
De Smoeshaan, Leidsekade 90 (District 4), tel. 25 03 68
Tisfris, St Antoniesbreestraat 142 (District 1), tel. 22 04 72
Traffic, Reguliersdwarsstraat 11 (District 4), tel. 23 32 98
Tramlijn Begeerte, Van Limburg Stirumplein 4, tel. 86 50 27
De Tuin, Tweede Tuindwarsstraat 13 (District 7), tel. 24 45 59
De Twee Prinsen, Prinsenstraat 27 (District 6), tel. 24 97 22
De Twee Zwaantjes, Prinsengracht 114 (District 7), tel. 25 27 29
Twiggy's, Marnixstraat 166 (District 7), tel. 24 60 87
Vandenberg, Lindengracht 95 (District 7), tel. 22 27 16
De Vergulde Gaper, Prinsenstraat 30 (District 6), tel. 24 89 75
Vivelavie, Amstelstraat 7 (District 4), tel. 24 01 14
Vondelpaviljoen, Vondelpark (District 2)
Waterloo, Zwanenburgwal 15 (District 1), tel. 20 90 39
Weber, Marnixstraat 397 (District 4), tel. 22 99 10

Welling, Johannes Verhulststraat 2 (District 2), tel. 662 01 55
Wildschut, Roelof Hartplein 1 (District 2), tel. 73 86 22
Witteveen, Ceintuurbaan 256–258 (District 8), tel. 662 43 68
De IJsbreker, Weesperzijde 23 (District 8), tel. 668 18 05
De Zwart, Spuistraat 334 (District 5), tel. 24 65 11

5 · Shopping

Shopping in Amsterdam can provide an embarrassment of riches. This may not be apparent at first glance, but as this guide will show you, there are a multitude of possibilities that can make your visit to the city an experience quite out of the ordinary.

Amsterdam has the reputation of being the commercial, mercantile heart and leader of the country, a place it continues to hold despite fierce competition from other centres, notably Rotterdam, Utrecht, and recently Maastricht in the south and Groningen in the north. Like these cities, Amsterdam has a character of its own, so that on the surface what seems Dutch is really Amsterdam. Look beyond the tourist shops featuring Delft china, Dutch cheese and chocolates and Bols liqueurs. Although these are all certifiably Dutch, you don't have to make a visit to the capital to buy them. What is unique to the city is the cluster of shops around a focal point or street, each with its own ambience. Add to this an abundance of ateliers, design studios, antique shops, antiquarian bookshops and international brand names and you have what many have termed a cosmopolitan centre in a village. You begin to understand why Amsterdam is a Mecca for the country's consumers.

Before you start, a couple of pointers and caveats:

Shopping hours

The subject of much heated debate, hours continue none the less to be rigidly fixed as far as total hour limits, opening times and especially closing times are concerned. On Monday mornings you will find most shops shut, with the opening times varying from 12.30 p.m. to 1 p.m. Opening time on other days of the week is usually 9 a.m.; closing time on weekdays is 6 p.m. Late-night shopping is till 9 p.m. on Thursdays. On Saturdays shops close at 5 p.m. And nothing is open on Sundays. In the specific shopping districts as outlined below and which differ from the centre in feel, emphasis and history, there exists a certain latitude in the opening hours, based more or less on the whim and experience of the shopkeepers and prevailing custom, which in short means that these hours will most likely be later in the morning than in the more conventional shops – anything from 10 a.m. to 11 a.m. On Thursday evenings and Saturdays the main streets and shops are full of not only Amsterdammers but also suburbanites doing their weekly purchases.

Customer service

Most sales people can speak English, but don't be surprised if they are not as fluent as the proverbial Dutch language facility would lead you to believe. Therefore, it is best to keep queries to a simple level and unless you are dealing with experts in a given field, for instance antiques, diamonds or pewterware, avoid getting involved in convoluted conversations. Everyone understands money transactions. What is particularly nice about the Dutch is that they are willing to explain the monetary system to you and give you the correct change, so that you will not have the uneasy feeling that you are not being dealt with honestly or being taken advantage of because you are a foreigner. Service has become friendlier and more efficient in recent years, with more openness and willingness to please the customer than in the past, when so often it seemed that service was closer to indifference than to mere nonchalance. The change is rooted in economic forces, all too evident worldwide, job scarcity and competition. Despite these factors, salesmanship remains steadfastly unaggressive. And a remarkable number of the workforce in this sector are young. You may also come across another phenomenon when dealing with the service personnel: the Dutch pride themselves on being good bargain hunters, so don't be surprised if they sell you something with the comment that it is expensive or they send you to what may appear to you a competitor for an out-of-stock item. It is a natural reaction and not one tempered by greed.

Transport

It is advisable to take the tram to reach the more outlying areas described in this section (see pp. 265–7). Otherwise it is best to walk. Walking in itself requires a certain expertise, not the least dodging a few obstacles: the dog excrement, the parking pillars quaintly called *Amsterdammertjes*, the unevenness of the road surface and the narrowness of the pavements. Another nuisance is contending with the myriad forms of conveyances: trams, buses, motorists and above all cyclists. Once alerted, though, walking is definitely the transport to choose. This guide is laid out with this in mind.

THE SHOPPING DISTRICTS

The centre

This is usually the first stop for the tourist. With the Central Station at one end, the Dam in the middle and the Rijksmuseum roughly at the other end, it forms a north-to-south axis to the east-west trajectory of the Jordaan and the Waterlooplein. The **Damrak** (District 1), which is the main thoroughfare from the Central Station to the Dam Square, is paralleled by the **Nieuwendijk**, a pedestrian street. Next to the Warmoesstraat, the oldest part of the city, it is also the one offering the more tourist-orientated shops, with just a few exceptions. The canal boat trips, the curio shops and the less expensive shops catering for the young jostle one another. The atmosphere is downmarket and the area is usually crowded. The Hema, originally Holland's equivalent to the five-and-dime and now greater in scope, has one of its outlets here, several of which are dotted throughout the city. It has surprisingly functional children's clothes and well-designed household wares as well as reasonably priced wines. This area is also the hub of what most tourists fear: pickpockets and drug addicts. A bit of caution and common sense, however, are all that is needed. The fact that Berlage's old Stock Exchange, the Oude Kerk and the Nieuwe Kerk rub shoulders with the department stores and the red-light district speaks not only for the well-known Dutch sense of tolerance of live-and-let-live but also, it must be said, for their business acumen. So whatever you may have heard about crime on the streets of Amsterdam back home, be assured that it is perfectly safe to walk around here. The Dutch would not tolerate such significant danger to their livelihood to go unchecked.

In and around the **Dam Square** are located C&A, Peek & Cloppenburg and a major department store, De Bijenkorf. The first two offer good merchandise in the middle price range with quality and styles to suit. De Bijenkorf, which is the city's oldest department store, offers a more expensive and varied range of goods from sports articles to kitchen ware, from socks to ties, from Oriental rugs to books. The total shopping experience. Its annual and holiday sales are packed with shoppers, and on Wednesday afternoons, when the schoolchildren are free, the toy department is only for the intrepid. It is an Amsterdam institution.

The continuation of the Damrak is called the **Rokin** (District 1). Here are located upmarket boutiques such as Agnès B., the French designer; Puck and Hans, forerunners with their own fashion collection and importers of foreign designer clothes; and Jan Jansen, an important and fanciful Dutch shoemaker. Hajenius, the tobacconist, a temple of old-world charm with a serious approach to what has now become an almost taboo subject, is worth a visit even though you may have succeeded in breaking the smoking habit. On this street, which with its wide pavement is one of the easier promenades, are also to be found several fine art dealers, the auction house Sotheby's and the jeweller Bonebakker & Zn. The Maison de Bonneterie, with its interior well echoing turn of the century architecture, began as a fine ladies' clothing store and can be entered from this direction as well as from the parallel Kalverstraat. Now for both men and women, it has retained its reputation for quality goods. Ladies meet for lunch and tea and the mood is genteel.

The **Kalverstraat**, where the cattle used to be driven through to market, is *the* pedestrian shopping street of Amsterdam. From Dam Square to the Flower Market on the Singel, it is one continuous series of shops. It is there that all Amsterdam and sometimes it seems all Holland shop for articles ranging from posters to clothes to toys to cosmetics to fountain pens to shoes. The list is endless. The atmosphere is bustling and hectic and touched with not a little bit of mercantilism. Shops go in and out of business; the latest styles are followed to the letter; all incomes and all ages are catered for. It is the closest you will come across to a souk. On the side-streets such as the **St Luciënsteeg** (a good selection of designer boutiques), the **Heiligeweg** (leading to the Leidsestraat and offering a good mix of shops: clothes, rugs, table china and even hats) and the **Spui** (dividing the Kalverstraat in two and with a real jumble: old books, the Esprit fashion store, Hampe for musical instruments and the Athenaeum, a central literary venue for English-language books and newsprint) the activity is lower-keyed. At the **Flower Market** and the **Munt** are the large department store Vroom & Dreesman (in competition with De Bijenkorf) and of course the barges selling many varieties of flowers, bulbs and plants, many of which can be packed and sent abroad (with an eye to any Customs requirements). In the vicinity is another Hema outlet.

The Singel, as this canal is called, leads on to the **Leidsestraat** (District 4), another pedestrian shopping street where the only vehicles allowed are the Nos. 1 and 2 trams and bicycles. Before the boom years of the sixties, this was considered the fashionable venue in Amsterdam. All the classic shops were here and the area had a certain cachet. This is no longer true, but an occasional survivor stands out amidst the plethora of small boutiques and fast-food outlets. An example is Metz & Co., an expensive store featuring top design in interior decoration, Liberty fabrics, accessories and the like. Also in marked contrast to the hurly-burly of the street are Shoebaloo and Scheltema Holkema Vermeulen, the former a shoe store, the latter a large bookshop. Both are located on the **Koningsplein**, which then leads on to the Spui, the scene of social protest during the sixties and seventies. Walking further on it becomes the Nieuwezijds Voorburgwal (District 5); a way to reach the Dam by tram or foot.

The Oude Hoogstraat

From the Dam, take the Damstraat (District 1). It offers little that is of true interest and it is here that the mingling of unsavoury types might be a drawback. However, that impasse is relatively short and once the second canal is bridged you will be on the Oude Hoogstraat. On the corner is Capsicum, Amsterdam's premier cotton, silk and exotic fabric shop. Not cheap but worth a visit. Also worth a look is the antiquarian print and bookshop Kok situated across the street, an establishment of many years' standing. Further on the street becomes the Nieuwe Hoogstraat. An area recently revitalized by the modernization of the neighbourhood in the wake of the upheaval caused by the building of the metro system, it boasts a variety of boutiques. On the corner, across from the Head Shop, whose wares are on open display, is an excellent secondhand clothing shop, Puck; further on are designer ateliers, such as Colombine, whose fashion visions are original. Both the Oude Hoogstraat and the Nieuwe Hoogstraat are representative of small businesses, the majority under young management, with a sense of community focused on the activity of the street and resolved to promote their collective and individual enterprises. You will see shopowners going in and out of each other's shops and the welcome overall is friendly. Surrounded on the one hand by the Chinese quarter and on the other by the Rembrandt House and further on the Waterlooplein and the City Hall/Opera House complex (the so-called Stopera), the area is fast becoming a new shopping venue, with more shops along the St Antoniesbreestraat echoing the new entrepreneurial style. The prices are moderate and the clientele on the young side.

The Utrechtsestraat
Another former neighbourhood street now becoming more interesting to the visitor is this street beginning at the Rembrandtplein and ending at the Frederiksplein (District 4). Reached easily by No. 4 tram or preferably by walking from the Flower Market towards the river Amstel or from the Waterlooplein to the Rembrandtplein, it is a congested street but well worth a visit for its bookshops, especially De Verbeelding, specializing in art books, often at discounted prices, and A la Carte, where maps and travel take pride of place. In addition, Concerto, a new and used record shop; McPherson's, an eye-appealing shoe shop reflecting Amsterdam's new post-modern display concepts; Bobb's, the vintage watch dealer; and the household stores Ditjes en Datjes and La Cucina among others, all form part of an upwardly mobile district with a cleaned-up image, the result of a conscious effort to change what was once considered a borderline area with a shady night-life into an economic success story.

The P. C. Hooftstraat and Van Baerlestraat/Museumplein
Not far from the Leidseplein is perhaps the most chic and most expen-

sive street in Amsterdam, the P.C. Hooftstraat (District 2). Formerly of minor commercial importance, it has become a quality street. International designers are represented in shops like Reflections, the first to import Japanese and Italian trend-setters to the Netherlands. The store has another less expensive annex further down the street towards the Van Baerlestraat. If you are looking for quality and money is no object, this is the address. When the sale season is on, traditionally in January and July, the markdowns make for good bargain hunting. The street is rarely empty and Dutch is not the only language overheard; quite the contrary. The Van Baerlestraat, at right-angles to the P.C. Hooftstraat, continues on south-east towards the Museumplein and the Concertgebouw. Catering for the predominantly well-to-do who live in the neighbourhood and the monied tourist, it is an area of successful, business-wise merchants. The Society Shop, the Hobbit and the chain store Pauw all have separate stores for men, women and children carrying all the known international brand names. An optical shop, Oogappeloptiek, a top porcelain shop, Folke & Meltzer and an excellent sheet music store Broekmans & Van Poppel, its proximity to the Concertgebouw no accident, and further, several blocks down, Martyrium, books on remainder, are a few exceptions to the fashion world.

The Beethovenstraat

An exclusive neighbourhood, this short street which veers off from the J.M. Coenenstraat towards the southern part of the city is a microcosm of the upper range of the shops in the centre of the city. Maison de Bonneterie, for example, has a branch here, and should your hotel be in the vicinity many of your needs can be met by a stroll on its pavements.

Shopping in the centre will be familiar to the English and American tourists as goods will be of a recognizable style and price range. What characterizes all of the above shopping districts is variety and an abundance of goods. There is basically little lacking in Amsterdam and these generalized merchant streets make a conscious effort to meet consumer demand in as broad a spectrum as possible.

OF BUYING INTEREST

Diversity is the key word when shopping in Amsterdam. Real bargains can also be had and this is not entirely dependent on one's ability to haggle, an art that does come in handy in the markets. For the outer man or woman, shoes tend to be less expensive than in many countries. Because fashion is copied in many different fabrics, it is also possible to look chic without straining the purse. And Amsterdam follows fashion trends closely. Every tourist is acquainted with Amsterdam's vaunted **diamond industry**. Real tax breaks, certificates of guarantee, high quality, craftmanship and a professional, sober and above all honest reputation have made this a true buy even though rumour has it that perhaps Antwerp may be cheaper. The Amsterdam Diamond Centre is located on the Rokin (District 1), as is Bonebakker, mentioned before and an institution since the late eighteenth century. Most diamond-cutters, such as A. van Moppes & Zn. near the Albert Cuyp market (District 8), offer guided tours for individuals and groups and these are advertised throughout the city, thus making this industry most accessible for the tourist.

Old silver, pewter, antique glass and Chinese porcelain, old prints, books and maps testify to the city's mercantile might and the monopolies it held in its Golden Age. The Dutch lavished their wealth on their homes during this period and the legacy these burghers left is still to be found in an impressive number and variety of antiques. These are mostly to be seen on the Spiegelgracht (District 4) and its continuation, the Nieuwe Spiegelstraat. Running directly from the Rijksmuseum, as a sort of natural appendage to the art inside the museum, the art dealers made this *the* 'new' venue for **antiques** in the city, with the Rokin remaining the older established street. Don't let its size fool you; some of the most important pieces of silver, china and glass are to be found in what was before the museum was built an incredibly poor quarter of the city. As befitting the business conducted, the atmosphere is serious and the street is a quiet oasis.

Antiquarian bookshops with old prints, maps and first editions are sprinkled throughout the centre of the city and do not enjoy one specific concentration. Perhaps this is part of their charm, for locating them is just as much a joy for the connoisseur as the discovery of a real find. The Oudemanhuispoort (District 1), in the middle of the oldest building of the University of Amsterdam, is one of the traditional locations for old print and bookstalls. Not always well marked on street maps, it can best be reached by following the Kloveniersburgwal either from the Oude Hoogstraat end from which you turn right or from the Nieuwe Doelenstraat, a street originating at the Munt, and from which you turn left. This is indeed a very quiet corner in which to browse.

Should you have the impression that Amsterdam is steeped in the past and that good buys are only to be had from antiques, it must be said that much exciting activity is taking place in the realm of modern **jewellery design**. Sometimes startling and audacious but nevertheless unique are the works by Christopher Clarke, on the Molsteeg (District 6), an alley next to the main Post Office as you look in the direction of the Central

Station. Another name in this field is Hans Appenzeller on the Grimburgwal (District 1), the narrow street that begins at the Rokin at the equestrian statue of Queen Wilhelmina and continues away from the Kalverstraat. Neither is inexpensive, but the originality of thought is in itself worth the expense.

Markets

Worthy of a section to themselves, this is where the lively and astute sense of buying and selling characteristic of the Dutch and especially of the Amsterdammer is on view. The **Waterlooplein** (District 1), the famous flea market, has had a history of ups and downs and over the last few years was shunted aside to a nearby location while the City Hall/Opera House complex was being built. Now happily back in its original location, it is exhibiting a renewed vigour and locals have stopped disparaging the decline of the market, which means that there are bargains to be had. Easily reached by tram and metro, its stalls house anything that can be bought or sold, old or new.

Another market, but one that has become more expensive if the Amsterdam word of mouth is to be believed, is the **Noordermarkt** (District 7), perhaps the only thing open on Monday morning. Located in the Jordaan, a historic neighbourhood composed of an intricate web of streets crossing a series of canals, the best way to reach it is to walk, heading directly for the Noorderkerk, slightly to the west of the Central Station. Not often visited by tourists, it is, despite criticism, very typical and an occasion to get an insider's feel of the city. On Saturday morning another special market, a **bird market,** takes place in the same location. An open-air market is held every Sunday from noon on at the **Thorbeckeplein** (District 4), off the Rembrandtplein. The emphasis is on portrait painting, ceramics, watercolours, pottery and similar genre art. The exhibitions have their equivalent in every country and seem by unspoken consent to be relegated to Sundays.

For **stamp** and **coin** collectors, on Wednesdays and Saturday afternoons, the **Nieuwezijds Voorburgwal** (District 5) at its broadest point, not quite a square, but close, and, in the direction away from the main Post Office, is the meeting place. At first glance it seems strange to see men and boys – for these seem to be the chief collectors and dealers – stand around casually chatting. However, the quiet animation that informs the gathering gives an intriguing importance to the goings on. If you are interested, your welcome is assured in what for the uninitiated may incorrectly seem a closed club.

The **Rommelmarkt** on the Looiersgracht (District 7), near the main Police Bureau on the Marnixstraat and serviced by a number of transport lines, is a large expanse disguised as an enclosed market specializing in antiques, curiosities and memorabilia, with an occasional art gallery in between. Not strictly speaking a market, it is a place where dealers can set up stalls and sell a variety of wares.

Neighbourhood markets are located throughout the city and though you may not necessarily find a unique item and may mistakenly feel they concentrate only on foodstuffs, they are the site of local colour and viable trade for Amsterdammers. One of the most remarkable changes that has occurred over the years is to be seen in the food on sale, especially the vegetables and fish. For years the Dutch stayed fairly traditional in their tastes. With the immigration of large numbers of guest workers from the Mediterranean basin and the travels in the seventies by young and old alike now enjoying more dispensable income, the market for exotic and strange items grew. The canny Dutch business sense was quick to pick up on a new market, so aside from the new comestibles, there has also sprung up an accompanying market of fabrics, perfumes and jewellery. The **Albert Cuyp Market** (District 8) is the largest and most demonstrative of these new influences. Saturdays tend to be one of those days when it is wall-to-wall people, most taking a leisurely walk through the long street that stretches from the Ferdinand Bolstraat to the Van Woustraat. Shoppers stop to chat; stallers shout their wares. Open generally on a daily basis, there are a few stalls that only function on Saturdays, but these are the more traditional ones and are of minimal interest to the tourist, except perhaps for a glimpse into the life of the city's inhabitants.

Auctions

Dutch auctions have a flair and flavour all of their own. Informal in nature, with much chatting, laughing and badinage interspersed with many cups of coffee, you could be forgiven if you felt transported to the age of Frans Hals, when this was a daily occurrence. For the non-Dutch speaking tourist, the interest is principally in the ambience, though the good-naturedness of the proceedings would not preclude your participation. De Zwaan on the Keizersgracht could be a start. For the international auction-goer, however, two giants are located in Amsterdam, **Sotheby's** and **Christie's**. The best way to find out what is happening is to ring up. Open from 9 a.m. to 5 p.m. daily for evaluations and information, their auction dates vary, as do the viewing days. Usually, two or four days in advance are given over to viewing, during which you can make contact with the personnel should you want to place a bid. Sotheby's Amsterdam, Rokin 102 (District 1), tel. (020) 27 56 56 and Christie's Amsterdam, C. Schuytstraat 57 (District 2), tel. (020) 64 20 11.

PARTICULAR PURCHASES

A random look around Amsterdam and outside the conventional venues begins to give you the idea that shops are organized according to an almost medieval concept but one transported to the twentieth century. Shops that sell exclusively one type of goods tend to cluster together; those carrying a specific narrow range of wares conform to a concept or market. Thus you can have a shop that sells only toothbrushes and everything that has to do with dental hygiene, something unheard of in say the USA. The Witte Tandenwinkel, on the Runstraat (District 5), is a case in point; everything, including free advice, is under one roof.

There are shops that specialize in plants and flowers, which on the face of it doesn't sound so remarkable. But what is remarkable is the intensity and depth of the merchants' knowledge. Gerda, on the same street, has a clear motivation and attitude which can be seen in the authorative way the flora is presented. Ivy, on the Leidseplein (District 4), is another. Although your hotel room may not be the place to put a full-grown ficus, the flowers on sale at these two addresses will make you want to take a vaseful of your favourite blooms home with you.

Comic strips may have been something you were denied as a young child or you may have an enviable collection of your own. On the Kerkstraat, off the Leidsestraat (District 4), Lambiek is a paradise for the aficionado.

On the Wolvenstraat (District 5), the Knopenwinkel sells nothing but buttons; across the street is Kerkhof, the braid, lace, and trimming store. It is not only amazing that these shops still exist but that they make a living, and a good one, in the city.

Books and toys for children are also accounted for because the Dutch dote on their children and have a special concern for them. On the Bloemdwarsstraat (District 7), another Jordaan street, and on the Nieuwezijds Voorburgwal, in the Kinderboekwinkel, books in English can be purchased for all age groups, as they can in the American Discount Book Center, and the recently opened W.H. Smith bookshop, both on the busy Kalverstraat. As far as toys are concerned one of the oldest firms, Merkelbach in the Bilderdijkstraat, Amsterdam-West (no district number), has an assortment to please adults as well as children.

A flat landscape, a windswept land and, naturally, you will come across a kite shop or two. There are three in Amsterdam, one on the Nieuwe Hoogstraat (District 1), the second on the Gasthuismolensteeg (District 5), a small street whose name changes to the Hartenstraat, which then becomes the Reestraat, and the third in the Tuindwarsstraat, in the Jordaan (District 7). Light to pack, they can be bought as decorative and attractive gifts and don't necessarily need to be flown to be enjoyed. The Dutch are tea drinkers, a tradition that dates from the seventeenth century when the fledgling nation's travellers and colonizers brought it from the Orient. Coffee shoon followed. Geels & Co. on the Warmoesstraat (District 1), parallel to the Damrak and close to the Oude Kerk, is worth a visit for the smell of coffee alone. A tea and coffee specialist, Keijzer, is to be found on the Prinsengracht near the Westerkerk (District 7) and across from the Anne Frank House. For the knitter, the Afstap, on the Oude Leliestraat (District 6), is a useful address.

Both A. Coppenhagen on the Bloemgracht (District 7) in the Jordaan and Kralerlei on the Overtoom carry an amazing collection of beads.

Even though this is the age of the computer, the fountain pen is making a comeback. Akkerman, on the Kalverstraat (District 1), is the oldest address in the city; other smaller shops are beginning to stock them too.

On the Kloveniersburgwal (District 1), opposite the Nieuwmarkt, is an ancient establishment, Jacob Hooy, the apothecary that carries a wealth of natural health products, herbs and remedies that harken to the past.

Banga Klamboe, on the Prinsengracht, imports mosquito netting; not through a mistaken idea that Amsterdam is in the tropics but simply because in early summer the mosquitoes can be deadly.

Next to Obsession, a clothing shop on the Gasthuismolensteeg (District 5) which only sells designs by the Italian Ettore Massari, is another strictly one-product store, in this case boomerangs.

And lastly, clogs. Two shops, one on the Nieuwezijds Voorburgwal (District 1), De Klompenboer, and another on the Nieuwe Hoogstraat (District 1), 't Klompenhuisje, carry the traditional Dutch clogs as well as the more decorative ones to hang on your wall.

What all these shops have in common is the enthusiasm of the shopkeepers and the depth of their knowledge. The Dutch don't like to think of themselves as superficial; this is evident in the way in which they tackle the merchandise they sell and accounts for the specialization in these shops. An attendant reason is the perception of a gap in the market and the realization that a living can be made by providing the supply to fit the demand. Although this type of mercantilism is not unique to Holland, it is the way in which it is manifested that makes it typical of the country and of Amsterdam in particular. It is a continuation of a historic and traditional way of conducting business. The pride that comes across in the attention to detail and decoration and display goes hand in hand with this attitude. Also the variety of small shops that flavours the city gives what is, after all, the capital the sense of being a small village where the merchants know each other and the city dwellers also take pleasure in adding to their knowledge of where you can go to buy what.

ALTERNATIVE SHOPPING

Like most Dutch people, Amsterdammers are thrifty. They also know value for money. The number of **secondhand shops** in the city owe their being to this concept. However, do not be misled into thinking that what is on sale is of inferior quality or simply recycled merchandise that no one wants. The secondhand shops have become so sophisticated that it is sometimes difficult to recognize them as such. Additionally they have made an impact on the clothing consciousness of the public, for instance, so that what is old is not necessarily relegated to the junk heap but has become a style statement. The Dutch have a deep respect for the past, not only in a nostalgic sense but in a living sense, surrounded as they are by history. And nowhere more so than in Amsterdam, where the old quarters are constantly being restored and polished. The variety of old wares, postcards, books, knicknacks and dolls, to cite some imperishables, is observable in the little shops in the older section of town. Should you be in Amsterdam on 30 April, the Queen's Day, and when the whole country can buy and sell at will without a licence, you will experience at first hand the interest in used items that is part of the Dutch psyche.

Going back in history, the market mentality of places such as the Waterlooplein and the Noordermarkt allowed merchants to sell salvaged goods just like any other flea market round the world. Then came the sixties and seventies, when a certain chic was attached to old clothes. The bundles became stalls and the stalls became shops. A whole small industry came into being for mending and cleaning. An appreciation of craftsmanship in execution and design grew, as well as the desire to express an individual personality.

The **Waterlooplein** (District 1), once the main site of Jewish street trade, remains the largest venue for secondhand goods, not just clothing. The atmosphere here is very much that of the traditional flea market, with the humour, noise and attitude one has come to expect, even if there has been an effort to introduce new and unused downmarket items. Pots and pans, lamps and bric-à-brac abound and some have been lucky enough to find treasures in piles of old newspaper and photo albums. An incredible find was recently made in just such an instance when a member of the Anne Frank House Foundation recovered the long-lost letters and pictures of the dentist who had sheltered with the family. His wife, who had been unaware of his whereabouts until the end of the war when the story became known, had died and her possessions had ended up in the market.

The **Noordermarkt** (District 7), the weekly Monday market, has a more modest variety of clothing and discarded and refound articles. This is the venue for the small merchant and the feeling is informal.

The area in which the Noordermarkt is located is the **Jordaan**, a very special location described in the guide elsewhere. As its history would suggest, it is an enclave within the city and one which lends itself to the kind of secondhand shops that pop up, such as Petticoat on the Lindengracht. Many students live here and the shop prices in the neighbourhood reflect the size of their wallets. Since this was also for a long time a working class/artist/artisan area, the nostalgia for this era lingers on despite attempts at gentrification. And since most of the shops tend to go in and out of business as a matter of course, the best guide to the area is yourself, walking shoes and curiosity.

From the Rozengracht, the boundary of the garden-named streets of the Jordaan, to the Elandsgracht and sealed off on one side by the Lijnbaansgracht (District 7) and the Nieuwezijds Voorburgwal (District 5) on the other, is another area. The fact that the streets are small and similar can be misleading, but the inhabitants are often people in the professions and the shops reflect a different income level. This can be seen by the tone of the speciality shops that are interspersed amid the old and recovered goods and the fact that the choice canal-side dwellings and business offices are on the canals which form the large bands crossed by these streets. Their names change at each crossing of the canals and unless you speak Dutch you may be unaware that they are almost all animal names. A good way to take in the number of stores on each street is to wind your way from either the Royal Palace or the Spui ends, looping around the canals.

Two examples of alternative clothing shops are Lady Day, on the Hartenstraat (District 5), which has been in business for a long time, confirming the fact that reconditioned clothes have indeed made a solid place in the fashion world. The clothes are actually old-new, never used but recycled for today's fashion sense. The other, Jo-Jo Outfitters on the Huidenstraat (District 5), carries mostly men's clothing with some women's apparel. The quality is good and the prices are reasonable. The style exhibited in both is classic. Somewhat outside the conventional is Zipper, a secondhand store on the Huidenstraat that has become so successful that it has a small chain in the city. Despite a trend by the young shopper, the target group of these shops, to favour trendy places like Sissy-Boy on the Kalverstraat (District 1) and its other outlet on the Van Baerlestraat (District 2), Laura Dolls on the Wolvenstraat (District 5) is a tried and true member of the recycled category that is doing well.

Falling outside the definition of antique shops but yet having an allure for the collector are a series of shops carrying a jumble of old articles.

One such, Jan Best, is located on the corner of the Huidenstraat. Here the good, the bad and the indifferent are arrayed in such a manner that your reward is just as much in the seeing of it as in the purchase.

When one's income is limited or one's appetite for reading is unlimited, used books can be bought at both the Book Exchange and Book Traffic, the former on the Kloveniersburgwal (District 1), the latter on the Leliegracht (District 6). The interesting thing about these shops is that they will accept your books in exchange for a purchase as well as buy your old books. The selection is very wide and English dominates the titles.

Outside the realm of secondhand goods but forming an important part of alternative shopping are the myriad ateliers in the city. Fashion-school graduates set up their own businesses, very often a one-room shop, and offer their designs as alternatives to mass consumption. The promise of success and the desire to make an impact motivate them to continue in their pursuits. Although competition is tough the climate is favourable enough for them to keep trying. Some of them, like Fred de la Bretonière, the shoemaker on the St Luciënsteeg (District 1), started out simply and have gone on to become solid business successes. The Prinsenstraat (District 6), near the Jordaan, is where Margriet Nannings has established her designer studio, as has Liesbeth Royaards; both of them make quality clothes that are still affordable. The Dutch visual sense is strongly developed and the integration of design into daily life is one of the characteristics that you will discover as you walk round the city. Not only do Amsterdammers display care in the home, and for the tourist this is evident from the fact that windows act as frames for what goes on inside, but they are actively interested in the latest developments in this field. Shops mirror this concern: architects are enlisted to put a modern stamp on interiors as part of the design statement the shop wants to make. Design studios with glass, ceramics, furniture, lamps, and kitchen and table accessories are an accepted source for world-class objects outside the large commercial houses. Bordering on being galleries, they are in many ways the trendsetters for the look of the city. One of the most influential is Het Binnenhuis on the Huidenstraat (District 5). These are sometimes one-off, sometimes serial works and, as expected, expensive.

Quack en Overberg on the Keizersgracht (District 5) next to Metz & Co. is a design studio concentrating on lamps. Very often restoring old pieces from useless fixtures, the owners refit the pieces to usable stands, repair and re-chrome them for very reasonable prices.

With ties going back to the Orient from the days when the Dutch traders and the East India Company dominated this world market, it comes as no surprise that Amsterdam has so many Oriental art stores.

Not quite galleries and not quite antique shops, they fall into a category of their own. Baobab on the Elandsgracht (District 7) and Astamangala on the Kerkstraat (District 4) off the Utrechtsestraat are two that specialize in what could be best termed ethnographic art.

Other alternative shops to those as described above are located in the older section of Amsterdam. The goods sold in them do not always represent an alternative lifestyle, but they form part of a community of independent shop-owners selling the odd thing or two that does not easily fit into any category. They span the Jordaan and are tucked away in the what for lack of a better name can be called the between-canal area. You can also find them if you walk the side-streets off the Spiegelgracht district and the Utrechtsestraat. These offshoots do not necessarily conform to the character of the main street, so that they tend to be havens for the small shop-owner who has a collection of old postcards, costumes and discarded china and is content to make a modest living. There is even off the Noordermarkt (District 7) a shop that supplied the spectacles for the Oscar-winning film *The Last Emperor*. These are old fashioned frames that once again have become modish. The ingenuity of which this speaks is truly characteristic of Amsterdam. Taken as a whole, then, alternative shops are not significant in number but they add another dimension to shopping in the capital and give an old-world flavour to the rest of the city which is bent on joining the twenty-first century. It is this mingling of styles and diversity that is at once the charm and the strength of the city.

6 · Museums and Art

Apart from its canals, seventeenth–century painting is arguably Amsterdam's greatest blessing as a tourist centre. Its collections are quite rightly world-famous, and without them there would be considerably less reason for visiting the capital of the Netherlands.

The city's museums, of which there are a great many, would seem on the face of it to be in excellent shape. In fact, however, space needs to be found for still more museums, in order to relieve the pressure on storerooms, which are full to overflowing, and to be able to exhibit and preserve the collections' treasures more adequately. One day national and local government will have to provide the considerable funds required for the purpose. There are, for example, already vague plans for the urgently needed expansion of the Stedelijk Museum.

It can scarcely be maintained that the Netherlands state has been particularly lavish in the past in preserving the nation's artistic heritage (with the exception of the building of the Rijksmuseum). Things invariably proceeded with a certain amount of reluctance and delay. The collections so proudly displayed in Amsterdam are generally the result of private initiatives. Without the individuals concerned, what is on offer would be nowhere near as extensive or as attractive to visitors from abroad.

In the following pages the principal Amsterdam museums are dealt with in alphabetical order. (For a description of the remaining museums the reader is referred to the English-language guide to museums obtainable from VVV offices in Amsterdam.)

If you intend to visit a large number of museums, it might be worth while purchasing an annual season ticket (*museumjaarkaart*). These are obtainable from VVV offices and from museum ticket-offices. Individual ticket prices are 15 guilders for those of twenty-six and under and 30 guilders for those above. The annual season ticket gives one free admission to most museums in Amsterdam for a whole calendar year.

ALLARD PIERSON MUSEUM

Address: Oude Turfmarkt 127 (District 1)
Opening times: Tuesday–Friday, 10 a.m.–5 p.m.; Saturdays, Sundays and national holidays, 1–5 p.m.

Allard Pierson (1831–96), from whom this archaeological museum takes its name, was a poet, philosopher and professor of Art History, Aesthetics and Modern Literature at the University of Amsterdam. An exceptionally fine portrait of him, painted by Jan Veth (1864–1925), hangs by the stairs leading up to the exhibition rooms. Opposite are a number of plaster casts of Classical sculptures, including the caryatids from the Acropolis in Athens, part of the large collection once owned by the Rijksmuseum.

However, the museum's collection of antiquities has no direct connection with Pierson; the nucleus of it is made up of the collection of C.W. Lunsingh Scheurleer, acquired in 1934. Although the space available is not particularly large, the rooms are crammed with exhibits. The Egyptian section is invariably the most popular.

AMSTERDAMS HISTORISCH MUSEUM/ AMSTERDAM HISTORICAL MUSEUM

Address: Kalverstraat 92 (District 5)
Opening times: 11 a.m.–5 p.m. daily

The Amsterdam Historical Museum, containing the most important collection of Amsterdam art outside the Rijksmuseum, has been housed since 1975 in the former municipal orphanage (Burgerweeshuis), in a quiet spot right in the heart of the city. Besides all kinds of historical artefacts, the museum has an enormous collection of paintings, comprising an interesting set of so-called 'group portraits'. This kind of portrait is an almost exclusively Dutch phenomenon which began to appear around the middle of the sixteenth century and continued into the eighteenth century (many examples were also produced in other towns in the Dutch Republic). With their assembled groups of ladies and gentlemen, they are an almost literal pictorial equivalent of the well-ordered, corporative society of the Dutch Republic. The sitters are mostly either the regents, or the governors (male and female) of institutions such as the orphanage, the prisons (including the so-called Spinhuis, where inmates were forced to spin), the lunatic asylums and the leper houses, or members of the corporative guilds and militia (*schutters*). These militia were voluntary organizations responsible for the city's defence which had assumed the task of keeping public order.

The museum has a variety of these works, including some exceptionally fine examples (often executed by such pre-eminent masters as Rembrandt and Bartholomeus van der Helst). The most brilliant stroke of invention in the layout of the museum is the so-called 'Militiamen's Gallery' (Schuttersgallerij), a kind of covered thoroughfare through which one can walk without entering the museum itself, whose walls are lined with group portraits of militia companies. Two English-language booklets on group portraits are on sale in the museum.

The museum proper is of course devoted more to the history of the city than to its artistic heritage as such. **Rooms 1 to 4** deal with the first phase of the city's history, from the oldest known document, the 'toll privilege' granted in 1275 by Floris V, count of Holland, down to the end of the sixteenth century. Here one finds the earliest map of the city by Cornelis Anthonisz (1500–1553); alongside the decorative drinking-horns used by the militiamen is the first militia piece by the same master, a double portrait by Dirck Jacobsz. (1497–1567) and two fragments of an 'Adoration of the Magi' by Pieter Aertsen (1509–75), which only partially survived the Iconoclastic Fury of the mid sixteenth century.

Room 5 is devoted to the voyages of discovery and to navigation. One can follow the abortive voyage (1596–97) of Willem Barentsz, who attempted to reach the East Indies via the North Pole – making an enormous detour to avoid the Dunkirk pirates – but got no further than Nova Zembla in Siberia; and the circumnavigation of the globe achieved between 1598 and 1604 by Olivier van Noort (albeit almost eighty years after Magellan had managed the feat). **Room 6** contains Artus Quellinus's designs for decorations in the Town Hall, as well as an original model of the building complete with decoration of 1648. Also a view of the Town Hall – one of many he painted – by Gerrit Berckheyde (1638–98).

In **Room 7** there is an allegorical painting by Gerard de Lairesse (1640–1711). On the way to Room 8, from the window looking out on to the Militiamen's Gallery, a pleasant painting by Govert Flinck (1615–60) can be seen, in which the militiamen, with their stockings round their ankles, are celebrating the Peace of Munster (1648), the end of the Eighty Years' War (the Netherlands' struggle for independence from Spain). At the top of the stairs is an excellent group portrait by Gerbrandt van den Eeckhout, depicting the governors of the coopers' and cellarmen's guild (1673).

Room 8 has a large painted view of the wharves of the Dutch East India Company by Ludolf Backhuysen; from the windows there is a good view of the militia paintings of Nicolaes Pickenoy. **Room 9** is devoted to Amsterdam artists; there are preliminary studies by Lievens and Bol for the Town Hall and small historical pieces by Pieter Lastman and Jan Tengnagel (1584/5–1635). In addition there is a portrait of the Sybrand de Flines family by Jan Weenix (1640–1719), much better known for his still-lifes with dead game, and a splendid 'Woman Selling Vegetables' by Michiel van Musscher.

Room 10 deals with the religious life of the inhabitants of the city. It is striking that the Calvinists did not, either in the city or elsewhere, prove great church-builders; having denied access to the Catholics, they evidently found room enough in the great medieval churches. Catholics were forced to resort to the so-called 'undercover churches' (*schuilkerken*); these were semi-clandestine rooms where mass was celebrated – there were considerably more of these than there were Protestant places of worship. One can, incidentally, still see what such a 'church' looked like in **Museum Amstelkring** (Oudezijds Voorburgwal 40; opening times Monday–Saturday, 10 a.m.–5 p.m.; Sundays and national holidays, 1–5 p.m.). As we have seen, there were seventeenth-century painters who specialized almost exclusively in church interiors; there is a splendid example here of the work of the accomplished Emanuel de Witte (1617–92).

In **Room 11** one can see the regents in their Sunday best. A wax sculpture of a beggar is set amid the luxury of the male and female governors of the spinning-house in paintings by Dirck van Santvoort (1638) and Bartholomeus van der Helst (1650). In addition there is one of the most beautiful works of Ferdinand Bol, 'The Regents of the Leper-House' of 1649. Compare this with Cornelis Troost's regents of almost a hundred years later (1740), a creditable enough painting but still far below the level of the Bol. The feeding and dressing of the orphans is the unusual theme of a work by Rembrandt's versatile pupil Jan Victors (1620–after 1676). This type of group portrait was generally hung in the regents' boardrooms, just as the militiamen adorned their headquarters (the so-called *Doelen*, or rifle-ranges) with paintings of themselves.

In **Room 12** we find ourselves in the eighteenth century. Right at the entrance is Jacob de Wit's 'Patroness of Amsterdam'. There is also a personification of the art of painting by the same artist, on a panel which formed the door of a so-called 'art cupboard' for storing drawings and prints. We can recognize the same cupboard in a family portrait by Tibout Regters (1710–68). In addition there is a rather mediocre painting of the headquarters of Felix Meritis ('Happy through Achievement'), the Amsterdam society for arts and sciences set up in the eighteenth century.

Room 13 is arranged as if to demonstrate that the eighteenth century did occasionally produce some good painting: flower still-lifes by Jan van Huysum (1682–1749) and Rachel Ruysch (1664–1750), a historical piece by Nicolaas Verkolje (1673–1746), and a fine painting by George van der Mijn (1723–63) of a woman and child in a garden (in accordance with an age-old custom the child is wearing a protective helmet).

Rooms 14 to 17 are devoted to daily life in the eighteenth and nine-teenth centuries and to such topics as industrialization. Descending the staircase to the exit, one sees a large townscape of Amsterdam in the snow by George Breitner, the Dutch impressionist, who so often cap-tured life in the city with both paint-brush and camera.

The Amsterdam Historical Museum has a separate exhibition area which features interesting temporary exhibitions. Attached to the museum is a restaurant called 'David and Goliath', with large wooden statues of David and Goliath and a shield-bearer. They are relics of the pleasure gardens of Het Oude Doolhof, evidently a kind of theme park located at the confluence of the Prinsengracht and Looiersgracht between 1625 and 1862. The statues are partially articulated: Goliath's head turns and his eyes roll.

ANNE FRANKHUIS/ANNE FRANK HOUSE

Address: Prinsengracht 263 (District 6)
Opening times: Monday–Saturday, 9 a.m.–5 p.m.; Sundays and national holidays, 10 a.m.–5 p.m.
Season ticket not valid, admission 5 guilders.

This building, where Anne Frank hid for two years and one month dur-ing the German occupation in the Second World War, was bought by her father in 1940 to house his spice business. A year or two later, when the situation had become really desperate for the Jewish population, Otto converted the unused rear portion of the house (the so-called *achterhuis*) into a hiding-place. Here the young Anne wrote her famous diary. When the family was discovered and arrested by the German po-lice on 4 August 1944, her diary was left behind in the *achterhuis*.

Anyone who has difficulty in climbing steep stairs should be advised against a visit, as should those who are at all claustrophobic: the Anne Frankhuis is small and crowded with visitors. In the summer it is not un-usual to find queues outside the door.

The property is administered by the Anne Frank Foundation, which is committed to the fight against such phenomena as discrimination and anti-Semitism. To this end the Foundation regularly organizes exhibi-tions in the rooms at the front of the house.

FILMMUSEUM

Address: Vondelpark 3 (District 2)
Opening times: Tuesday–Friday 10 a.m.–5 p.m.

The Filmmuseum is located in a magnificent building on the edge of the
Vondelpark. It has a fairly small collection of items connected with the
film industry, such as of course cameras, projectors and lights; in addition
there are posters and some furnishings rescued from demolished cinemas.
The museum's actual film collection is shown in organized seasons at
regular times in a small theatre.

JEWISH HISTORICAL MUSEUM

Address: Jonas Daniël Meijerplein 2–4 (District 3)
Opening times: 11 a.m.–5 p.m. daily; closed on Yom Kippur

This museum was installed quite recently in an old complex of four so-
called 'High-German' synagogues, among them the oldest public synagogue in Western Europe (built in 1670–71). The complex is opposite
the Portuguese Synagogue on the Jonas Daniël Meijerplein in the former
Jewish quarter of Amsterdam, where Rembrandt lived for many years.
As the name indicates, the museum is devoted to the culture of the Jewish community, which found its way to tolerant Amsterdam from Central Europe and Portugal around 1600. The principal themes are Judaism
(with a wealth of religious paraphernalia), social organization, the eman-
cipation of the community in the nineteenth century, the rise of Zion-
ism, and occupation and deportation (1940–45).
The museum contains a number of interesting works of art by among
others Jan Voerman (1857–1941) and better-known artists such as Lion
Cachet, Jozef Israëls, his son Isaäc Israëls, and Thérèse Schwartze. There
are regular temporary exhibitions in the separate exhibition area. Kosher
dishes are served in a congenial café-restaurant.

KONINKLIJK PALEIS/ROYAL PALACE ON THE DAM,
FORMERLY THE TOWN HALL

The former Town Hall, now the Royal Palace on the Dam (District 1),
is perhaps the most imposing architectural monument in the Nether-

lands. The museum season ticket is not valid here, but admission is only 2 guilders 50. In the summer season, from about the end of May till the beginning of September, there are guided tours on Wednesdays from 12.30 p.m. onwards. Off season there is one tour per week, on Wednesdays at 2 p.m. Since these times occasionally change at short notice and the palace may be closed when the Queen has an official reception, it is advisable to inquire at VVV offices if and when the the building is open to visitors.

Because the palace is still used for official functions, only part of it is open to the public. Nevertheless visitors can always walk round the imposing ground floor, beginning with the great **Burgerzaal**, or Citizens' Chamber. Its floor is inlaid with marble maps of the eastern and western hemispheres and part of the night sky. Above the entrance is the Amsterdam city patroness, seated between personifications of Strength and Wisdom. Directly opposite her, on the other short wall of the chamber, is a statue of Justice spurning Greed and Envy. In the niches of the entrances to the south and north galleries the four elements (earth, air, fire and water) can be seen. These sculptures were executed by Artus Quellinus; the Antwerp sculptor was specially recruited for the decoration of the Town Hall, because of the absence of a respectable sculptural tradition in the Dutch Republic.

The **Schepenzaal** (Alderman's Chamber), where important cases were tried (with a painting above the mantelpiece by Ferdinand Bol), and the Chamber of Commissioners for Minor Cases (Kamer van Commissarissen van Kleine Zaken) for minor infringements, lead to the south gallery. The painted decorations here depict the struggle of the Batavians (the former inhabitants of part of what is now the Netherlands) against the Romans, by, among others, Jan Lievens (1607–74), a friend of Rembrandt's, and Jurriaen Ovens (1623–78), one of Rembrandt's pupils. For a short while in 1662, in the place where Ovens's painting now hangs, there was a work by Rembrandt on the same theme, the famous 'Oath of Claudius Civilis', now in the Nationalmuseum in Stockholm. Shortly after completion of the work Rembrandt appears to have run into difficulties with the town council over the commission, the precise nature of which is still unknown. The upshot, however, was that the painting was removed.

We now walk in the direction of the Dam and enter the **Burgemeesterszaal** (Mayor's Chamber), which contains two canvases, another Bol and one of the last works of Govert Flinck (1615–60). Both these celebrated paintings, containing scenes of Roman valour and virtue (derived from Livy), are much better than photographs would lead one to believe. Next door is the Mayor's Office, or **Burgemeesterskamer**, with a similar picture by Jan Lievens. From the corridor leading off it there is a glimpse of the Tribunal Chamber (**Vierschaar**), of which more will be said shortly. The corridor leads via the Chamber of Justice (**Justitiekamer**) to the Council Chamber (**Vroedschapskamer**), nowadays also called the 'Moses Chamber'; the *vroedschap* was an advisory body to the mayor. It was here that Princess Juliana abdicated in favour of the present Queen Beatrix in 1980. The room contains a sizeable canvas by Jacob de Wit depicting the 'Selection of the Seventy Elders by Moses'; the Old Testament scenes above the mantelpieces are by Jan van Bronckhorst (1603–70) and Flinck. From here one emerges into the north gallery, hung with paintings by the Fleming Jacob Jordaens (1593–1678).

Finally comes the Tribunal Chamber. It is a rather macabre touch that the visitor's route is approximately the same as that once followed by those sentenced to death. Death sentences were pronounced in the Tribunal Chamber, and ceremony demanded that this should take place in the open air (the present glass windows are of more recent date), so it is understandable that the decoration here is not painted but in marble. The impressive judgement scenes are again by Artus Quellinus.

MUSEUM FODOR

Address: Keizersgracht 609 (District 4)
Opening times: 11 a.m.–5 p.m. daily

Situated opposite the Museum Van Loon, Museum Fodor is named after the former occupier, the art collector Carel Joseph Fodor (the name appears to be of Hungarian origin). On his death in 1860 Fodor bequeathed his house and art collection to the city of Amsterdam. Unfortunately, his extremely interesting collection is no longer on display in the present museum; since 1948 it has been kept in the store of the Stedelijk Museum.

Fodor collected drawings and etchings by Rembrandt in particular and in addition owned nineteenth-century works by among others Géricault (1791–1824) – including a study for the latter's celebrated 'Raft of the Medusa' – and Dutch Romantics like Barend Koekkoek (1803–62), Johannes Bosboom (1817–91), Andreas Schelfhout (1787–1870) and Ary Scheffer (1795–1885). It is something of a disgrace that the collection should not be exhibited in its entirety somewhere in Amsterdam.

The Fodor Museum itself is now devoted to contemporary works by Amsterdam artists. It has no permanent collection, but puts on regular temporary exhibitions. Once a year, in the summer, Amsterdam City Council's art acquisitions for the year are shown.

MUSEUM OVERHOLLAND

Address: Museumplein 4 (District 2)
Opening times: 1 a.m.–5 p.m. daily

This is a new and very individual museum. It was opened on 20 February 1987 in a very handsome former private house built in 1925 by the architect J. de Bie Leuveling Tjeenk (whose name is even longer than that of the architect who clearly inspired the building: Frank Lloyd Wright). The museum is worth a visit for the building alone. It should be added that the museum season ticket is not valid and that the price of admission is fairly steep (8 guilders); Museum Overholland is privately owned.
The museum has no permanent collection, but mounts temporary exhibitions of paper-based modern art (drawings, graphics, etc.). The choice is not adventurous, but of high quality. Up to now work has been exhibited by artists such as Cézanne, Gerhard Richter, Arnulf Rainer, Roy Lichtenstein, Frank Stella and Ellsworth Kelly. It is located behind and to the side of the Vincent Van Gogh Museum.

MUSEUM VAN LOON

Address: Keizersgracht 672 (District 4)
Opening times: Mondays, 10 a.m.–5 p.m.
Season ticket not valid; admission 5 guilders

Run by the Van Loon Foundation, this museum, like the Museum Willet-Holthuysen, occupies a majestic canal-side mansion. The Van Loon family, from which it takes its name, moved here relatively recently. The seventeenth-century building was bought by one Hendrik van Loon as recently as 1884 for his son; a member of the family apparently still occupies the first floor. The rest of the house is open to the public on Mondays only.
When you go in, be sure to buy the little information folder, which will tell you about the succession of bankcruptcies which befell the previous owners of the house. One exception was the painter Ferdinand Bol (1610–80), who lived in the house for a while. Bol married a rich wife,

with the result that when he moved here he was able to stop painting. Today the interior of the house consists of eighteenth and nineteenth century furnishings, re-creating its likely appearance at that time. Of particular interest is the large collection of portraits of members of the family. At the entrance you will see the portraits of Willem van Loon, who in 1602 laid the basis of the family fortune when, together with other merchants, he helped found the mighty United East India Company, and of his wife Petronella. The East India Company controlled trade with the Indies (the present Indonesia) and other areas, and was so profitable that an artist like Pieter Saenredam, on the strength of the dividend from a small number of shares, was able to limit his painting output to one work a year.

Besides a splendid ivory sculpture attributed to the Italian sculptor Alessandro Algardi (1595–1654), the Van Loon Museum possesses portraits by Jurriaen Ovens (1623–78), Dirck Santvoort, Michiel van Musscher, Tischbein and Charles Howard Hodges (1764–1837), the English artist resident in Holland. In addition there is a self-portrait by Hodges' pupil Cornelis Kruseman (1797–1857). One rarity is a portrait by the French painter Alexandre Cabanel (1824–89), like Bouguereau virtually unrepresented in the Netherlands. Finally there is a good painting by Thérèse Schwartze (1851–1918).

However, the most important items are two works by Jan Miense Molenaar (1610–68), a pupil of Frans Hals: a small family portrait of the Van Loons, which may also symbolize the five senses, and a magnificent, crowded depiction of the wedding of Willem van Loon (another member of the family) and Margaretha Bos in 1637.

MUSEUM VINCENT VAN GOGH

Address: Paulus Potterstraat 7 (District 2)
Opening times: Tuesday–Saturday, 10 a.m.–5 p.m.; Sundays and national holidays, 1–5 p.m.

The National Vincent Van Gogh Museum is a quite recent foundation. It was opened – after a deal of special pleading – in 1973. Plans for a separate museum to exhibit the extensive collection of Van Gogh's works date back years. The first preliminary drawings for the museum were made as early as 1963 by the celebrated Utrecht designer and architect Gerrit Rietveld (1888–1964).

The museum is one of the most frequently visited in the country. Vincent van Gogh is a 'popular' artist, not only on account of his work, but also because of his tormented life, to which he put an end in 1890. Van Gogh was born in 1853 in the village of Zundert in the south of the Netherlands. Though he died quite young, his output is quite astonishing considering that he produced his enormous *œuvre* in the last ten years of his life! Part of his work – more than two hundred paintings and four hundred drawings – was in the possession of his brother Theo, who died shortly after Vincent. Subsequently the collection was administered by Theo's widow, who bequeathed it to their son, V.W. van Gogh. Although Vincent achieved great renown very soon after his death and his work fetched high prices, the collection fortunately remained intact. Nowadays Van Gogh's paintings command top prices on the art market.

The collection of the National Van Gogh Museum, then, is not the result of state interest, but of pressure exercised from outside. Its richness is the result of a determined private initiative.

The first floor gives the visitor a good impression of the chronological development of the artist's work: from his early, closely observed, Dutch work (with as its climax 'The Potato-Eaters' of 1885) up to his last intense period at Arles in the South of France. Works by French artists such as Corot, Manet, Pissarro and Toulouse-Lautrec also form part of the permanent collection.

On the second floor is the print room, which is often used for temporary exhibitions, as is the third floor. These exhibitions, often excellent, are in principle related to the work of Van Gogh.

The museum has an extensive bookshop and a canteen with rather slow service (season ticket holders wanting a meal are best advised to go to the neighbouring Stedelijk Museum).

MUSEUM WILLET-HOLTHUYSEN

Address: Herengracht 605 (District 4)
Opening times: 11 a.m.–5 p.m. daily

The imposing mansion housing this museum was built in about 1687 on what is today a quiet stretch of the Herengracht. In 1855, after changing hands several times, the property came into the possession of one Pieter Gerard Holthuysen. His daughter Sandrina Luise Geertruida, married to the connoisseur Abraham Willet, finally left the house and its contents to the city of Amsterdam, with the express wish that it be opened to the public under the name 'Museum Willet-Holthuysen'. Government agencies in the Netherlands are frequently reluctant to accept such bequests, but in this case it would indeed have been more sensible to accommodate Willet's art collection in a larger existing public collection. However, this was forbidden under the terms of Sandrina's offer.

Museum Willet-Holthuysen seems never to have attracted large numbers of visitors. In fact, it is neither one thing nor the other; the visitor is not sure whether to concentrate on the interior with its ninetenth-century furniture, the collection of paintings or the collection of applied art (glass, ceramics and silver).

At the entrance to the museum, at the end of the corridor next to the kitchen, a slide-show (with a choice of Dutch or English commentary), briefly setting out the story of the house and its occupants, can be seen. On the first floor there are a number of valuable works by Michiel van Musscher (1645–1705), and Jan van Mieris (1660–90), a scion of a famous Leiden family of painters, and Johann Friedrich Tischbein (1750–1812). There is a striking small copy of Michelangelo's 'Day' from the Medici Chapel in Florence (possibly acquired by the Willets on one of their Italian trips). On the ceiling of the smoking room there is an interesting painting by Jacob de Wit (1695–1754), which incidentally originates from another house in Amsterdam, and a painting above the mantelpiece by the same artist.

Along the stairway leading to the second floor are three large Italian sculptures representing Venus, Juno and Paris respectively (eighteenth century; origin unknown).

Abraham Willet and his wife had an appealing but not extravagant collection of paintings, including two fine nineteenth-century copies of Frans Hals, as well as works by the Romantic painter Charles Rochussen (1814–94) and Jacob and Willem Maris (1837–94 and 1844–1910 respectively), members of the Hague School. Unusual for Holland are two French paintings by William-Adolphe Bouguereau (1825–1905), whose reputation is again rising since the opening of the Musée d'Orsay in Paris. A final curiosity is a painting of Abraham Willet himself portrayed as a seventeenth-century militiaman by André Mniszech (1823–1905).

The museum as a whole affords an interesting picture of an extremely rich couple with average aesthetic interests.

REMBRANDT-HUIS/REMBRANDT'S HOUSE

Address: Jodenbreestraat 4–6 (District 1)
Opening times: Monday–Saturday, 10 a.m.–5 p.m.; Sundays and national holidays, 1–5 p.m.

This house was built in 1606, the year of Rembrandt van Rijn's birth.

Later, from 1639 onwards, when Rembrandt was prospering financially, he was to live there for almost twenty years. He purchased the house for the then considerable sum of 13,000 guilders. However, Rembrandt was not a good manager of money: he went bankrupt in 1657–8 and was forced to sell the house and his possessions. From the inventory drawn up at the time we can more or less deduce how things looked. It emerged, for example, that Rembrandt had his studio on the upper floor and that below, in the actual living quarters, there was a small treasure-house of more than a hundred paintings, a sizeable collection of drawings by a variety of masters, and a large number of exotic curiosities, for which the painter obviously had a particular liking.

In 1906 – the tercentenary of Rembrandt's birth – the property was purchased for conversion into a museum. On the basis of the old inventory, K.P.C. de Bazel (the architect of the monumental Algemene Handels-maatschappij building in the Vijzelstraat) restored the interior of the Rembrandt House more or less to what it had once been. At present, 245 of the approximately 280 etchings made by Rembrandt are on permanent display under subdued lighting.

As is well known, Rembrandt was a master of etching technique; notice, for example, the delicate detail of large prints like the so-called 'Hundred Guilder Print' or the 'Ecce Homo'. In a separate room there is an illustrated description of the etching process.

In addition there are a number of Rembrandt's drawings, as well as several paintings by two artists associated with him. Presumably the reason for their presence is that these painters – Pieter Lastman (Rembrandt's teacher, 1583–1633) and Jan Pijnas (1583–1631) – together with others, are often labelled with the anachronistic term *pre-Rembrandtists*.

Until recently Rembrandt was regarded as an odd-man-out in the Dutch school, because like the above-mentioned artists he produced so many historical paintings (with Biblical or mythological themes), whereas it was 'genre painting' with its scenes 'taken from life' that was considered so typical of the Dutch. Although this turns out not to be the case – historical painting was just as normal in the Dutch Republic as in Italy – the term pre-Rembrandtists still occurs here and there in attempts to reconstruct a kind of artistic genealogy for Rembrandt.

Once your eyes have adjusted to the dim light, you will see that Pieter Lastman especially was an excellent painter (and draughtsman). On the other hand, two works by Gerbrandt van den Eeckhout demonstrate that even a Dutch pupil of Rembrandt was more adept in the typical group portrait (as seen for example in the Amsterdam Historical Museum) than in his history paintings here.

RIJKSMUSEUM

Address: Stadhouderskade 42 (District 2)
Opening times: Tuesday–Saturday, 10 a.m.–5 p.m.; Sundays and national holidays, 1–5 p.m

The word *rijksmuseum* simply means a museum owned and run by the Netherlands state. So that the Vincent van Gogh Museum, for example, is also a *rijksmuseum*. At the opening of Cuypers' great building in 1885, a large variety of different 'national museums' had to be housed in it: besides the Museum of Paintings, there were also the National Collection of Works by Modern Masters, the National Collection of Prints and Drawings, the National Museum of History and Art and the National Collection of Plaster Casts and Sculpture. With the exception of the latter these collections are still in the care of what the Dutch themselves also call the 'Rijksmuseum' for short. Regrettably, the collection of plaster casts of famous sculptures, such as can still be seen, for example, in the Victoria and Albert Museum in London, has been lost.

At the time, the Netherlands state made what was by its standards a huge investment in this complex. No expense or effort was spared. It was originally full of lavish decorations, but these have in the course of time been gradually eliminated because of successive new-fangled ideas on the aesthetic (meaning, in practice, less elaborate) presentation of the collections, and also on account of the extensive modifications required to house the collections, which soon began to fill the storerooms to their total capacity.

Initially there was a library attached to the museum, and two educational institutions, the National College for Teachers of Drawing and the National School for Applied Art; these institutions also disappeared from the building in the course of time. The intention underlying the state's investment is thus clear: the creation of a huge museum complex that would meet all conservation needs in the coming century.

Nowadays, when our views on museums and the presentation of collections have drastically changed, the building makes a different impression, namely that of an enormous provincial museum (magnificent here and there it is true, but provincial none the less). Though it may not be immediately apparent, the spacial and financial resources of the Rijksmuseum are quite inadequate. Recently the board of management took the step of closing certain rooms in the morning or afternoon because of staff shortages. The budget for new acquisitions of paintings is depressingly low: 270,000 guilders, a sum that has remained the same for thirty years and is nowhere near sufficient to enable the museum to compete on the international art market. Despite a plethora of modifications to the building – some rooms have now been restored more or less to their original state for the sake of historical authenticity – the museum is bursting at the seams, or at least certain important parts of the collection are unsatisfactorily presented. The modifications do, though, have an unexpected charm: because of its labyrinthine complexity, a trip round the museum is rather like a magical mystery tour through a grand treasure-house of historical exhibits.

Most attention will be paid here to the painting collection, which as usual is ordered more or less chronologically. It was built up from great collections already in existence at the time of the museum's opening – the Van der Hoop collection, for example, or the important parts of the Amsterdam Municipal collection – together with many private bequests, and purchases made in the course of the museum's hundred-year existence, with or without sponsorship.

Fifteenth- and sixteenth-century art

Obviously with an eye to groups of tourists wishing to see the most famous items in as short a time as possible, the museum has lined the so-called Gallery of Honour leading directly to the 'Nightwatch' with Rembrandt's other masterpieces. After a visit to the adjoining room containing the four Vermeers, one can leave again, having walked no more than a hundred metres.

Needless to say, that route will not be followed here; we shall begin at the beginning. **Rooms 201–206** cover the fifteenth and sixteenth centuries. In the fifteenth century the finest paintings were of course produced in Flanders, in the Southern Netherlands. The art of Jan van Eyck and his contemporaries is unfortunately entirely absent here. It should perhaps be made clear at the outset that the painting collection is by no means an international one. It is focused entirely on North Netherlands work, more or less in the same way that the Uffizi in Florence contains virtually only Italian art. In both cases, though, it must be conceded that what is on display is of phenomenal quality.

Geertgen tot St Jans (1465–95), a painter from Haarlem, is without doubt the most significant master of the period. The museum has two paintings by him: an 'Adoration of the Magi' and a marvellous panel with a colourful representation of the 'Tree of Jesse'; this latter work, purchased in 1956 as a Geertgen tot St Jans, was for a long time attributed to Jan Mostaert, but according to the caption is now once again accepted as Geertgen's work. Also important is the work of the so-called Master of Alkmaar, represented by the 'Seven Works of Mercy'. This already brings us to the beginning of the sixteenth century, whose high point is Lucas van Leyden (1489–1533), as the name indicates a resident of Leiden, and especially renowned for his engravings. An exceptional new acquisition is the 'Wedding at Canaan' by Jan Vermeyen (1500–1559). Vermeyen possessed what was for his time unusual skill in handling chiaroscuro effects.

Jan van Scorel (1495–1562) and his pupil Maarten van Heemskerck (1498–1574) are the most important masters of the second half of the sixteenth century. Both went to Italy to learn the art of painting. Van Scorel, from Utrecht, even seems to have spent a year as curator of the Vatican's collection of Classical sculptures, under the Dutch pope Adrian VI (1521–2). Some of the pair's figure paintings do show, it must be said, that they never entirely mastered the depiction of the human body in motion. This helps to explain why Dutch painters tended to be praised more for their meticulous depiction of different materials, their portraits, and later their landscapes and still-lifes. The portraits of Antonius Mor van Dashorst (1512–75; he spent a condiderable time in Spain and hence is more commonly known as Antonio Moro) show that this praise is well deserved, as do the flower still-lifes of Balthazar van der Ast (1593/4–1657) and Ambrosius Bosschaert (1573–1621), and the fantasy landscapes of Joos de Momper (1564–1635) and Paulus Bril (1554–1626) – the last-mentioned artist was also long resident in Italy.

Seventeenth-century art

Approaching the rooms containing seventeenth-century art, we should mention two important transitional figures: Cornelis Cornelisz van Haarlem (1562–1638) and Abraham Bloemaert (1564–1651).

In the following room, **208**, a number of pupils of Bloemaert appear in their own right: Gerard van Honthorst (1590–1656), Hendrik Terbrugghen (1581–1629) and Jan van Bijlert (1603–71); together with Dirck van Baburen (1595–1624) they form the first generation of important seventeenth-century artists. As a group they are known as the Utrecht Caravaggists, since they all went to work in Italy and fell under the spell of the prevailing fashion for Caravaggism. Like all followers of Caravaggio, they consistently use half-length figures, often painted with strong chiaroscuro effects. There are also a number of group portraits, a typically Dutch genre (for a fuller account, see p. 81). The 'Thin Company' is a painting by Frans Hals (1580–1666), born in Antwerp, and Pieter Codde (1599–1678). Frans Hals was one of many refugees who fled to the North during the revolt of the Netherlands against Spanish dominion; the Northern Netherlands gained independence, while the Southern Netherlands had to wait for centuries. Many Flemings fled because of religious persecution or because they saw their livelihood being threatened by hostilities. Those who made their way to the large towns in the North were often highly trained craftsmen, and they added in no small measure to the prosperity of the Republic. It is odd that Codde of all people should have collaborated on 'The Thin Company', as his style is totally different from that of the exuberant Hals – an example of it can be seen in **Room 210**.

In addition there are gallant companies by Dirk Hals (a brother of Frans; 1591–1656) and Willem Buytewech (1591–1624). It is no coincidence that there should also be a small work by Jan Miense Molenaar (1610–68): he was a pupil of Frans Hals and married another pupil more faithful to Hals' free style, Judith Leyster (1609–1660).

Next comes the first of the rooms featuring Rembrandt (1606–69). As you will notice, the 'Rembrandt' theme runs like a thread through the collection as exhibited. In this room his early paintings are brought together with works by painters connected with him at the time: Pieter Lastman (1583–1633) and Jan Lievens (1607–74). Lastman was Rembrandt's teacher, and in his first efforts the pupil imitated the master's style. These are small, preciously painted works, usually based on some Biblical theme. Jan Lievens was at this time a close associate of Rembrandt's. In his autobiography the celebrated statesman and author Constantijn Huygens, whose splendid portrait by Lievens hangs in this room, mentions them in the same breath: Huygens regrets that they do not wish to go to Italy to 'imbibe the art of these great geniuses ... [Rembrandt and Lievens] say that they have no time to waste on a pilgrimage, bearing in mind that they are at the height of their powers. Moreover, they maintain that given the present rage for collecting among princes north of the Alps, the best paintings are to be seen outside Italy.'

The seventeenth century, then, is the age of collections. Art was no longer made to order for a specific purpose, but was produced for collections. This led to the emergence of a large number of new genres, and with them a large number of specialists. Dutch painters often concentrated exclusively on a single genre: some painted nothing but still-lifes, others only landscapes, still others only church interiors (there were even artists who painted only still-lifes with fish, thus creating a sub-speciality). All these specialities are represented in the following rooms: **Room 214** contains church paintings by Pieter Saenredam (1597–1665), one of the first to produce such 'views' of actual churches. One of the paintings, the 'Church at Assendelft', comes from the Van der Hoop collection. In addition there are landscapes by Salomon van Ruysdael (1600–1670), Jan van Goyen (1596–1656) and Albert Cuyp (1620–91). Cuyp's work was once much sought-after in England, which is why so few of his paintings have remained in the Netherlands. There is also an interesting river by moonlight by Aert van der Neer (1603/4–77). Finally, there is the curious figure of Torrentius (1589–1644), who appears to have been the leader of a kind of sect. His only known painting, a still-life incorporating an allegory on temperance, hangs in this room.

The reader should not overlook the side-annexe leading off this room, containing paintings by the previously mentioned Judith Leyster, Gerrit Houckgeest (1600–1661), as well as a splendid little 'Pan and Syrinx' by Caesar van Everdingen (1616–78). **Room 215** contains works by typical portraitists: the great Bartholomeus van der Helst (1613–70) and Dirck Santvoort (1610–80). The splendid portrait of the portly young Andries Bicker by Van der Helst is worth noting. This room also features work by some of Rembrandt's pupils, including Govert Flinck (1615–60) and Ferdinand Bol (1616–80), who were later to be given important commissions for the decoration of the new Town Hall, now the Palace on the Dam. Bol's portrait of the elderly Elizabeth Bas was once thought to be a Rembrandt. Also represented are the most gifted of Rembrandt's pupils, the short-lived Carel Fabritius (1622–54) who moved to Delft and was tragically killed in the explosion of the town's gunpowder store; and Jacob Backer (1608–51), less well known, but in the same class as the others.

In **Room 216** we see the first examples of Dutch painting's most famous theme: the recording, mostly on a small scale, of some domestic, anecdotal scene. The prolific Jan Steen (1626–79), whose self-portrait hangs here, is one of the most celebrated genre painters (works of this type are known as genre paintings). Steen's representation of the celebration of the feast of St Nicholas (Sinterklaas or Santa Claus) is very charming. Steen is famous for the fairly disorderly state of his interiors; from this derives the Dutch expression 'a Jan Steen household' to describe a chaotic home, which may well be the only case of a painter's name being used in such a phrase.

In **Room 217** there is a wonderful portrait of a girl by the Haarlem painter Johannes Verspronck (1597–1662) and also the famous painting of the mill at Wijk bij Duurstede by Jacob Ruisdael (1628/9–82), a cousin of Salomon Ruysdael.

The two small rooms (**219**) that follow are among the finest in the whole museum. There are further works by Jan Steen, among them the shop of the laughing baker Oostwaard, the 'Woman Fish-Seller' by Adriaen van Ostade (1610–84), and a young lady pulling off her stockings, also by Jan Steen. According to one theory she, like the others, is practising a profession – the oldest in the world; this theory is based on the fact that in the seventeenth century the word 'stocking' was synonymous with 'prostitute'. Such activities took place far from the respectable neighbourhoods of Amsterdam, such as depicted in the work of Gerrit Berckheyde (1638–98) and Jan van der Heyden (1637–1712). Van der Heyden is also an important figure in the history of fire-fighting, having been credited with the invention of the fire-engine.

In **Room 220** we find a different kind of landscape painting. These are much sunnier, rockier and more exotic than those evoking the flat countryside of the Netherlands. They are by a group of painters known as the Italianists, which includes among others Nicolaes Berchem (1620–83), Adam Pijnacker (1622–73) and the versatile Karel Dujardin (1622–78). In the same room there is a self-portrait by the latter artist which is among the finest in the whole collection. In the following room (**221**) there are more paintings of the same type. One genre not yet mentioned is animal painting; here – rather tucked away – there is a well-known example, 'The Threatened Swan' by Jan Asselijn (1615–52). Someone subsequently attempted to make the swan at bay into a political symbol by painting texts on the painting: on the eggs we find 'Holland', the swan supposedly represents the 'State Pensionary' (at the time the highest government official), protecting the eggs against 'the enemy of the state' (the barking dog). Finally there are works by Frans Post (1612–80), the first painter of tropical landscapes.

The following room contains the work of the next generation of pupils of Rembrandt: Aert de Gelder (1645–1727), Nicolaes Maes (1634–93), Gerbrandt van den Eeckhout (1621–74) and Philips Koninck (1619–88). De Gelder particularly was an accomplished artist.

That is even more true of the painter found in the next room, Gerard Dou (1613–75). Dou was Rembrandt's first pupil and went on to train a renowned school of painters in Leiden, known as the *Leiden fijnschilders*, or 'delicate painters'. For a long time connoisseurs were not particularly fond of the very detailed but rather 'slick' and 'impersonal' style of Gerard Dou and his Leiden acolytes; today attitudes are very different. In their own day – the second half of the seventeenth century, when Dutch painters were beginning to attract far more attention abroad – artists like Dou and Frans van Mieris the Elder (1635–81) became 'world famous' and earned fortunes from their work. A third painter in the same vein, Adriaen van der Werff (1659–1722), was also immensely rich. He came not from Leiden, but from Kralingen (now a district of Rotterdam). 'The Sick Child' by Gabriël Metsu (1629–67) is an appealing and hence extremely popular painting.

Gerard Terborch (1617–81) lived some distance away from the province of Holland, in the eastern town of Deventer, but was still widely renowned. The Grand Duke of Tuscany once requested his self-portrait, just as he had those of Van Mieris and Dou. Terborch's work is rather like that of Johannes Vermeer (1632–75) from Delft: subdued interiors with well-dressed figures. Sometimes appearances can be deceptive: one painting hanging here, which Goethe in one of his works erroneously called 'A Fatherly Warning', is in fact a brothel scene.

In the last room (where it can get very crowded) before the 'Nightwatch' room we find the four famous Vermeers: 'Woman Reading a Letter', 'The Love-Letter', 'The Alleyway' and 'The Milkmaid'. Among Vermeer's fellow-townsmen were Pieter de Hooch (1629–84) and Emanuel de Witte (1617–92).

After passing a room containing a small permanent exhibition on Rembrandt's 'Nightwatch', we come face to face with the 'Nightwatch' itself. Don't let the fame and dark radiance of the great painting, again hanging in the place it occupied at the opening of the museum in 1885, stop you looking at the other militia paintings collected here. Although the 'Nightwatch' gives the impression of depicting an action or an event, it in fact consists of a series of portraits, like the other group portraits in the vicinity, by Van der Helst, Flinck and a painter of German origin, Joachim von Sandrart (1606–88).

The Gallery of Honour brings us back to the point of departure, the room selling books and catalogues. This gallery contains the great Rembrandt masterpieces: the celebrated 'Jewish Bride' (the identity of whose subjects is still not known); 'The Syndics', one of the master's last great works from 1661; 'The Denial of St Peter'; and the wonderful 'Anatomy Lesson of Professor Deyman'.

Rembrandt is again surrounded by his pupils. The tour ends with group and family portraits by Abraham van den Tempel (1622/3–72) and Karel Dujardin, who here shows himself capable of more than 'delicate painting' and Italianate landscapes. Gerard de Lairesse (1641–1711), represented by a large painting, came from Liège and after going blind wrote what is probably the thickest treatise on art in history.

The painting section of the museum has up to now dealt only with the Dutch sixteenth and seventeenth centuries. The Rijksmuseum has far too small a collection of foreign art, and the best items are rather tucked away behind the wall where the 'Nightwatch' hangs: they include works by Fra Angelico, Piero di Cosimo, Veronese, Lodovico Carracci, Goya, Jordaens and Rubens.

Eighteenth- and nineteenth-century art

Those wishing to see Dutch eighteenth- and nineteenth-century art must venture into the great labyrinth of the Arts and Crafts section. Although the Arts and Crafts and Sculpture departments are the largest in area in the whole museum, their collections will not be dealt with at length here. The museum does, though, have some wonderful examples of applied art. To mention some of the finest: the Delftware (**Rooms 225/6**), the Meissen porcelain (**Rooms 169 to 172**), the rooms containing Empire, Art Nouveau and Art Deco furniture (**Rooms 33 and 34**), including pieces by the architect H.P. Berlage and the Belgian Henry van de Velde (1863–1957).

Sculpture exhibits include fifteenth-century wood-carvings, with, for example, work by the German Tilman Riemenschneider (**Rooms 240 to 247**); Italian miniatures and terracotta pieces (**Room 249**); works by Adriaen de Vries (1545–1626), a Dutch sculptor of international standing (**Room 250**); and portraits and designs by Artus Quellinus or Quellien (1609–68) for the Amsterdam Town Hall (see also p. 85). Having finally reached the section on eighteenth and nineteenth century painting by a circuitous route, you first enter a small room containing a bench, where suddenly smoking is allowed (as it is also in the museum canteen, which has improved in recent years).

Next comes a long corridor giving access to the so-called **Drucker Extension**. This is named after a Mr and Mrs Drucker, from whom the greater part of the museum's nineteenth-century art derives. In the corridor there is a sort of brief recapitulation of the last quarter of the seventeenth century; there are again works by Adriaen van der Werff, Frans van Mieris, Gerard de Lairesse, and also some fine pieces by Caspar Netscher (1639–84), a pupil of Terborch's, and Godfried Schalcken (1643–1706), famous for his striking rendering of burning torches (perhaps a trivial subject, but a difficult one to paint).

Schalcken was a pupil of Dou, himself a pupil of Rembrandt. The Golden Century of Dutch painting did indeed last a hundred years and spanned three generations. What follows in **Room 136** is far less impressive. Cornelis Troost (1696–1750), a painter and actor, is probably the best-known eighteenth-century artist, and there are a great many of his works on show. It will gradually become apparent that the genres and themes of the seventeenth century were quietly perpetuated for a hundred years more: group portraits, still-lifes, genre paintings. Perhaps the best painter of this century is George van der Mijn (1723–63). This is said with some hesitation, as very little of his work is known. In this room there are two portraits, and if you go, via **Room 139** – with a collection of splendid pastels by the Swiss painter Jean-Étienne Liotard (1702–89) – to the next room, where a stairway suddenly appears out of nowhere, you will find a magnificent group portrait by Van der Mijn.

The stairway leads down to another collection housed in the extension: the **Asiatic Art Section**. You can often wander round here all on your own. Almost no one goes there; not because it is not worth while, but because no one knows about it. If you don't descend the staircase but turn left, there are two more rooms of (late) eighteenth-century art.

The nineteenth century saw a revival of the arts in the Netherlands: art academies were set up, the Prix de Rome was instituted (and still exists), and there' was an amazing upsurge in the number of artists (not that the quality immediately improved). Later in the century the so-called Hague School, a group consisting predominantly of landscape and marine artists, emerged. The best of them were the three Maris brothers, J.H. Weissenbruch (1824–1903) and H.W. Mesdag (1831–1915), who spent the fortune he acquired on his marriage to Sientje Mesdag-van Houten, herself also a painter, on collecting contemporary art (especially French) and with this set up one of the first Dutch museums (the Museum Mesdag in The Hague, which still exists). The work of Josef Israëls is also famous; because of his sombre palette and the importance accorded him he was often called the nineteenth-century Rembrandt.

The last room (**149**) is devoted to the Amsterdam artist George Breitner (1857–1923), who has links with the Hague School.

The visitor is advised against trying to take in the whole Rijksmuseum in one go. The **Print Room** has quite frequent exhibitions, usually from its own (excellent) collection of drawings and prints. The **Dutch History Section**, in which a good deal of attention is paid to the sea battles of the seventeenth century (unfortunately with explanatory texts in Dutch only), is in need of smartening up. It contains paintings by Honthorst (a family portrait of the stadholder Frederik Hendrik), who is accorded too little attention in the main section; naturally the maritime painters Willem van de Velde the Elder (1611–93) and Willem van de Velde the Younger (1633–1707); also well-known portraits of William the Silent (by Adriaan Key, 1544–89) and his descendant William III, stadholder of the Dutch Republic and king of England (by Godfried Schalcken, and predictably candle-lit). Somewhat out of the way there is one of the most famous pictures of the nineteenth century, the enormous 'Battle of Waterloo' by J.W. Pieneman (1779–1853).

SCHEEPVAARTMUSEUM/MARITIME MUSEUM

Address: Kattenburgerplein 1
Opening times: Tuesday–Saturday, 10 a.m.–5 p.m.; Sundays and national holidays, 1–5 p.m.

In 1990, if everything goes to plan, a full-sized replica of an East Indiaman will tie up at the quay of Amsterdam's former 'Naval Warehouse' (Zeemagazijn), which now houses the National Maritime Museum. This so-called 'return boat', which was used in the Indies trade, is being copied using the construction drawings of the former *Amsterdam*, built in 1748, which sank in a sudden storm off Hastings in 1749.

The Naval Warehouse itself, commissioned as early as 1657 by the Admiralty (the supreme regional command of the fleet), was built 'in nine months', and served as an equipment depot; from here ships were supplied with sails, rigging, cannon, provisions, etc.

The museum, located here since 1981, offers an extensive survey of the history of Dutch shipping. Spacious and quiet, the Maritime Museum has an exceptionally rich collection of books and catalogues on sale, and a pleasant, though as regards selection rather small, canteen (in view of the fact that the museum is some way from the centre and is almost entirely surrounded by water, this will hopefully soon improve). Before going upstairs to the exhibition, it is worth while glancing at the so-called 'royal sloop'. This vessel, richly decorated and covered in gold leaf, was used until 1962 by the royal family.

The first floor gives an extensive overview of the vicissitudes of the East India Company's ships and of the Dutch fleet of warships in the seventeenth and eighteenth centuries. The second floor deals with shipping in the nineteenth and twentieth centuries.

A large part of Amsterdam's wealth in the sevententh century was based on shipping and on her position as a European entrepôt for wood, spices, chinaware and suchlike. In 1672 the Republic was attacked by no less than four European states simultaneously: England, France, Munster and Cologne. After the indecisive sea battle of Kijkduin a year later, this Dutch commercial empire, which had once had more merchant ships than the rest of Europe put together, went into a long but steady eclipse. Even at the time the Delft painter Johannes Vermeer complained that as a result of the hostilities both he and his eleven under-age children had suffered a severe drop in income.

Naturally one's attention is drawn first and foremost to the museum's many splendid model ships, but there is also a collection of seascapes by recognized specialists such as Hendrick Cornelisz. Vroom (1566–1640), the inventor of the genre, Ludolf Backhuysen (1631–1708), Willem van de Velde the Elder, represented by some typically detailed pen-and-ink drawings, and his son Willem van de Velde the Younger (the best of the bunch). One notable item is a painted account of the Battle of Gibraltar (1622) by Cornelis van Wieringen (1580–1633), a pupil of Vroom's. For this large, but not outstanding, work the town council paid what was then the enormous sum of 2,400 guilders! In addition there are paintings of famous naval heroes, among them the well-known portrait of Michiel Adriaansz. de Ruyter by Ferdinand Bol and a *tronie* – or 'mug-shot', as it was called at the time – of Piet Hein. Dutch school-books recount the story of De Ruyter's sortie up the Thames during the Second Anglo-Dutch war (1665–7) and his ramming of a chain stretched across the river. Piet Hein captured a Spanish fleet laden with silver off Cuba; the song of the 'Silver Fleet' is still sung at football matches. The second floor contains exhibits devoted to the magnificent dining rooms and cabins of pre-war steamships, and there is a dining table designed by Lion Cachet (1864–1945).

It is a shame that the captions are almost exclusively in Dutch; on the other hand, a great deal of nautical jargon is used which is not always comprehensible even to Dutch-speaking laymen.

STEDELIJK MUSEUM /MUNICIPAL MUSEUM

Adress: Paulus Potterstraat 13 (District 2)
Opening times: 11 a.m.–5 p.m. daily

It is a much-heard complaint that Amsterdam (or the Netherlands, for that matter) has no representative museum for the nineteenth century. But what about a museum of the twentieth century, which is after all almost over?

In the Stedelijk Museum, Amsterdam does possess an excellent museum for modern art, but it cannot be said to give a comprehensive overview of the development of art history in our century. Although the museum, opened in 1895, is quite spacious, it has no room for a permanent exhibition of all its holdings. The storerooms, on the other hand, are full of excellent collections: late nineteenth-century art; posters, applied art and design; Dutch pre-Second World War art. The collection of international post-war art, acquired under the directorship of Willem Sandberg, was (and to some extent still is) famous.

The Stedelijk Museum uses its exhibition space almost exclusively for temporary exhibitions, which means that there is no point in surveying the whole collection. The visitor can assume that the splendid collection of the artists of the Dutch De Stijl group, with Piet Mondriaan (1872–1944) and Theo van Doesburg (1883–1931) as its most important representatives, will be on display in its entirety. Under the previous director, Willem Sandberg, an important collection of works by the Russian painter Kasimir Malevich (1878–1935) was built up; part of this is also usually on exhibition. A great late work by Henri Matisse is always on show, as is an installation by Edward Kienholz, the so-called 'Beanery', which is too large to be constantly dismantled (on the left, by the entrance to the canteen).

Americans (with the exception of Mark Rothko) have always been well represented in the museum's collection. Barnett Newman's 'Who's Afraid of Red, Yellow and Blue' was for a long time considered the Stedelijk's answer to the 'Nightwatch', and was surrounded by works by Kenneth Noland, Frank Stella (not a particularly good example of his work) and above all Ellsworth Kelly. Since they and their artistic descendants have been somewhat overshadowed from the beginning of the 1980s onwards by European New Painting, they have been much less in evidence in the museum.

The Stedelijk is a particularly lively place – even when there is nothing special to see – with the nicest and largest cafeteria in the Netherlands.

Modern Dutch art

Dutch post-war art is not of any special international importance, perhaps precisely because it is so internationally orientated – and perhaps also because it is so easily possible to trace these international developments in the Stedelijk Museum. Italy, for example, has no such museum for modern art and hence has no sounding board, which tends to make Italian artists more inward-looking; yet Italian art has an enormous international reputation.

For a small country, the Netherlands has an almost inordinate number of art schools (two important ones, the Rijksacademie and the Rietveld Academie, are located in Amsterdam). These schools train a large number – probably too many – artists, who then face an uncertain future.

Until recently professional artists profited greatly by the so-called Visual Artists' Scheme (Beeldende Kunstenaars Regeling). Briefly, the scheme meant that work by artists adjudged to be of high enough quality was purchased by the state for a particular sum. Subsequently calculations were made as to how long the artist could support himself on that amount, which determined the date at which he could again call on the scheme. Although intended as a bridging arrangement to help up-and-coming talents become established, the scheme became a structural part of Dutch artistic life. Moreover, it cost the state more and more money, as more and more emerging artists began to make use of it. One sad aspect of the scheme was that the specially constructed storerooms gradually filled up with works which obviously no one was interested in owning. For all one knows they may be languishing there still, unseen by anyone.

In the mid-1980s the scheme was abolished; artists now have to make do with temporary bursaries and subsidies for the purchase of materials.

Another Dutch institution is 'Art on Loan'. For a deposit the public can acquire a work of art on temporary loan, which must be returned after a set period. This can be repeated indefinitely, and from the total sum saved in this way the borrower can eventually become the owner of a work from the 'Art on Loan' collection.

Another possibility is to take out an interest-free loan from the Dutch government to finance the purchase of a work of art from a recognized gallery. One condition, however, is that the work should be by a living Dutch artist. Thanks to – or maybe in spite of – such state support, this country does have a few artists of stature. To make a random selection from the last twenty years: Karel Appel, Constant, Bram van de Velde, Armando, Jan Dibbets, Ger van Elk, Peter Struycken, Lucassen and Stanley Brown, and, more recently, Henk Visch, Marlene Dumas, Rob Scholte, Emo Verkerk, Peer Veneman and Lydia Schouten. The work of these artists is generally represented in the Stedelijk Museum, or otherwise in the leading Amsterdam galleries, a list of which is on p. 106.

Those visiting Amsterdam in the right week can attend the large Dutch art trade fair, the **Kunst-Rai** (held in the Amsterdam Rai Trade Fair complex), where everything can be seen in one go. Foreign galleries are also represented at this fair; each year a different country plays host. Finally, the **Nieuwe Kerk** (Dam) and Berlage's **Stock Exchange** (Damrak) occasionally mount shows devoted to modern art or photography, and the **Flemish Cultural Centre** (Vlaams Cultureel Centrum, Nes 45) has exhibitions of Flemish artists.

TROPENMUSEUM/TROPICAL MUSEUM

Address: Linnaeusstraat 2
Opening times: Monday–Friday, 10 a.m.–5 p.m.; Saturdays, Sundays and
national holidays, 12–5 p.m.

This museum was founded in 1910 as the 'Colonial Museum' with the
aim of building a collection of exhibits 'which relate to the present
condition of the peoples of the colonies, to disseminate knowledge of
the domestic lives, mores and customs and the social development of
those peoples'. Except for the fact that the Netherlands no longer has
any colonies, the museum still adheres to its original educational task.
The interior of the building in which the museum is housed is one of
the finest in Amsterdam. Its large hall is surrounded by three tiers of galleries; the hall itself is used for temporary exhibitions.
The museum is organized into five large sections: South-East Asia, South
Asia, the Middle East, Africa and Latin America. In addition there are
small sections organized around such themes as 'Man and Technology',
'Man and the Environment' and 'World Trade'. The visitor to the museum cannot escape the penetrating smell of spices.
The Tropenmuseum tries to reproduce the daily lives of the peoples of
the tropics as realistically as possible by reconstructing fragments of their
environment (houses, shops, temples). In an exhibiton on the Yemen in
1989 they went as far as to install a genuine merchant in the reconstructed Yemeni village. Unfortunately no special attention is paid to objects
of an artistic nature. Visitors are recommended to cast at least the odd
glance at the architecture of the museum itself; the sculptings on the capitals of the columns and on the keystones are worth looking at.
The Tropenmuseum is a little way out of the centre, but is close to the
large Artis zoo, with its *Zoological Museum*.

GALLERIES

Galleries for the visual arts
Galerie A, Joh. Verhulststraat 53 (District 2)
Akinci, Singel 74 (neo-geometric art) (District 6)
De Appel, Prinseneiland 7 (District 4)
Art & Project, Prinsengracht 785 (District 4) (very important: Gilbert
and George, Jan Dibbets)
Barbara Farber, Keizersgracht 265 (District 6)

Brinkman, Kerkstraat 105 (District 4)

Collection d'Art, Keizersgracht 516 (Lucebert, Freymuth, Armando) (District 4)

De Drie Gratiën, Weteringstraat 39 (erotic art) (District 4)

Espace, Keizersgracht 548 (one of the oldest in the city) (District 4)

Van Gelder, Planciusstraat 9a (J.C.J. van der Heyden, Rudi van de Windt) (District 4)

Hans Gieles, Rozenstraat 59 (very recent art) (District 7)

Van Krimpen, Prinsengracht 629 (important gallery) (District 4)

The Living Room, Laurierstraat 70 (Frank van de Broek, Rob Scholte) (District 7)

Lumen Travo, Nieuwezijds Voorburgwal 352-IV (District 5)

Mokum, Oudezijds Voorburgwal 334 (realist art) (District 1)

Onrust, Prinsengracht 627 (very small, very pleasant, next door to Van Krimpen) (District 4)

Paul Andriesse, Prinsengracht 116 (important, certainly for the young, 'established' generation: Mol, René Daniels, Henk Visch, Marlene Dumas) (District 7)

Riekje Swart, Van Breestraat 23 (possibly the oldest in the city, very highly respected: Walter Dahn, Dokupil, Milan Kunc, especially drawings) (District 2)

Van Rooy, Kerkstraat 216 (architectural drawings) (District 4)

Torch, Prinsengracht 218 (photography) (District 7)

Fons Welters, Bloemstraat 140 (sculpture) (District 7)

Wetering Galerie, Lijnbaansgracht 288 (District 4)

Galleries for design and applied art

Galerie Binnen, Keizersgracht 82 (Italian furniture: Memphis, Ettore Sottsass) (District 6)

Leidelmeyer, Nieuwe Spiegelstraat 58 (very important: Art Nouveau and Art Deco) (District 4)

Lodewijk van Walraven, Korte Leidsedwarsstraat 157 (1960s design) (District 4)

Galerie Ra, Vijzelstraat 80 (jewellery) (District 4)

De Witte Voet, Kerkstraat 149 (ceramics) (District 4)

7 · Architecture

The enormous diversity of architecture in Amsterdam is the result of seven centuries of experiment with a city in which people both work – especially in international commerce – and live. The unique feature of Amsterdam is that the many different phases of development over the centuries survive side by side. In the centre, within the area bounded by the Oude Schans and the Nieuwezijds Voorburgwal, there is a tightly packed late-medieval quarter which, relatively speaking, has changed most in appearance over the centuries. This is surrounded by the impressive seventeenth-century ring of canals (Singel, Herengracht, Keizersgracht, Prinsengracht and Lijnbaansgracht), which evokes the grandeur of the Golden Age and to this day is one of the most popular locations for prestigious homes and offices.

Next there is the Jordaan, which in the seventeenth century saw the first social housing projects, in the shape of the many *hofjes*, or almshouses belonging to charitable institutions, and the band of nineteenth-century speculative building beyond the ring of canals (Oud-West, the 'Pijp'), now being extensively renovated. Berlage's world-famous 'Plan Zuid' is a large-scale general urban development plan dating from before the Second World War, though largely executed only after that dismal period. Finally, there are the new building projects in the south-east and north of the city, which began with the Bijlmer in the 1960s. At present the emphasis is on inner-city renewal and a few small-scale new building projects on disused industrial sites and in the docklands.

While elsewhere in the world whole cities were in certain periods swept away to make room for the ideas of new urban planners – and sometimes still are – in Amsterdam the existing districts were in the main left intact, so creating a city which has become a Mecca for architecture enthusiasts. Everyone interested in the history of architecture comes to Amsterdam to see the two great themes: the seventeenth-century Amsterdam of the architects De Keyser, Van Campen and Vingboons, with its typically Dutch treatment of Classicism, and turn-of-the-century Amsterdam, where Berlage, De Klerk and Duiker are the prophets of a new architecture.

MIDDLE AGES AND GOTHIC

The architectural history of Amsterdam begins at the end of the thirteenth century. The medieval town consisted of wooden structures, of which only two examples survive, in more or less reconstructed form: at **Zeedijk 1** (District 1) and in the **Begijnhof** (Béguinage; entrance in the Spui, District 5). Amid these wooden buildings stood a few late-Gothic churches. The **Oude Kerk** (District 1; begun in 1300) is an example of a church which has 'grown' organically over the centuries. The **Nieuwe Kerk** (District 6) was built approximately a century later. Both churches were stripped of much ornamentation at the end of the sixteenth century during the Iconoclastic Fury. Afterwards the buildings were adapted to new religious thinking. In the seventeenth and eighteenth centuries some of the foremost artists, such as the sculptor Rombout Verhulst (1625–96) and the silversmith Johannes Lutma (1585–1669), worked on the Nieuwe Kerk.

The medieval town was surrounded by a wall, of which a number of towers and a gatehouse are the most striking remnants. The **Montelbaanstoren** (Montelbaan Tower, on the Oude Schans canal, District 1) and the **Munttoren** (Mint Tower, on the Muntplein, District 4) acquired a new function and at the beginning of the seventeenth century were capped with Renaissance spires by Hendrick de Keyser. The most important city gate, **Sint Antoniespoort**, was converted into a weighing-house (**Waag**, Nieuwmarkt, District 1) as early as the middle of the sixteenth century and later into an anatomical theatre. In 1989 the French architect and furniture designer Philippe Starck turned it into a cultural centre.

URBAN EXPANSION IN THE SEVENTEENTH CENTURY

The expansion of seventeenth-century Amsterdam was funded principally by wealthy patricians, who also controlled the town council. It was in this prosperous climate and at a time of huge population growth that the Amsterdam authorities decided to launch a canal-building project on the marshy ground just outside the medieval city. Between 1610 and 1670 the land was prepared in different stages for building in a radial form. Two people, Frans Hendriksz Oetgens and Hendrick Jacobsz Staets, were solely responsible for the concentric expansion.

It is typical of the whole development that no account was taken of existing watercourses; the costly plan was executed on purely aesthetic grounds. The plots of land, called *kavels*, were sold literally piece by piece. It was the merchants who originally had their offices and residences on the crowded business thoroughfares and quays who decided to have houses constructed in the new areas. Very rich merchants would even buy two *kavels* of land, so as to be able to build houses twice as wide as those of their neighbours.

By the time the initial ring of canals was completed in the first quarter of the seventeenth century, from the Brouwersgracht to the Leidsestraat, a district had meanwhile been laid out beyond it, the Jordaan. Here it can be clearly seen that a decision was taken on cost grounds not to change existing waterways, and the whole district is on a smaller scale.

A start was also made on the construction of the **Western Islands** (Bickerseiland, Realeneiland). These islands had a more industrial function: wharves and warehouses were sited on them. (The building of the railway line to Haarlem in 1839 led to their becoming cut off from the rest of the city.) Not until the second half of the seventeenth century was the ring of canals extended as far as the Amstel. Shortly afterwards a section on the other side of the river was built up as far as the Plantage.

THE RENAISSANCE AND HENDRICK DE KEYSER

When in the second half of the sixteenth century most houses were fronted with stone, a quite unique Renaissance style developed in Amsterdam, with Hendrick de Keyser (1565–1621) as its principal representative. De Keyser was a member of one of the more active artistic families based in Amsterdam at the beginning of the seventeenth century. His very extensive body of work is Italian-inspired, as can be seen from the copious use of columns on the gables. The **Bartolotti House** of 1617 (Herengracht 170–172, District 6, now a theatre museum, open to the public) and the **Huis met de Hoofden** (House of Heads) of 1622 (Keizersgracht 123, District 6, now the Municipal Conservation Office, open to the public) are the most important examples. The style is whimsical, with many miniature columns and pinnacles, while the overall shape is a variant of a traditional house with a stepped gable. Both typify the influence of mannerist architect of Hans Vredeman de Vries (1527–1606), who won enduring fame through his architectural model books.

CHURCHES AND HENDRICK DE KEYSER

Hendrick de Keyser also built a number of new churches. He could now experiment with innovatory ground-plans, because the form of worship practised by the new Protestants had different architectural requirements from that of the Catholics. The **Zuiderkerk** begun in 1603 (Zandstraat 17, District 1, at present the Information Centre for Urban Renewal, open to the public), adorned with a multitude of columns and pinnacles, is now situated in the middle of a delightful new building project, which owes its existence to the building of the underground system. Theo Bosch's **Pentagon** of 1984 (Zuiderkerkhof) is one of the finest recent examples of social housing.

The **Westerkerk** begun in 1620 (Westermarkt, District 6, tower open to the public) is much more restrained in character. The austere interior, with its white walls and sandstone columns and edging, reveals a later development in De Keyser's style. The 85-metre-high tower, with the imperial crown at the top, consists of smaller and smaller square sections stacked on top of each other, surrounded by columns.

His last church is the **Noorderkerk** of 1620 (Noordermarkt, District 7, restricted opening). The ground-plan, very advanced for its time, has been completely adapted to the requirements of Protestant worship. The inside of the church, with its concentric rows of pews, is in a poor state of repair, but is certainly worth a visit.

CLASSICISM IN THE SEVENTEENTH CENTURY

Around this time the flourishing Amsterdam publishing trade was distributing architectural manuals by the leading lights of the Italian Renaissance of the fifteenth and sixteenth centuries (Palladio, Scamozzi and Serlio) throughout Europe. These contained detailed models for the new style in architecture – Classicism. Amsterdam, then experiencing a period of explosive growth, had an ample supply of what was required for the development of a new architectural style: money and space. Seventeenth-century Amsterdam was an affluent city where businessmen strove to impress each other by commissioning beautiful architecture and contemporary art.

Jacob van Campen and Classicism
In the work of Jacob van Campen (1595–1657) one can see the transition from Dutch Renaissance to the Dutch Classical style of the Baroque. Whereas elsewhere in Europe the Baroque was wildly exuberant, in Holland we find a more restrained treatment. If we compare it with seventeenth-century painting we find the same restrained exuberance, but also unprecedented quality. **Rembrandt van Rijn's House** of 1633 (Jodenbreestraat 4–6, District 1, see also p. 91) shows how Van Campen first designed a gable in traditional brick, though much more austere than those of Hendrick de Keyser. The pediment topping the gable and a further one above the door are Classical elements.

At the height of Amsterdam's prosperity Jacob van Campen gained the commission for the construction of the **Town Hall on the Dam** (since Napoleon's time the Royal Palace, open to the public, see p. 85). There had been a competition for the award of the commission, and a violent controversy erupted: the building of the Town Hall for the hub of world trade was naturally a much sought-after commission. The rivalry led to intense dispute and the eventual absence of the architect from the beginning of the construction in 1648.

The construction of the Town Hall necessitated the removal of a large part of the medieval town centre with its dilapidated buildings and old town hall (shown in a painting in the Rijksmuseum based on a drawing by Pieter Saenredam of 1641). Internationally acclaimed artists were commissioned to work on the many decorations. All the marble carvings were executed by the studio of Artus Quellien or Quellinus (1609–68), the teacher of the Rotterdam-born Englishman Grinling Gibbons (1648–1721).

The Town Hall became one of the principal meeting-places for the patrician class. They would stroll in their best attire through the Citizens' Chamber and along the wide corridors in order to be seen and to conduct 'business'.

The Vingboons and Stalpaert

Two architects of note who also received commissions were the brothers Philips (1608–78) and Justus Vingboons (1621–98), members of another very active artistic family of the time, who produced extremely austere Classical designs. Philips was the principal loser in the Town Hall competition won by Jacob van Campen.

At **Oude Turfmarkt 145** (District 1) is the house designed by Philips for the composer Jan Pieterszoon Sweelinck. It has a Classical gable with a traditional placing of windows and door. Gone are the ebullient gables of previous years: here we find a stark arrangement of columns and windows. The roof-ridge was once fronted by a stepped gable, now replaced by a neck gable, while the sloping edge of the roof is camouflaged by stone scrolls. Each floor of the house-front belongs to a different Classical order recognizable from the capitals: sober Doric on the ground floor, furled Ionic in the middle and Doric again at the top. Originally the house was one of a pair, but the front of the adjoining property was replaced in the late nineteenth century by one of the ugliest examples of so-called 'neo-Renaissance' style.

In 1655 Philips built a splendid private residence, **De Mayer House**, at Oudezijds Voorburgwal 316 (District 1, not open to the public). The front has a slightly protruding middle section with Doric and Ionic columns and a richly decorated pediment. The row of houses he subsequently built for the merchant Jacob Cromhout on the Herengracht (364–370, now the **Bible Museum**, open to the public) shows his method of working with sandstone and with the different orders of columns on the house-fronts. At attic level we find a typically Amsterdam feature, the so-called *œil-de-bœuf*: a circular window surrounded by sandstone decoration (a cartouche).

Between 1660 and 1662 Justus built the imposing **Trippenhuis** on the Kloveniersburgwal 29 (District 1). The Corinthian columns are decorated with capitals made of leaves and the gable is in natural stone. The house looks as though it has been built as a single dwelling, but is in fact divided exactly in two. This means that the middle window is false, masking the dividing wall. A nice detail is that the Trip brothers' trade (arms-dealing) is alluded to in the cannon-shaped chimneys.

Daniël Stalpaert (1615–76) built the Naval Storehouse (**Zeemagazijn**, Kattenburgerplein 1, now the **Maritime Museum**, see p. 102). Stalpaert was also an adherent of the severe Classical style of the mid seventeenth century. The Naval Storehouse is a large, square arsenal, with protruding middle sections and pediments designed by Artus Quellinus. It is especially its location on the open harbour front that makes it an impressive structure.

Synagogues in the seventeenth century

In the course of the sevententh century many Jews from all over Europe found sanctuary in Amsterdam. Two complexes of buildings are situated close to each other on the Mr Visserplein (District 3). The oldest is the **High-German Synagogue** of 1670 by Elias Bouman (1635–86), a tall, sober building with a well-preserved interior. Together with a smaller synagogue and the splendid **New Synagogue** with a charming skylight by G.F. Maybaum of 1752, it now forms the **Jewish Historical Museum** (see also p. 85). The museum was opened in 1987 and in 1989 won the international Museum Prize for the impressively designed interior by the architect Abel Cahen and the firm of BRS Premsela Vonk. It shows how efficient modern architecture can ensure that a building works as a whole, while respecting the individual components. The street between the two buildings has been covered with a glass roof and now serves as an entrance hall.

Opposite stands the **Portuguese-Israelite Synagogue** of 1675 by Elias Bouman. A huge square block with tall windows and a balustrade along the edge of the roof, it is set in the middle of a site ringed by small houses. Unfortunately the building is seldom open.

Social housing in the seventeenth century

Another example of a modern conversion of a group of historical buildings is the **Municipal Orphanage**, which has become the **Amsterdam
Historical Museum** (Kalverstraat 92; see also p. 81). It has a richly
decorated entrance-way of 1581 on the Kalverstraat, an enormous Classical girls' courtyard with colossal Ionic columns, and a boys' courtyard
containing a loggia with fourteen Doric columns. These imposing
spaces, together with the nearby Begijnhof, are among the most tranquil
spots in the city.

Seventeenth-century architects were already engaged in the construction
of the oldest forms of social housing. Charitable institutions for the care
of orphans and the elderly were set up from an early period. Architects
like Vingboons and Stalpaert were involved with either the first mass-
produced housing (Reguliersdwarsstraat) or with so-called *hofjes*
(almshouses). Daniël Stalpaert's *hofje* of 1650 in the Karthuizersstraat
61–191 (District 7) is a good example of such a project. It consists of a
large number of one-room dwellings on two floors built round a courtyard. Above the entrance is a Classical element: a pediment bearing the
Amsterdam coat-of-arms.

In 1681 the architect Hans Pertersom built an old people's home at Amstel 51 (District 3, now **Amstelhof**), with its thirty-one sets of windows
still the widest house in Amsterdam. It is a sober Classical building with a
pediment only over the central main entrance. The main entrance has a
pair of Ionic columns, the two side-entrances Doric columns.

FRENCH INFLUENCE

During the eighteenth century few changes were made to the city itself.
Economically Amsterdam was no longer the force it had been in the seventeenth century. However, there was no question of financial hardship
in the business community. There was a move towards further adorn-
ment of houses, influenced particularly by the French Louis styles. Classical restraint gave way to sumptuous gable-tops and roof ridges outside
and lavish attention inside. Stucco came into fashion, or alternatively
painters were commissioned to imitate stucco-work in *grisaille* – painted
panels in grey and white.

The finest example of this is to be found in the house built by Philips
Vingboons in 1638 at Herengracht 168 (District 6, now part of the
Theatre Museum, open to the public), which was completely modernized inside in the eighteenth century. The stucco-work in the hall was
executed in 1727 by the great master in the field, Jan van Logteren. The
hall neatly demonstrates the kind of French-inspired visual tricks that

were played on visitors at the time. After passing through a door placed at the extreme left, one enters a hallway which gives the impression of being entirely symmetrical; there are double doors on both sides. The right-hand doors lead into unexpectedly richly decorated rooms featuring an Arcadian landscape by the decorative artist Isaac de Moucheron and *grisailles* of the elements and seasons by Jacob de Wit (1695–1754), a painter also much employed in the Town Hall in the eighteenth century. The left-hand doors lead to nothing but a broom cupboard.

Another fine example of a Louis XIV house-front is the **Van Brienen Family House** of 1728 (Herengracht 284, District 6, viewable only by appointment), now the headquarters of a private conservation organization, the Hendrick de Keyser Association. The house has a sandstone front retaining the original disposition of the windows and a lavish roof ridge with a balustrade and decorative vases. The interior is in Louis XVI style and there is a symmetrically planned garden with a particularly beautiful summerhouse.

The section of the Herengracht between the Leidsestraat and the Vijzelstraat is rightly known as the **Golden Curve** (District 4) – it has the finest eighteenth-century buildings in the whole canal ring. Almost all the houses are wider than usual, either as a result of two houses being joined together or because of the purchase of two adjacent plots a century earlier. The houses are all faced with sandstone, a material which had to be transported long distances and was hence much more expensive than brick, which was immediately available. **Herengracht 475** (1730) by Hans Jacob Husly (1702–76) and **Herengracht 485** (1739) by Jean Coulon (1680–1756) have the familiar feature of a double set of steps crowned by a balustrade leading to the front entrance. A little further on at numbers 493 and 527, both of 1770, are two examples of Louis XVI style, where one can see a revival of austere Classical lines.

LOUIS XVI

Amsterdam assimilated the Rococo and Louis XV periods only in a few minor gable decorations. The style may have been a little too frivolous for wealthy Amsterdammers. The neo-Classicism of Louis XVI clearly had more of an appeal. It bore the marks of the fact that for the first time people were beginning to look at the Greek models for themselves. Of course, non-Greek decorative elements still appeared – the stone laurel-wreaths or bow-shaped wood-carvings round the small windows above the doors of many canal-side houses of the period, for instance.

The most spectacular building of the period is the headquarters of the **Felix Meritis** society (Keizersgracht 324, District 7, now the Shaffy

Theatre, open to the public), built in 1788 by Jacob Otten Husly (1738–96). With its huge height and gigantic half-columns, it is actually too large for its surroundings. Its pediment is decorated with splendid wood-carvings. In those days it was the cultural centre of Amsterdam.

In the late eighteenth and early nineteenth century the city architect Abraham van der Hart (1747–1820) especially was responsible for the construction of many orphanages and workhouses. The **Maagdenhuis** of 1783–7 (Spui, District 5, open to the public) is one such massive edifice, whose sole decoration, on the pediment, is by the sculptor Anthonie Ziesenis.

THE DEVELOPMENT OF THE PLANTAGE IN THE EIGHTEENTH CENTURY

The most important eighteenth-century town-planning development was the conversion of the Plantage (District 3) into a luxurious residential and recreational area. Where now the Plantage Middenlaan runs past the Artis Zoological Gardens, there was once a long lane leading southeastwards, along which rich businessmen built their country houses. Only one such house has survived, **Frankendael**, at Middenweg 72 (gardens open to the public). The villa has a lavishly decorated entrance with Louis XVI ornamentation and a fountain featuring sculptures of river gods.

Some Amsterdammers went further afield to build their country houses, and many had villas constructed along what is still a peaceful tributary of the Rhine, the Vecht.

LOUIS BONAPARTE AND THE BEGINNING OF THE NINETEENTH CENTURY

The nineteenth century, which elsewhere in Europe provided so many architectural fireworks, brought little benefit to Amsterdam, which by the early nineteenth century had become a complete economic backwater. Louis Bonaparte, who was made King of Holland by his brother Napoleon in 1806, had meanwhile bought the Town Hall from the town council for a pittance in order to use it as his palace. Concerned by the plight of architects with nothing to build, he sent a number of them to France for proper training.

T.F. Suys (1783–1861), who built the **Mozes en Aäronkerk** on the Waterlooplein (District 1), had studied with the French architect Charles Percier (1764–1838), and the towers of his church are clearly inspired by those of St Sulpice in Paris. Another French-trained architect was J.D. Zocher (1791–1870). Zocher was the father of a family of landscape architects who were to change the look of towns throughout Holland by removing town walls virtually everywhere and converting the ramparts into parks. These parks were laid out in the eighteenth-century landscape style imported from England, which aimed at as close an approximation as possible to natural landscape. The landscape style contrasted sharply with the formal garden design which had set the tone since the Middle Ages. Gardens – and up to the nineteenth century one saw gardens in Amsterdam only at the rear of canal-side mansions – invariably had a strictly geometric layout. One of the most elegant formal gardens can be seen at the back of the **Museum Willet-Holthuysen** (Herengracht 605, District 4; see p. 90).In Amsterdam Zocher's sons laid out the Vondelpark and Zorgvliet cemetery on the Amstel just outside the city, both in landscape style.

RESIDENTIAL BUILDING IN THE NINETEENTH CENTURY

The most important new district to be built in the nineteenth century was the 'Pijp' (District 8). It is a typical example of speculative building, with the hypocritical 'liberal' authorities opting for a plan which affected as few major landowners as possible – an alternative plan had been drawn up which envisaged a network of avenues and parks round the ring of canals, and would have given Amsterdam the grandeur of a Vienna. Nevertheless, the district has its own distinct atmosphere, and one street which by chance turned out wider than the rest, the **Albert Cuypstraat**, contains the pleasantest vegetable market in the city.

One architect who worked innovatively on social housing was P.J. Hamer (1812–87). In the Jordaan he designed a number of pleasantly appointed blocks of flats built round inner courtyards. The blocks were commissioned by the first institutions to concern themselves on a larger scale with philanthropic housing for the working class. The two complexes, both on the **Lijnbaansgracht** (63–65 and 174–179), and the adjacent streets, were recently restored. Though neither project is exactly spectacular from the outside, their distinctive inner courtyards are open to the public.

In one of the few parks which were actually laid out, the **Sarphatipark**, there is a monument to the man whose name it bears, Dr Samuel Sarphati (1813–66), sometimes called the father of modern Amsterdam. Sarphati had ambitious construction plans and hoped that Amsterdam would eventually regain its place among the leading capitals of Europe.

His projects were designed to create employment. The developments around the **Frederiksplein** (District 4) and near the **Amstelhotel**, built by C. Outshoorn (1812–75) in 1867, are reminiscent of Sarphati's plans: large public and commercial edifices interspersed with residential building. An exhibition hall, the **Paleis voor Volksvlijt** (Palace of National Industry), the most spectacular building erected in the Netherlands in the nineteenth century, occupied a dominant position in the middle of the Frederiksplein, approximately where the twin towers of the Netherlands National Bank now stand. The Palace burned down in 1929 and it was long after the Second World War before the last vestiges were cleared away. It is regrettable that a building every bit as imposing as the Grand Palais in Paris or London's Crystal Palace should not have been rebuilt.

ECLECTICISM

At the end of the nineteenth century an odd mixture of revived architectural styles appeared, which is not to everyone's taste – eclecticism, Neo-Gothic, neo-Renaissance and neo-Classicism were used side by side. The most characteristic feature of this period is the emergence of completely new types of building. Technological advances had created a need for buildings to house gasworks or grain silos. In the centre of town new offices and shops were built. On the corner of the Keizersgracht and the Leidsestraat (District 5) J. van Looy (1852–1911) put up an insurance office, which is now the department store **Metz & Co.** Commissioned by the New York Life Assurance Company (whose name can be seen on the front of the building) it was executed in an impeccable 'Baroque' style. In 1933 Gerrit Rietveld (1888–1964), one of the Netherlands' greatest architects (responsible for among other things the Rietveld-Schröder house in Utrecht), who did not build much in Amsterdam, added a cupola and a shop front to a house at Keizersgracht 449 (now Café Walem). In 1886 Van Looy built a bookshop at Damrak 62 (District 1, at present the **Allert de Lange** bookshop). Here too the front of the building reveals its function: a sculpture of the seventeenth-century poet Vondel, after whom the Vondelpark is named, is set in a niche above the main entrance.

The Neo-Renaissance **Stadsschouwburg** (Municipal Theatre) on the Leidseplein (District 4), by J.L. Springer (1850–1915) and A.L. van Gendt (1835–1901), is rather like an iced cake with frills, and also protrudes too far into the square. The interior on the other hand is a pleasantly intimate neo-Classical theatre space full of pillars, golden statuary and plush.

This is also an age of other new types of building, such as circuses and riding schools. At Amstel 115–125 (District 3) the **Oscar Carré Circus**, based on a German model, was built in a very short space of time in 1887. A.L. van Gendt designed the **Hollandse Manege** (Dutch Riding School, 1881) at Vondelstraat 140, where from a splendid authentic café one can look out on to the interior of the school. The same architect built the **Concertgebouw** (Concert Hall, 1888) on the Museumplein (District 2). This is an imitation of a Central European theatre, and is world-famous for its acoustics. In 1987 the building was restored by the architect Pi de Bruijn and a completely new cellar and foyer wing were added.

At Plantage Middenlaan 53 (District 3) the Salm brothers built an **Aquarium**, with a gigantic neo-Classical portico, now part of the the Artis zoo.

P.J.H. CUYPERS

The **Rijksmuseum** (1885) and the **Central Station** (1889), built towards the end of the nineteenth century by the neo-Gothic architect P.J.H. Cuypers (1827–1921) under the influence of the Frenchman Viollet-le-Duc (1814–79), can be seen to herald the modern age. Viollet-le Duc and Cuypers respect the underlying construction of a building, revealing structural features as a kind of homage. This is why they revere the Gothic master-builders, who, though lacking the knowledge available to modern architects, succeeded in building the most impressive edifices. Cuypers built a large number of neo-Gothic churches in the Netherlands and carried out many restorations. The **Vondelkerk** of 1880 (Vondelstraat 120, District 2) is regarded as one of his finest creations. The building has a symmetrical ground-plan and stands in the middle of a square forming part of a complete quarter designed by him. In 1986 the church was converted into an office complex by A. van Stigt. Cuypers lived diagonally opposite the church in a house he built for himself in 1876 (Vondelstraat 77).

The building of the **Rijksmuseum** caused a great deal of controversy. A serious conflict had meanwhile arisen between the Catholics, who advocated neo-Gothic, and the Protestants, who in turn favoured the neo-Renaissance style. When Cuypers was given the important commission, cartoons appeared mocking the 'cathedral of the arts' which he was to build. Neither the Rijksmuseum nor the Central Station have many neo-Gothic features. What the two buildings do have in common is the combination of the various arts with technology. Both are lavishly decorated with sculpture and tile tableaux with symbolic motifs, those at the station referring to transport and those at the Rijksmuseum to the arts.

HENDRIK PETRUS BERLAGE

Following the same principles of visible construction and the combination of the various arts Hendrik Petrus Berlage (1856–1934), who initially used the various neo-styles of the late nineteenth centry, built the Stock Exchange on the Damrak (**Beurs van Berlage**, District 1, open during concerts and exhibitions), completed in 1903. No building in Amsterdam has ever been greeted with such a chorus of protest. Today it is internationally acclaimed as one of the most important monuments of 'modern' architecture. It is the first building in the world where such an obviously new style was used in combination with socially orientated art. Everywhere there are heavy symbolic pointers to the function of the building and its place in society.

The façade is constructed according to a mathematical scheme and the tower is inspired by Tuscan architecture. The building consists of a number of large halls with skylights. In 1988 one of them was converted into a concert hall for the Netherlands Philharmonic Orchestra; the great hall is now used for exhibitions and other events.

ART NOUVEAU AND AMSTERDAM

Art Nouveau, with the odd exception, passed Amsterdam by almost completely. The only true example of Art Nouveau style is the old headquarters of the insurance company E.L.H.B., now the head office of the environmental organization **Greenpeace** (Keizersgracht 174–176, District 6). It was built in 1906 by the architect G. van Arkel (1858–1918). Located opposite this building, which by Amsterdam standards is gigantic, at Leliegracht 44, is the only specialist architectural bookshop in the city, **Architectura et Natura**.

There is Art Nouveau to be seen in the (highly recommended) café of the **American Hotel** (Leidseplein, District 4) of 1902, by W. Kromhout (1864–1940). This architect, however, is more important as one of the precursors of a new, specifically Amsterdam, expressionist style – the Amsterdam School (see below).

That architects around the turn of the century were certainly aware of developments abroad is apparent from the **De Utrecht** building of 1905, on the Damrak (District 1) which J.F. Staal (1879–1940) and A.J. Kropholler (1882–1973) designed after a study trip to New York. It is a somewhat stunted skyscraper of the kind being built in America in the late nineteenth century. The sculpture on the front of the building is by Mendes da Costa. The staircase is also worth a visit.

LARGE-SCALE RESIDENTIAL BUILDING AND THE 'PLAN ZUID'

An Act of Parliament of 1901 gave the government great scope in stimulating building projects. Residential Housing Construction Corporations were set up and for the first time the compulsory purchase of land became possible. The corporations are to this day the largest builders in the city, which is the reason why Amsterdam possesses a large amount of rented housing.

The 'Plan Zuid' (covering the area south of the nineteenth-century urban expansion) is the first example of a development plan in which the designer, Berlage, allowed aesthetic considerations to play a part. In so doing Berlage hoped to achieve the same effect as in the ring of canals: a combination of the monumental and the picturesque. He worked with prospects of large buildings at the end of wide thoroughfares, such as skyscrapers at a fork in the road. This can be seen on the **Olympiaplein**, where the central point is a school of 1920 by H.A.J. Baanders (1876–1953) which is built above the roadway. Another nice point from which to observe how Berlage's plan worked is the area around the **Victorieplein**. Here, at the junction of two wide streets, stands the **Wolkenkrabber** (skyscraper) by J.F. Staal of 1930, the earliest true high-rise building in Amsterdam. In Berlage's expansion plans all the architectural styles of pre-war Amsterdam are represented, from the 'expressionism' of the Amsterdam School to the 'modernism' of the New Realists.

THE AMSTERDAM SCHOOL

The architects of the Amsterdam School were fortunate in finding a local authority which again and again opted for their style of architecture; they were able to realize several unique projects within the authority's various expansion plans. The style of the Amsterdam School is characterized by boundless imagination, both in the treatment of materials and in the division of space.

Their first experiment was the **Scheepvaarthuis** (Maritime House) of 1911–16 (Prins Hendrikkade 108, District 1, open to the public) by J.M. van der Mey (1878–1949). The architects P.L. Kramer (1881–1961) and M. de Klerk (1884–1923) collaborated on this odd building. It shows the architects' preoccupation with fanciful 'sculpture' in brick, which differs from contemporary Art Deco in France or Belgium by its use of more recognizable flower shapes. Later their work was to involve the use of inclined planes, as can be seen in the district all around the

Zaanstraat, north of the railway (1917–20); around the **Dageraad** in the P.L. Takstraat, south of Sarphatipark (1921–2); and on the **Henriëtte Ronnerplein** (1921–3). These are examples of virtuoso imagination in brick, which thanks to restoration are in splendid condition.

NEW REALISM BEFORE THE SECOND WORLD WAR

During the same period, there developed a style diametrically opposed to the Amsterdam School's joyful proliferation of forms. Under the influence of the American Frank Lloyd Wright a group had formed in the Netherlands around the architects Gerrit Rietveld and Theo van Doesburg under the name De Stijl. Simultaneously, in Germany, Walter Gropius became the centre of a similarly minded group at the Bauhaus. The representatives of De Stijl advocated functionalism in architecture and endeavoured to find a solution to the problem of building for large numbers of people: they explored ways in which human beings could best live in a building.

The **Openluchtschool** (Open-Air School) of 1930 (Cliostraat 36–40) by J. Duiker (1890–1935) shows how the architect, by using steel and glass, tried to make as much use as possible of sunlight. In good weather lessons could be conducted on the balconies, which extended the whole width of the classrooms, or even in the open air.

In the early 1920s a small district was built in East Amsterdam called **Betondorp** (Cementville), a functionalist project which no longer has a church at its centre but a library. This monument to New Realism was recently completely restored.

URBAN EXPANSION BEFORE AND AFTER THE SECOND WORLD WAR

In 1935 The Town Planning Department of the city council produced a comprehensive blueprint for expansion, the Algemeen Uitbreidingsplan, or General Development Plan. It foresaw a growth in the city's population to 900,000 inhabitants by the year 2000. A large portion of the plan was not put into effect until after the Second World War, though the immediate post-war climate was not propitious for high-quality architecture. The municipal authorities later decided also to build in Amsterdam North (Gool Plan) and in the south-east of the city (Bijlmermeer).

Forum

A group of young architects realized that the functionalist architecture of the post-war period had taken a wrong turn. It was necessary to restore the relationship between human beings and architecture. The most important figures in this group are Aldo van Eyck and Herman Hertzberger. As early as 1960 Van Eyck built the new **Municipal Orphanage** (IJsbaanpad 3, open to the public). This complex, inspired by African styles of construction, shows how architecture can become more human in scale. Unfortunately it is very poorly constructed and for years has been threatened with demolition. It will shortly be used to house the College for the Visual Arts.

In 1981 on the Plantage Middenlaan Van Eyck built the **Hubertushuis** (District 3), also called the 'Moederhuis', or Mothers' House. It is a crisis and support centre for single-parent families, appropriately using unintimidating materials and colour.

Herman Hertzberger's **student flats** of 1966 (Weesperstraat 7–57, District 3, open to the public) are an example of how communal areas can be used. The building interacts with the outside world through the large windows and through the public student restaurant on the ground floor.

In 1984 an ex-associate of Aldo van Eyck's, Theo Bosch, built the **Arts Faculty Building** of the University of Amsterdam (Spuistraat 210, corner of Singel and Raadhuisstraat, District 6). Despite its large scale the building, thanks to the use of light materials and serene shapes, fits nicely into its surroundings. But clearly the interaction of the worlds inside and outside the building does not always work. The lecture rooms have windows on to the corridors, which is not universally welcomed. The architect planned a number of entrances in order to create an accessible building; but this did not prove helpful for the protection of property. In this way ideas change, or the spirit of the age forces change upon us.

ECONOMIC AND SOCIAL CHANGES IN THE LAST TWENTY YEARS

Building Premiums

National and local government have played an important part in the last twenty years. Legislation at both levels has stimulated building by individuals, and so investors have become interested in smaller, higher-quality projects. The future purchasers receive high premiums, according to their income, for newly built houses or apartments. In this way whole areas are being renewed and large industrial complexes being converted for residential use.

The **Jordaan** especially is undergoing an enormous transformation. The district was built on a shoestring in the seventeenth century, retaining the existing pattern of ditches rather than following the concentric ring of canals which was built at about the same time. In this century the

Jordaan went steadily downhill, so that it was decided to concentrate on small-scale building projects to replace dilapidated housing or fill in gaps which had existed for years. There are now newly built projects everywhere and gaps continue to be filled as they appear.

Inner-city renewal
In the 1970s and 1980s a start was made all over the Netherlands with the improvement of the environment of the inner cities. In Amsterdam, with the building of the underground railway linking the suburb of the Bijlmer with the centre, a great hole was literally torn in the oldest part of the city around the Nieuwmarkt. Along the course of the underground, provision was made for new social housing. The rebuilding programme, completed at the end of the 1980s, has produced a very interesting area with a great diversity of architecture. Partly because of the appearance on the scene of the new **Town Hall-Opera House** complex (the so-called Stopera; see p. 126), the area has become very lively.

The nineteenth-century districts are also being given a facelift. Notably, the areas around the Kinkerstraat and the Van Limburg Stirumstraat in Oud-West have been changed beyond recognition by large-scale residential housing developments.

Squatters
In the 1930s the canal-side mansions of Amsterdam become too large for their occupants and were often converted, or rather gutted from inside, to make offices, and the residential function of the inner city largely disappeared. In the 1960s the offices moved to the outskirts of the city, thus creating large amounts of unoccupied property along the canals.

At this time the town authorities were devoting their attention to prestigious projects such as the the Stopera and the construction of the underground. Given the number of empty properties and the housing shortage, the council's priorities seemed incomprehensible to many, and the ever-growing population reacted in typically recalcitrant fashion: squatting campaigns were to dominate the 1970s. This led to violent conflicts between the squatters on the one hand and the landlords and the authorities on the other. The coronation of Queen Beatrix in 1980 was for many people an occasion to give vent to their discontent. This degenerated into a pitched battle between police and demonstrators all over the city.

It is in large part thanks to the squatters that attention has again been focused on the residential function of the inner city. In a short space of time the new occupants of the empty factories and office buildings were able to make their properties into habitable living quarters. Unfortunately many people remember only the bedsprings used to barricade the windows and the garish, anarchistic colours of the walls and window-frames. However, several occupied industrial complexes served as model renewal projects elsewhere in the country and abroad. The **Leeuwenberg**, a disused 1930s milk factory on the Zwanenburgwal (District 1), was due to be demolished because of the construction of the Town Hall. Recently the building was restored and given an outer insulating shell painted in glaring colours. The complex is still largely occupied by its first occupants, who rescued the unique property from the demolition men.

There is no doubt that many squatters failed to treat the architecture of the properties they occupied with respect. Many monuments were badly damaged, but the offices which had previously been located there had already wrought much havoc with their ruthless functionalism.

The inner ring of canals has become one of the most popular residential areas for smaller well-to-do households. The patrician mansions once considered too large by their occupants have been divided up into luxurious and very expensive flats. The international tendency for increasing numbers of people to enhance their quality of life and their preparedness to spend accordingly has not left Amsterdam untouched.

Government and industry

The Amsterdam municipal authorities have in recent years been greatly concerned to stimulate industrial building, and their efforts have met with success, as there is now a veritable building boom. The town council believes that developing high-quality architecture at easily accessible points in a ring around the city will attract new businesses. Moreover, it will provide an alternative for those who are in central accommodation which is bursting at the seams. At the same time the rail network around the city is being improved and a number of new stations built.

One of these stations, **Sloterdijk** (west of the centre), is certainly worth a visit. It was built in 1986 by H. Reijnders and is situated at the junction of two railway lines. On the one hand the architect has made use of high-tech effects, with steel construction playing a large part in the whole. On the other hand there is much decorative use of tiles. Around this station a whole new business centre is springing up. Nowadays all the country's leading banks and certain important international concerns set up their headquarters in centres like this. The head office of the **NMB bank** by Ton Alberts and Max van Huut, near the previously mentioned Bijlmer Station, is an example of particularly attractive unconventional architecture. For a building where several thousand people work it is the least energy-intensive building in the world. In a public competition one Amsterdammer characterized the exterior of the complex as halfway between a sand-castle and a group of galloping dromedaries. The interior is inspired by the anthroposophical ideas of Rudolf Steiner, expressed in the absence of right-angles and the abundance of natural shapes. For the moment the office staff seem happy to be surrounded by this organic architecture.

Less than a hundred metres away one can see buildings constructed on high-tech lines. The twin towers of **Centrepoint**, in which the venerable Elsevier publishing house is located, are like cold glass boxes. However, the interiors of the buildings are very attractively finished in warm colours.

Not much is happening in Amsterdam in the field of shop design. An exception is the high-tech conversion for the giant fashion chain Esprit of the **Afrikahuis** (Spui, District 1) by Ed. Cuypers (1859–1927) and the late nineteenth-century houses in the P.C. Hooftstraat 118 (District 2), which have been rebuilt, also for a large fashion company. The postmodernist American architect Robert Stern has here made striking use of early twentieth-century Art Deco. The entrance has been set into the shop-front like a gigantic tulip.

Bijlmer

South-East Amsterdam, usually called the Bijlmer, has been a constant headache for town planers. The district was designed according to ideas reminiscent of Le Corbusier's ideal city. Everywhere underground and vehicle traffic are kept separate from pedestrians and cyclists, all houses are built in parkland and the insides of the flats are among the most attractive in the city. The municipal authorities, however, by pursuing a strange policy of accommodating immigrants from the newly independent colony of Surinam in the area in the second half of the 1970s, very soon caused it to take on the look of a ghetto.

Ambitious plans have been drawn up to improve the quality of life in the the district. It is typical that it should have taken nearly twenty years for it to have its own centre. Only in the mid-1980s did a real town centre spring up round the underground station, where a number of banks established their headquarters in what was by Dutch standards spectacular architecture. Since then the residential quality of the area has improved.

Stopera

The previously mentioned Town Hall/Opera House complex on the Waterlooplein on the Amstel (District 1), built by Wilhelm Holzbauer and Cees Dam and officially opened in 1988, is the most important postwar building in Amsterdam. Even before the Second World War a competition was organized for a new Town Hall. Bernhard Bijvoet (1889–1979) was to have built an opera house in Amsterdam South. On his death the project was bequeathed to Cees Dam. A post-war competition for the construction of a Town Hall was won by the Austrian-born Willem Holzbauer, now an adopted Amsterdammer. However, as with many things in Amsterdam, there were years of in-fighting before the project was finalized. Eventually it was decided to combine the Opera House with the Town Hall, and the concept of a Town Hall-cum-Opera House came into being. What seemed to be a way of cutting costs turned out to be one of the most over-budget projects in the history of Amsterdam. No one knows precisely who has profited or lost by it and after a number of crises all the responsible politicians are installed and the building is functioning. The Opera House, with its enormous marble wall along the Amstel, nicknamed the 'set of dentures' by Amsterdammers, features, around the theatre designed by Bernhard Bijvoet, an enormous foyer with huge flights of steps. The dominant atmosphere is by Amsterdam standards unprecedentedly grand, but in our age seems to have gained acceptance. Three centuries earlier the Town Hall on the Dam had had a similar atmosphere in its Citizens' Chamber. The cultural élite of Amsterdam now saunter, champagne glass in hand, over the pink carpets.

The Town Hall, which surrounds the Opera House in an L-shape, is not particularly attractive from the outside: the side walls are too long. But the corner section on the Amstel is particularly fine. Much has been done with lighting effects from the interior of the building, and after dark there is a splendid view of the complex from the Munt Square. In the Town Hall there are a number of wedding rooms, which have been particularly attractively designed by various artists. It also houses a small bookshop (Stadsboekhandel) which has a great deal of information on the architecture of Amsterdam.

PRESENT ARCHITECTURAL ACTIVITIES

Amsterdam is a very active city when it comes to the development of architecture. Ambitious new residential housing projects are still under way in Amsterdam-East and in the city centre there are new developments in prospect. Underground garages are being constructed for car traffic, a difficult task in the marshy soil of the port. The bank of the IJ has not been properly developed since the laying of a railway line on an island facing the waterfront. Around the Central Station it is proposed to create a new area over the next few years, with a promenade along the water's edge. Many Amsterdammers regard this with some scepticism.

But the fact that Amsterdammers down the ages have concerned themselves with changes in the city is one of the most attractive aspects of Amsterdam. Architectural events and lectures by Dutch and foreign architects are regularly organized and well attended. The study of architectural history is highly regarded at the city's two universities and the Amsterdam Architectural Academy.

Amsterdam has a Municipal Bureau for the Conservation of Monuments (Keizersgracht 123), staffed by a number of architects and with an architectural history section, which advises on restoration and conservation projects. In the inner city there are more than 6,000 listed monuments. Recently a start was made on compiling a list of 'younger' monuments, dating from the nineteenth and twentieth centuries. In addition to the Municipal Conservation Office there are a number of private organizations which concern themselves with the purchase and restoration of historic properties. On many buildings one can find the sign of one of these organizations, the Hendrick de Keyser Association. Almost all of these properties have been let out for residential use.

On 1 July each year there is an Architecture Day, in which the accent is on older architecture.

8 · An Architectural Tour

The first part of this tour goes from the Central Station to the Wester-kerk, where there is a choice of two routes. Either route can be taken, and the walk completed by returning to the Westerkerk to follow the other route. The distances involved are considerable, and if need be can also be covered on a bike. They are, however, perfectly walkable, pro-vided one allows plenty of time. There is no shortage of congenial places *en route* to stop off at for coffee, tea or lunch. If you intend to go inside those buildings which are open to the public, you should reckon on a whole day for both walks.

Many of the buildings you will encounter on the tour have been dealt with above in their historical context, and these are referred to by page references. District numbers correspond to those used in Chapter 13 and to the map at the end of the book.

CENTRAL STATION TO THE WESTERKERK

The Central Station is located on an artificial island built across the old harbour front. This cut off what had previously been Amsterdam's direct access to the open sea. It is well worth while taking a brief look at the side of the station facing away from the centre of the city. There are two (free) ferries, the one on the far right for pedestrians only. This takes one across to a new project by the internationally known city planner Rem Koolhaas. It is a breathtaking trip and a must for all architecture fans.

The tour proper begins in front of the **Central Station** (1882–9, archi-tect P.J.H. Cuypers; p. 119), on the square which is the starting-point for many tram routes and where there is always live music provided by buskers The decorations on the station façade symbolize trade, industry and transport. The building stands like a gate at right-angles to the prin-cipal thoroughfare of central Amsterdam, the Damrak (District 1). This street follows the partly underground course of the river Amstel, as far as the Dam, where the city originated and from which it takes its name, and beyond it continues as the Rokin.

If you walk up the Damrak on the left-hand side, you will see to your left across the water one of the best-preserved rows of houses in the area, the back of what was once one of the principal shopping streets in Am-sterdam, the Warmoesstraat. You are now approaching the world-famous Exchange building. Just before it on the right, at Damrak 28–30, there is what by Amsterdam standards is an unusually high building. It was built in 1905 for the **De Utrecht** insurance company (p. 120) by two architects, J.F. Staal and A.J. Kropholler, just returned from an inspirational trip to the United States. It is a rather squat skyscraper whose front is heavily decorated with sculpture.

The **Exchange** (p. 120), built in 1898–1903 by H.P. Berlage, is now called the Beurs van Berlage, and the latter name is resplendent in gold lettering above the entrance to the concert halls recently made from part of the building. The Exchange is open to visitors. Very frequent exhibitions on architecture or design are staged in the Great Hall.

The front of the Exchange faces the Beursplein. Immediately on the left is the actual **Stock Exchange** (Effectenbeurs), built ten years after Berlage's building in a mock-historical style. The **Bijenkorf** department store (1913, J.A. van Straaten) was also built more than ten years after the Exchange, but in a style more reminiscent of the 1860s.

From the Beursplein one can look across at the **Allert de Lange** bookshop (1886, J. van Looy; p. 118), at Damrak 62. The neo-Renaissance front has decorations relating to the building's function. In the 1930s many literary works banned in Germany were published here. Allert de Lange is also the principal importer of Penguin Books in the Netherlands and consequently has one of the best English book sections in the city. Immediately adjacent is the former **Cineac** cinema (1926, N. Vreeswijk), now converted into an amusement arcade; this building has a fine tufa-stone façade and one of the earliest uses of neon lighting in Dutch architecture.

Arriving on the Dam, you can see on your left the National Monument (1949), erected to the memory of the victims of the Second World War. On your right stands the largest seventeenth-century building in Amsterdam: at the time the Town Hall, now the **Royal Palace** (1648, Jacob van Campen; p. 111). At first sight the palace may seem somewhat ponderous, certainly if one reflects that in the seventeenth century the surrounding buildings were no more than two storeys high. However, the façades are enlivened by decorations beneath the windows and on both front and rear pediments. But the building's true quality is to be found in its interior, which consists almost entirely of ornamental carvings in white marble by Artus Quellinus. One's first entry into the **Burgerzaal** (Citizens' Chamber) particularly is an experience unparalleled in many buildings in the world: the very high-ceilinged, light room stretches the whole length of the building. For a detailed description of the interior, see p. 85.

The walk continues to the right of the Palace past the **Nieuwe Kerk**

(New Church, begun at the end of the fourteenth century; p. 109). This Gothic church is rather squeezed into a corner of the square, with many buildings around it. Its fine interior contains examples of wood and stone carving and silverware from the Reformation onwards.

Behind and a little to the right of the Nieuwe Kerk, cross over and walk along a little alleyway, the Molsteeg, to the first canal, the Singel (District 6). Emerging from the narrow alleyway you are suddenly confronted with one of the widest bridges in Amsterdam, the **Torensluis**, which as the name indicates is actually built over a sluice gate. Halfway across there is a monument to the Dutch writer Multatuli (Eduard Douwes Dekker, 1820–87). Walk straight ahead to the next canal, the Herengracht. From the bridge one can see in the distance, at the beginning of the Leliegracht, one of Amsterdam's few Art Nouveau buildings, the former head office of the **E.L.H.B. insurance company**, now the headquarters of the environmental organization Greenpeace (1905, G. van Arkel; p. 120).

Go left along the right bank of the Herengracht. At Herengracht 164 there is an elegant mid-eighteenth-century building. **No. 168** is a house with an imposing sandstone façade (1638, Philips Vingboons; p. 114) and a splendid eighteenth-century interior with a stuccoed hallway and rooms with hand-painted decoration. Together with the **Bartolotti House** (1617, Hendrick de Keyser; p. 110), built during the Dutch Renaissance, at No. 170, this houses the Netherlands **Theatre Museum**. Past this row of houses turn right into the Raadhuisstraat. This street was created in 1894 when a swath was cut through the rows of gabled houses in order to give access to the increasing volume of traffic. The façade on the left incorporating an arcade was built by the architect of the Concertgebouw, A.L. van Gendt. Following the gentle curve of the Raadhuisstraat, you reach the **Westerkerk** (1620, Hendrick de Keyser; p. 111), whose tower can be climbed. At the back of the church there are three large marble triangles set into the pavement, known as the Homonument. This is a monument to homosexuals executed by the Germans during the Second World War.

From the Westerkerk you can choose between two routes, and start afresh from this point later. Both routes end with groups of buildings by architects of the Amsterdam School.

ROUTE 1: THE JORDAAN

From the Westerkerk one can walk through the Jordaan (District 7) as far as the Spaarndam quarter, featuring architecture by the Amsterdam School. To do this, pass the church tower and the Anne Frank House, take the first bridge over the Prinsengracht, and then proceed along the left bank. The first bridge you come to crosses the Bloemgracht. Turn left along this canal and take the first cross-street on the right, the Eerste Leliedwarsstraat, one of the most attractive thoroughfares in the Jordaan. Walk along it until you reach the Westerstraat, a filled-in canal often used as an open-air market. Turn left and follow the Westerstraat to the end. On your left you will see a mid-nineteenth-century **residential block** (1862, P.J. Hamer; p. 117) which is certainly worth a visit. Be sure to have a look at the inner courtyard of this recently restored monument to social housing.

At the end of the Westerstraat turn right along the Lijnbaansgracht, the outermost canal of the ring. The difference between the degree of opulence found along the first canal, the Singel, and this canal is plain to see. Take the next street on the right and you will see, at Karthuizersstraat 61–191, one of the earliest examples of social housing in Amsterdam, a *hofje* or almshouse for single women (1650, Daniël Stalpaert; p. 114). Immediately after the *hofje* turn right, which will bring you back to the Westerstraat. Turn left again and go as far as the Noordermarkt, dominated by the badly neglected **Noorderkerk** (1620, Hendrick de Keyser). Now follow the Prinsengracht as far as the Brouwersgracht. At the corner of the Prinsengracht and the Brouwersgracht is a café with two stepped gables which serves very good beer. From this picturesque spot you can see the many warehouses along the Brouwersgracht which have been converted into homes. Go along the left bank of the Brouwersgracht as far as the filled-in Palmgracht. Turn left and you will see the entrance of the **Rapenhofje** (1648), with its idyllic courtyard.

Back on the Brouwersgracht take the next bridge and walk through to the Haarlemmerstraat. Turn left and continue as far as the Haarlemmerplein, with its neo-Renaissance former city gate the **Haarlemmerpoort** (1840, C. Alewijn), since converted for residential use. You are now within walking distance of a quarter built entirely in the style of the Amsterdam School (p. 121). Go under the railway bridge and follow the railway line. When you reach the Spaarndammerplantsoen with its little post office, you are in the heart of the quarter built between 1912 and 1920 by Michel de Klerk for the residential housing corporation Eigen Haard.

ROUTE 2: NINETEENTH-CENTURY AMSTERDAM

Starting from the Westerkerk you can also take a walk through nineteenth-century Amsterdam, ending at another development designed by the Amsterdam School, the **Dageraad**.

From the Westerkerk take the Keizersgracht (District 5) as far as No. 224. This building bears the name **Saxenburg** (1765) and now forms part of the Pulitzer Hotel. It is a fine example of French influence on Dutch architecture in the mid eighteenth century. At No. 324 is the very large **Shaffy Theatre**, formerly the Society Felix Meritis (1788, Jacob Otten Husly; p. 115). It now houses an avant-garde theatre, a cinema and a restaurant.

Continue as far as the bridge, where you cross and enter the Huiden-straat. When you reach the Herengracht, immediately round the corner you will find four houses with sandstone façades (1662, Philips Ving-boons; p. 112). These house the **Bible Museum**. A little further on, at **Nos. 380–382**, there is a very un-Dutch-looking nineteenth-century house (1890, A. Salm).

Continue as far as the Leidsegracht, a canal which offers what is perhaps the most beautiful and serene view in Amsterdam. Follow the Leidse-gracht as far as the Keizersgracht, turn left and walk along the left bank of the canal as far as the Leidsestraat. At **No. 449** is a seventeenth-century mansion given a new shop front by Gerrit Rietveld (p. 122) in 1938. It now houses the modern café-restaurant Walem. Its garden contains a superb eighteenth-century summerhouse. On the corner of the Leidsestraat are the large premises of the **Metz & Co.** department store, built by J. van Looy in 1891 in neo-Classical style for a life assurance company (p. 118). The roof is crowned by a glass cupola designed by Gerrit Rietveld, from where one has a splendid view of the city.

Take the Leidsestraat in the direction of the Leidseplein (District 4). One is immediately struck by the **Stadsschouwburg** (Municipal Theatre; p. 118) in the middle of the square (daily guided tours in the summer months). Diagonally opposite is the former department store **Hirsch** (1911, A. Jacot), now an office complex. The **City Theatre** (1936, J. Wils) is by the same architect as the Olympic Stadium of 1928.

You now pass the **American Hotel** (1898–1902, W. Kromhout; p. 120), whose interior is well worth the price of a cup of coffee. Cross the bridge and walk straight ahead into the Vondelstraat, past the **Marriott Hotel** (1975, S. Schaafsma). Two hundred metres along the Vondelstraat on the corner to your left is the striking **Villa Oud Leyerhoven** (1885, P.J.H. Cuypers).

Further along you cross the Eerste Constantijn Huygensstraat (District 2) and enter an area where the greatest Dutch nineteenth-century architect lived. P.J.H. Cuypers has left his mark on the quarter: he designed its layout, the **Vondelkerk** (1880; p. 119) and a number of private houses. At No. 140 is the entrance to the **Hollandse Manege** (Dutch Riding School, 1881, A.L. van Gendt; p. 119), whose foyer is worth a look.

From the church square enter the Vondelpark. Immediately on your left is the **Vondelpark Paviljoen** (1881, P.J. and W. Hamer), now housing the Filmmuseum. Not far away is the monument to the seventeenth-century poet whose name the park bears, with a pedestal by P.J.H. Cuypers. Further on is the round **Theehuis**, built in 1936 by H.A.J. Baanders in the style of the New Functionalism.

Leaving the park at the beginning of the Van Baerlestraat, where a bridge crosses it, turn right and cross the P.C. Hooftstraat, a sophisticated, fashionable street full of attractive modern shop-fronts. On your left, on the corner of the Paulus Potterstraat, the **Stedelijk Museum** (Municipal Museum) comes into view. This modern art museum is housed in a building in the historicist style (1895, A. Weissmann). Continue along the Van Baerlestraat and on your right you will see the **Concertgebouw** (Concert Hall, 1888, A.L. van Gendt), with round the corner a new wing by Pi de Bruijn (1988). With your back to the Concertgebouw you can see the **Rijksmuseum** (1885, P.J.H. Cuypers; p. 119) in the distance at the end of the Museumplein, and on your left the **Van Gogh Museum** (1973, G.T. Rietveld and Partners).

Continuing along the Van Baerlestraat you come to the Roelof Hartplein, containing a number of buildings in the style of the Amsterdam School from a slightly later period. **Huize Lydia** (1922–7, J. Boterenbrood) and the **Openbare Bibliotheek** (Public Library, 1928, B. van den Nieuwen Amstel) are good examples.

You now proceed along the Roelof Hartstraat, which across the bridge becomes the Ceintuurbaan. Some way along this is the **Sarphatipark** (District 8), named after the great mid-nineteenth-century town planner. The park, laid out in landscape style, contains a fine monument to Dr Sarphati. Here one can cross over into the Albert Cuypstraat market. All the streets here present the same picture of nineteenth-century speculative building: tall, pinched houses in streets which are too narrow.

At the end of the park you cross the Ceintuurbaan and enter the Tweede Sweelinckstraat. Walk to the end of it, turn right into the Van Ostadestraat and take the second turning on the left, the Henrick de Keijserstraat. Named after the greatest seventeenth-century architect, this street runs into the Burgemeester Tellegenstraat, which in turn curves and comes out into the **P.L. Takstraat** (1921–2, P.L. Kramer; p. 121). Here one can see the architecture of the Amsterdam School at its best. Fanciful façades in brick, tiles and window-frames. The corner buildings inscribed with the name 'De Dageraad' are delightful. On either side of the P.L. Takstraat are two small squares built in the same style (1921, M. de Klerk). This is the end of the long tour.

You can now return to the centre of town along the Van Woustraat (tram to the Central Station) and the Utrechtsestraat, past the the head-quarters of the **Nederlandse Bank** (1968, M.F. Duintjer). You can get off at the Rembrandtplein and turn right along the Amstelstraat towards the new **Stadhuis/Muziektheater** (1988, W. Holzbauer, C. Dam, B. Bijvoet), popularly known as the Stopera (p. 126). Close by are the seventeenth and eighteenth-century **synagogues** on the Mr de Visser-plein (p.113), and the **Nieuwmarkt**, where there some attractive examples of recent inner-city renewal (p. 124).

9 · The Performing Arts

There is so much to do in Amsterdam, with thousands of concerts, theatre, ballet and opera performances every year, that it is difficult to know what to choose and where to start. And there is also the added problem that tickets for some of the more popular events may sell out quickly. The best course of action for anyone arriving in the city with the aim of fitting in as much entertainment as possible is to head straight for either the VVV Box Office, which is housed in an attractive white building right opposite the main entrance of the Central Station, or the AUB Ticketshop, which is located in a corner of the Stadsschouwburg on the Leidseplein. Both are full of leaflets, brochures and lists of forthcoming events and the English-language fortnightly listings magazine *What's On in Amsterdam*. Best of all, they are staffed with knowledgeable and helpful people who will provide advice and make the bookings. Tickets booked at these offices carry no extra cost.

FILM

It is easy to dismiss the Netherlands as a film country. With its modest output, it certainly does not immediately spring to mind as having a strong film industry. Budgets are minuscule and what subsidies are available from the Production Fund and the Netherlands Film Fund amount to around 12 million guilders (3.5 million pounds) a year. Many Dutch films find no favour even with their indigenous audience and those that do prove commercial, and are subsequently picked up for international release in countries like the United States, always end up on the art house circuit.

And yet it would be wrong to think that the Netherlands makes no contribution to international cinema. Throughout the years Dutch film makers in just about every category have seen their names on the credits of internationally successful films. Perhaps the greatest fillip to date for this reservoir of talent was *RoboCop*, a fast-paced action film with overtones of satire which reached the top of American box-office successes in 1987. Much of its success was due to the sure and imaginative direction of Paul Verhoeven. Asked to say which fellow director he most admires, Ken Russell nominated Verhoeven for *RoboCop*, which he considers 'a

masterpiece. It manages to achieve the two cardinal aims of a film director – to entertain and enlighten at the same time.'

Verhoeven is one of the few Dutch film-makers who has managed to
achieve international success with Dutch productions, picking up an Oscar nomination for *Turkish Delight* in 1973 and winning the 1979 Gold-
en Globe for *Soldier of Orange*. The latter also starred three Dutch actors
whose names have since travelled outside the Netherlands.

Rutger Hauer was immediately offered the role of the rebellious 'replica'
in Ridley Scott's *Blade Runner* and has since become the Netherlands'
most visible film export, closely followed by Jeroen Krabbé (*The Living
Daylights*, *Crossing Delancy*, with cameraman Theo van de Sande, and
Melancholia) and Derek de Lint (*The Unbearable Lightness of Being* and
Stealing Heaven). De Lint attracted American attention with his central
role in *The Assault*, director Fons Rademaker's Oscar-winning film version of a popular Dutch novel.

Two of the country's top actresses, Renée Soutendijk and Monique van
de Ven, have achieved international recognition with leading roles in
American mini-series and the names of cameramen like Jan de Bont,
who filmed *The Jewel of the Nile* and *Ruthless People*, and Robby Müller,
who works regularly with Wim Wenders (*Paris, Texas*), continue to feature prominently on the credits of major films.

Perhaps the most consistently successful of the film-makers producing
Dutch films is director Dick Maas, whose *The Lift*, *Flodder* and *Amster-
damned* all attracted reasonable audiences outside the Netherlands. Huub
Stapel, who starred in all three, began to receive offers from America and
more than held his own in his first outing in the television film *The Attic*.

Festivals

While Dutch film-makers look, and often move, abroad, their foreign
counterparts flock to the country in large numbers for two important
events: the *International Film Festival* in Rotterdam at the end of January,
and the *Dutch Film Days* in Utrecht in September. Both invite guests
from home and abroad, but many more come at their own expense.

The Rotterdam Film Festival was founded in 1972 by Huub Bals, who
served as its director until his sudden death in 1988. A year later the Italian Marco Müller was appointed as his successor, which was regarded as
something of a coup. Bals' aim was to introduce Dutch film-goers to the
latest trends in world cinema. The formula worked. From modest begin-
nings in a back street, the festival now occupies most of the cinema
screens in Rotterdam for ten days. Over the years it has introduced
many previously unknown film-makers and cultures. Wim Wenders,
Rainer Werner Fassbinder, Jim Jarmusch and Otar Yosseliani were all

discovered via Rotterdam, as was the new generation of directors from China.

The Dutch Film Days were founded in 1981 as a meeting place for Dutch film-makers. All the films produced in the Netherlands in the previous year are screened and there is a programme of retrospectives, symposia and talk shows. The closing night is an Awards Gala when the Golden Calf, the Dutch equivalent of the Oscar, is given for outstanding achievements.

Cinemas

Amsterdam is the home of two beautiful cinemas. The extraordinary interior design of the **Theater Tuschinski**, with its Art Deco lamps, Chinese silk, oriental patterns, carved woodwork and Japanese drawing room, were all the idea of Abram Tuschinski, a poor Polish waistcoat-maker who arrived in Rotterdam on the way to America but stayed to open his first cinema in 1909. Twelve years later the exotic palace which was to become his monument was erected. It has all been lovingly preserved, despite the high cost. In 1984 for instance sixty women in Morocco wove a new carpet following exactly the original pattern and colours. It weighed 1,500 kilos and cost millions. These days Tuschinski is open for tourist trips round the building, which attract hundreds of visitors. There aren't many cinemas in the world which can boast an audience without showing a film.

You can find Theater Tuschinski in the Reguliersbreestraat (District 4). Tours take place in July and August on Sundays and Mondays at 10.30 a.m. Tickets from the box office cost 5 guilders, which includes a showing of the Amsterdam promotion film.

The Movies (Haarlemmerdijk 161, District 6) is smaller and more intimate. Its policy is to show well-made commercial art films which in the opinion of the former owner, Pieter Goedings, have something special to offer the public. That his opinion is more often than not valid is shown by the number of people who turn up on the off-chance, knowing their evening will at the very least prove interesting. The Movies was built in 1928 when the Haarlemmerdijk on which it is situated was *the* shopping street. After the war and with the trams rerouted, it gradually lost its sheen. When Goedings took over sixteen years ago, the Movies had reached its lowest point. He has had the building completely restored to its former glory and its café must be one of the most beautiful examples of the Amsterdam School.

Other art houses include **Desmet**, Plantage Middenlaan 4a (District 3), **Kriterion**, Roetersstraat 170 (District 3) and **Rialto**, Ceintuurbaan 338 (District 8).

All films are shown in original languages with Dutch subtitles. All cinemas display at their box offices current lists of what's on where, taken from the local newspaper. Programmes change on Thursdays. Tickets can be bought in advance within the film week for the small fee of 50 cents. The Netherlands is fairly up-to-date with its releases and often ahead of other countries. It may be possible to see a major new film in Amsterdam well before it reaches London.

Most of the main commercial cinemas are to be found on and around the Leidseplein.

CLASSICAL MUSIC AND OPERA

There has been quite a lot of controversy over the past few years within the ranks of the Royal Concertgebouw Orchestra and the Nederlandse Opera, two major Dutch cultural institutions based in Amsterdam. Then there was the furore which erupted over the construction of the city's newest theatre, the Muziektheater (or Stopera), which opened in 1986, and over the extension to the hallowed Concertgebouw, on which work began that same year. All of which suggests the rigour of these two aspects of cultural life in the Dutch capital.

Royal Concertgebouw Orchestra

The Royal Concertgebouw Orchestra, which ranks among the world's top five, occasioned many press notices in 1988, not only because it celebrated its one hundredth anniversary but also because of the departure of conductor-in-chief Bernard Haitink to the London Royal Opera House. His replacement proved a complete break with tradition: the Italian Riccardo Chailly, the first non-Dutchman to be entrusted with what many people worldwide consider to be an orchestra with a quintessentially Dutch sound.

It was on 3 November 1888 that the Royal Concertgebouw Orchestra gave its first concert under the baton of Willem Kes. He banned tables, chairs and waiters from the auditorium and insisted that the public was seated in rows and encouraged to be punctual, while at the same time moulding the orchestra into one seamless whole. But it was the arrival in 1895 of the then unknown twenty-four-year-old Willem Mengelberg which marked the beginning of the high reputation the orchestra holds to this day and the creation of its distinctive 'voice'. Mengelberg's half-century tenure was the period when composers like Richard Strauss, Debussy, Mahler, Ravel, Stravinsky, Schönberg and Milhaud came to conduct the orchestra.

When Mengelberg left in 1945, Eduard van Beinum took on the task of leading the orchestra through the difficult post-war years. He died suddenly in April 1959 during a rehearsal. The twenty-nine-year-old Haitink was invited to take over, together with the more experienced Eugen Jochem, and three years later was appointed conductor-in-chief. In those early years, Haitink listened carefully to concerts under Jochem's direction and noticed that virtually everything was played in a Bruckner or Brahms style, with heavy strings and woodwind, something he worked hard to change. During nearly twenty-five years with the orchestra, Haitink upheld and enhanced its reputation and came to be considered one of the world's most important conductors of symphonic repertoire.

Concertgebouw

If one secret of the orchestra's fame is in the continuity afforded by just a handful of conductors-in-chief in such a long history, a second ingredient is the remarkable sound quality of the concert hall from which it takes its name. The acoustics of the Concertgebouw are among the best in the world, which makes it popular with international musicians. Since its inauguration in 1888, the building has played host to just about every style of music imaginable, to congresses, parties, balls and church services and, between 1920 and 1940, to boxing competitions.

With so much happening on a foundation based on 2,186 piles sunk into the soft Amsterdam soil, it is hardly surprising that by October 1983 reports on the state of the building had become alarming. Drastic action was called for, and if there was to be upheaval why not take the opportunity to build a large basement to provide better facilities for musicians and administrative personnel and to renovate the interior and build an extension to give better access for the public?

Work on the foundations began in 1985. While the Concertgebouw provided a full programme of concerts, new piles were driven into the soil beneath the building and, most amazing of all, the 10,000-ton edifice was moved from its rotten wooden piles on to the solid new ones. By then it was June 1986, and work began on the interior restoration and the construction of the extension. As architect Pi de Bruijn's glass gallery took shape, the criticism of Amsterdammers grew with it. Some talked of an ugly parasite of glass and concrete and others felt that the main entrance should not be moved from the front of the building. But on 11 April 1988, the day of a gala concert celebrating the centenary, the last scaffolding was finally removed and many people looked with greater appreciation at the glass gallery.

Luckily no lasting damage has been done to the façade of the building.

Beurs van Berlage

While all this was exercising the attention of press and public alike, Amsterdam was quietly getting on with the acquisition of a new venue for classical concerts. Since its first auditorium, seating 700, opened in May 1988, the concept of the Beurs van Berlage has undergone a radical change. This Italian-inspired building, designed by the architect Berlage, was opened in 1903 as the Beurs or Stock Exchange. When the various exchanges began to move out at the beginning of this decade, it was decided to convert the building into a concert hall and exhibition centre. The Beurs is now the home of the Netherlands Philharmonic, arguably the Netherlands' most versatile orchestra, with 150 concerts each season besides the task of accompanying the Nederlandse Opera.

New music

The Netherlands is a fertile breeding-ground for music. There are large numbers of symphony orchestras and conservatories, and much attention is paid to chamber music, both old and new. In the early music field Dutch musicians are well known for their concern for authenticity of performance. In modern music too there are several active specialist ensembles, such as the Asko Ensemble, the Schönberg Ensemble, the Dutch Wind Ensemble, the Hague Percussion Ensemble and the New Ensemble.

De IJsbreker (Weesperzijde 23, District 8) plays an important role in the Dutch new music scene. This music centre is in an attractive part of Amsterdam, on the Amstel, and is housed in a building designed in 1885 by Van Gendt, the architect of the Concertgebouw. Apart from the concert hall (with 150 seats), it has a splendid café and a pleasant terrace overlooking the river.

De IJsbreker is in a certain sense unique, focusing entirely on new music. In the chamber music room, featuring mainly soloists and small ensembles, there are about two hundred concerts a year. Not only the most influential Dutch ensembles but a representative selection of top-flight international musicians play there: on average about half the performers are from abroad. Important composers like John Cage, Elliott Carter, Yannis Xenakis, Mauricio Kagel and György Ligeti have brought their works to the IJsbreker.

Besides concerts, the IJsbreker organizes a number of projects each year which focus on a particular musical instrument. During these events, which attract a great deal of national and international interest, there are performances, workshops, master classes and lectures. The IJsbreker's programmes are publicized on posters throughout the city. In addition complete up-to-date information is available the whole year round (in the summer also in English) on the IJsbreker Music Line (tel. 93 90 93). Concerts begin at 8 p.m. and bookings can be made on 668 18 05.

Muziektheater and Nederlandse Opera

It was the former cramped conditions of the Nederlandse Opera and one of the two principal ballet companies, Het Nationale Ballet which led to Amsterdam's most controversial plans for a new theatre: a combined Town Hall and Opera House, the **Stopera**, offering the very latest in stage technology.

The outcry was immediate: over the removal of a long-established daily market (now back on part of its original location), over the amount of demolition needed to create the huge site, over the design of the building and, most particularly, over the enormous budget. No one knows, or is saying, exactly how many hundreds of millions of guilders the Muziektheater cost because so many things had to be redone to get them right that civil servants lost count. The result though, is that Amsterdam now boasts the largest theatre in the Netherlands, with seating for 1,689 people in the auditorium plus rehearsal and office space. With its salmon-pink and marble interior and 14-metre-high curved foyers, designed by Willelm Holzbauer and Cees Dam, the Muziektheater does offer maximum comfort to audiences and every possible facility for opera productions.

Since the **Nederlandse Opera**, the largest and most expensive of Dutch cultural institutions, moved to the Muziektheater in 1986, it has undergone considerable upheaval. With an international-size opera house at its disposal, the company began to expand and experiment by inviting controversial theatre directors to try their hands at opera. The resulting productions undoubtedly improved the international standing of the Nederlandse Opera, drawing glowing reviews in foreign publications. At home the reactions were mainly favourable and performances sold out. There was one snag. Large-scale productions with expensive directors cost a great deal of money and arguments began to surface between the artistic and the finance directors.

By June 1988 there had been a change at the top. The man now entrusted with combining adventurous programming with the restrictions of the budget is Pierre Audi, whose appointment as artistic director was warmly welcomed in Amsterdam. Despite little experience with opera, Audi would seem to bring the right credentials to the job. In 1979 he founded the Almeida Theatre in London with some friends, and as their artistic leader won for this small, precariously financed theatre an international reputation for presenting modern drama and music.

Audi has declared his intention of reinstating the Opera Studio to provide experience for young, promising singers in smaller productions – a sound move for a company which has never been able to afford the great names of opera but which prides itself on developing its own stars.

CONCERT HALLS FOR CLASSICAL MUSIC AND OPERA

Concertgebouw, Concertgebouwplein 2–6 (District 2), tel. 71 83 45. Bookings from one month ahead. It also has its own programme of visiting orchestras and soloists.

Muziektheater (Stopera), Waterlooplein 22 (District 1), tel. 25 54 55. Bookings from one month ahead. It also has its own programme of visiting dance and opera companies.

Beurs van Berlage, Damrak 213 (District 1), tel. 27 04 66. Bookings from one month ahead.

Hotel Pulitzer, Prinsengracht 315–331 (District 5), tel. 22 83 33. On Sunday mornings the hotel organizes concerts in the Garden Room or – weather permitting – in the hotel garden.

Stichting Cristofori, Prinsengracht 579 (District 5), tel. 26 84 85 or 26 84 95. In August – usually on the last Friday in the month – this foundation, together with Hotel Pulitzer, organizes an open-air piano concert on the Prinsengracht. In addition there is on average one performance a week of piano or chamber music on the foundation's premises, and there are guided tours of the workshop, where upright and grand pianos are made and repaired.

Programmes of recitals in the **Engelse Kerk**, Begijnhof 48 (District 1), tel. 24 96 65; the **Oude Kerk**, Oudekerksplein 23 (District 1); in the **Sonesta Koepelzaal**, Kattengat 1 (District 6), tel. 23 98 96; and the **Waalse Kerk**, Oudezijds Achterburgwal 157 (District 1).

THEATRE

There was a time when Amsterdam theatres closed their doors for the summer months and the Dutch season ran from September to March. It still does of course, but impresarios and theatre managers have realized that there is a large market for international productions in the English language or where language is no barrier. And not just for the tourists, since the Dutch themselves will happily spend an evening practising their grasp of a foreign tongue. The result is that theatres remain open all year round. The **Stadsschouwburg**, **Nieuwe de la Mar** and **Carré** are among the venues that plan special summer seasons while not neglecting international programming during the rest of the year.

There is a saying that 'if it's on at Carré then it must be good'. It is not entirely true of course. This famous Amsterdam theatre, which bears comparison with the London Palladium and New York's Madison Square Garden, has had its fair share of stinkers over the years. But in general the theatre built in 1887 by Oscar Carré to house his circus can be relied upon for quality and has become something of a centre for international productions. Carré prides itself on being able to accommodate any type of production. The seats in the section directly in front of the stage can be removed to form a circus ring or a theatre-in-the-round. Each Christmas the elephants and big cats return for a spectacular circus, leading the artists who appear there in other musicals and revues to remark that the building has never lost the smell of animals. Since much that is of interest in Carré, such as the stables and the stage facilities, is normally hidden from the audience, the theatre has begun behind-the-scenes tours.

Dutch theatre makers cannot be said to have set the world alight, but two inextricably entwined names ensure that the country does have an international standing. It is now twenty-three years since Ritsaert ten Cate founded the **Mickery** to present and make theatre and in that time he has provided a platform for the best of the new theatre. He has not always got it right but he has spotted the potential of such now established groups as Station House Opera, the Wooster Group and Neue Slovenische Kunst. In 1988 Ten Cate turned the Mickery Theatre over to **Frau Holle**, a society for theatre making, and began presenting Mickery productions elsewhere, in and outside Amsterdam.

English-speaking theatre

Given that the Dutch are linguists and that so many English and Americans live in the city, it is not surprising that English-speaking theatre groups tend to spring up and wither away like weeds. Their output though is patchy, with the quality often underlining just why the actors and directors are working here rather than in their native country. After all, real talent would have been snapped up at home.

Best of the current bunch is the **Stalhouderij Theatre Company**, which provides the opportunity to see recent American theatre by playwrights like Sam Shepard and Lyle Kessler in the original language. It also has the always watchable young American actor Joe Weston. If the productions at the Stalhouderij are from the traditional side of theatre, the venue is most definitely improvisation. A former stable on one of the small side-streets in the Jordaan, the Stalhouderij proudly declares that it is Amsterdam's smallest theatre. The front door leads directly into the auditorium with seating for forty people and the stage demands the tightest of direction. Upstairs is a bar. It may not be the most comfortable of places but no one falls asleep!

Theatre festivals

Festivals are the other aspect of Amsterdam theatrical life, the most famous being the **Holland Festival**, which takes place in June and also includes music, opera and dance. It was founded in 1947 when the Netherlands had been cut off from international culture for five years by the war. Its aim is to introduce new forms of expression of a high standard and for the past several years it has focused its attention on a particular country each year.

The annual **Stagedoor Festival** in November began life as a platform for immigrant theatre. It has developed into a major international event for professional and amateur companies and now includes dance and music as well as theatre.

July is the month when the most extraordinary performances take place in the strangest of places during the **Zomerfestijn**, an international theatre festival for what traditionalists would call fringe and avant-garde.

Theatres

Theater Carré, Amstel 115–125 (District 3), tel. 22 52 25. Bookings from one month ahead. Tours of Carré with an English-speaking guide are available only for groups at the moment, but there are plans to extend the service. They take place every day and cost 2.50 guilders per person. For information and bookings tel. 02510-41745.

Stadsschouwburg (Municipal Theatre), Leidseplein 26 (District 4), tel. 24 23 11. Bookings from one month ahead.

Nieuwe de la Mar Theater, Marnixstraat 404 (District 4), tel. 23 34 62. Bookings from one month ahead.

Mickery, Herenmarkt 12 (District 6), tel. 23 49 68. Bookings from one month ahead.

Frau Holle, Rozengracht 117 (District 7), tel. 20 23 27.

De Stalhouderij, 1e Bloemdwarsstraat 4 (District 7), tel. 26 22 82. Bookings from one month ahead.

Fringe theatres whose programmes are worth checking include **De Balie**, Kleine Gartmanplantsoen 10 (District 4), tel. 23 29 04; **Bellevue**, Leidsekade 90 (District 4), tel. 24 72 48; **De Engelenbak**, Nes 71 (District 1), tel. 23 57 23; **Frascati**, Nes 63 (District 1), tel. 26 68 66; **De Kleine Komedie**, Amstel 56 (District 4), tel. 24 05 34.

The **Open Air Theatre** in the Vondelpark (District 2) runs a summer programme of music and theatre in June, July and August. Ring 73 14 99 for details or see the programme board at the park gates.

BALLET AND DANCE

It may well be indicative of the general level of Dutch ballet that the name of one of its most famous and respected choreographers is that of the Czech Jirí Kylián. For the past sixteen years he has been artistic director of the Nederlands Dans Theater where just five of the thirty-two dancers are Dutch. The proportion is better at the Netherlands' other leading ballet company, Het Nationale Ballet, where 40 per cent of the dancers are Dutch, but it still does not say much for the level of training provided for children at the various Dutch ballet academies. The quality of a ballet education is not as high as that of other Western countries and yet the Netherlands nurtures a host of varied dance companies and internationally known dancers, choreographers and companies.

Het Nationale Ballet and the Nederlands Dans Theater

The two companies of international standing are Het Nationale Ballet, which has the Amsterdam Muziektheater (the Stopera) as its home base, and the Nederlands Dans Theater (NDT), housed since 1987 in the new Danstheater in the Hague. Although Het Nationale Ballet provides romantic and modern classical with some contemporary dance and the NDT explores and extends the boundaries of modern dance, the companies are united historically.

The NDT, which has been described in the international press as daring, inventive, dynamic and physically exciting, was formed in the spring of 1959 when a rebel group of dancers from Het Nationale Ballet left in order to free themselves from traditional dance patterns. Among them were the then unknown ballerina Alexandra Radius, Han Ebbelaar, who later became her husband, and the young choreographer Rudi van Dantzig. The first performance took place in September of the same year in Belgium, so setting the scene for what has become a widely travelled company. Also involved in those early years was the young Amsterdam dancer Hans van Manen, whose work, together with that of foreigners like Glen Tetley, did much to ensure the company would be successful. This period saw the emergence in Amsterdam of Het Nationale Ballet with the task of perpetuating romantic classical ballets while developing contemporary dance. The repertoire still reflects that spectrum, since 1969 under the artistic leadership of Van Dantzig, whose own works are often spectacles of ideological dance and movement. Toer van Schayk provides ballets inspired by the visual arts, and Van Manen, back at the NDT since his contract with Het Nationale Ballet ended in 1987, contributes his inventive and abstract choreography.

Of all the names associated with Dutch ballet and dance perhaps the most famous is that of Alexandra Radius, whose technique, fluency and expression has been compared to that of Margot Fonteyn. A lyric classical dancer who surprised everyone in the early years with her ability to interpret the very different demands of modern dance, Radius began her career in 1957 at Het Nationale Ballet. Together with her husband Han Ebbelaar, she danced as soloist with the American Ballet Theatre from 1968 to 1970 before returning to Het Nationale Ballet. Since then she has appeared throughout the world and has partnered some of the great names in ballet including Rudolf Nureyev and Peter Martins. Sadly but not surprisingly after nearly three and a half decades, Radius has recently announced her intention of retiring, although, like Fonteyn's, her influence is bound to continue for some considerable time.

Dance for children

Encouraging an interest in dance among children was Hans Snoek's specific aim when in 1945 she founded **Scapino Ballet**. In those days, the important thing was to provide characters with whom youngsters could identify, and the narrator, Scapino, provided a focal point for the young audience. When Snoek left the company in 1970, Scapino disappeared from the stage and the dance had to speak for itself. Under artistic director Armando Navarro the dancing has improved, the company is now a cohesive unit and the repertoire has expanded now that established choreographers have begun creating ballets for the company, among them Jiří Kylián, Hans van Manen and Nils Christe, whose work with companies like the Danish Royal Ballet and the Royal Winnipeg Ballet in Canada has brought him international recognition. These days the standard is such that whole families enjoy Scapino's performances.

Most dance companies are concentrated in the main cities in the west of the Netherlands, but one of the most interesting new developments hails from the north. **Reflex** was founded in 1985 in Groningen, an event which went unnoticed in a country where dance companies appear and disappear every year. Then in June 1986 the dancer and choreographer

Yoka van Brummelen took on the job of director and six months later had persuaded the influential New York choreographer Nina Wiener to become artistic adviser. The company now has two of her works in its repertoire and she has recently created a piece especially for it. Reflex has developed quickly, attracting praise from reviewers and touring throughout the Netherlands and abroad. Its young and agile dancers have the ability and passion so necessary for interpreting modern dance and choreographies by Toer van Schayk, Bob Foltz and Hans Tuerlings are already in its repertoire.

INFORMATION ABOUT BALLET AND DANCE

Het **Nationale Ballet**, Waterlooplein 22 (District 1), tel. 551 89 11.
Nederlands Dans Theater, Schedeldoekshaven 60, The Hague, tel. 070 – 360 99 31.

Scapino Ballet, Luchtvaartstraat 2, tel. 15 39 16.

Reflex, Moesstraat 7, Groningen, tel. 050 – 71 98 88.

Spring Dance is an international festival of modern dance and movement held each April in Utrecht. Information from Spring Dance, Lucas Bolwerk 24, Utrecht, tel. 030 – 33 13 43.

Holland Dance Festival, with a programme combining internationally renowned companies and promising new groups, takes place in The Hague every two years in September. Information from the Holland Dance Festival, Kleine Gartmanplantsoen 21, tel. 27 65 66.

10 · Pop Music and Jazz

POP MUSIC

Amsterdam is what one could call a cultural melting pot, and that is perhaps most clearly apparent in the wide spectrum of music the city has to offer. Music from all over the world can be heard daily at one or other of the Amsterdam venues, from American rock to reggae and African or Latin American music.

Anyone arriving in Amsterdam by train is immediately confronted, on the square in front of the Central Station, with one of its most characteristic musical phenomena: the busker. A motley array of folk guitarists, blues singers, percussion groups and even complete bands with drum kits and small amplifiers populate the streets of the city in summer, not only the Station Square, but also the Dam and the countless café terraces around the Leidseplein.

Amsterdam pubs, for example in the Jordaan, are still a bastion of tear-jerking Dutch popular songs. Dutch pop music has no such tradition: most groups base themselves on English and American models and also sing in English. Pop music in Dutch, despite a brief period of popularity in the early 1980s, has never really taken off.

Dutch pop and rock groups are pretty insignificant in international terms. For that reason any success abroad (such as Golden Earring and Herman Brood & His Wild Romance had in the past) tends to be blown up out of all proportion by the Dutch (music) press. But pop groups are more or less obliged to go abroad, as the home market for pop is far too small. Only a handful of bands can earn their living by making music, and many musicians live on the dole.

The most important organization engaged in trying to improve the pop climate in Holland is the **Stichting Popmuziek Nederland** (Wibaut-straat 214, Amsterdam, tel. 668 22 55). It is partly due to this excellent organization that a number of the principal venues staging concerts by Dutch bands receive a subsidy from the Ministry of Welfare, Health and Culture. The Stichting Popmuziek Nederland was also the driving force behind the first course for pop lecturers, a novelty in the Netherlands: for some years pop music has been a subject at a number of music schools. Of course, real pop musicians have no use for such courses: traditionally pop music does not fit into the straitjacket of a musical academy. The bulk of pop musicians, unless they come from the more intellectual jazz or fusion areas, are still self-taught. In any case that is true of the **Amsterdam Guitar School**, led by guitar bands like Claw Boys Claw, Fatal Flowers and Tröckener Kecks, hugely popular in their home town, who owe their reputations less to their records than to their exciting live gigs.

Dutch pop may be marginal in international terms – which, however, says nothing about the quality: Amsterdam venues feature a wide choice of interesting Dutch bands – but Amsterdam is still one of the most important musical centres in Europe. The Netherlands is regarded as a testbed for young, promising British and American bands, for whom a gig in Amsterdam may be a springboard to success in the rest of the European mainland.

World music

The summer is the time when the accent shifts to African and other non-Western music. Then Amsterdam emerges as not only a lively pop city but as an important centre for world music – the blanket name for more or less every kind of music not falling directly under the heading of 'pop', whether it comes from the Balkans, the Ivory Coast or the South Pole. Since the beginning of the 1980s there has been a growing interest in music from Turkey and Morocco, north African rai and other African music, which was given an important boost by musicians from Guinea and Ghana who had settled in the city.

The Surinamese and especially the Antillan population of Amsterdam imported not only their own musical culture but also introduced salsa, which had a great vogue in Amsterdam, particularly in the 1970s. The second generation of Surinamers seem less interested in their own cultural heritage than in the rap which originated in New York. Young black rappers largely set the tone of the flourishing Amsterdam hip-hop culture. The only real hip-hop centre in town is **Akhnaton** (Bakkersstraat 12, District 1, tel. 24 33 96), which attracts a young and mostly black crowd. Local rap crews perform regularly. (For venues featuring world music, see p. 152.)

Paradiso and the Melkweg

The two principal pop centres in Amsterdam are Paradiso and the Melkweg, which are a stone's throw from each other. Amsterdam may be a metropolis, but in some respects it is more like a huge village. The area within the canal ring is small, and both Paradiso and the Melkweg are off the Leidseplein, the most important entertainment centre in Amsterdam.

Paradiso, Weteringschans 6 (District 4), tel. 26 45 21/23 73 48, housed in a former church, offers an all-year-round programme of the big names on the pop scene – as long as the particular act does not justify a gig in a stadium or sports arena. Prince, for example, long before he achieved superstar status, made his Dutch début in Paradiso. The décor of the two halls, a small upper hall and a larger lower hall with a balcony, is sombre and functional, and drinks are relatively cheap. The programming, which shows a good feel for possible new trends, is always up to the minute. You won't often find unsubtle, commercial pop here.

Concerts begin at about 9.30 p.m., and admission is not expensive, varying from 10 to 15 guilders. On a first visit to a venue there is a small extra charge for membership, which is valid for a month.

De Melkweg, Lijnbaansgracht 234a (District 4), tel. 24 17 77, has a similar set-up, being like Paradiso a product of the turbulent 1960s, the time of the anarchist-inspired Provo and Kabouter movements. The Melkweg, or Milky Way, was regarded until the late 1970s as the last bastion of hippiedom. Located in an old dairy (hence the name) on a narrow canal behind the Leidseplein, it was a big attraction and a meeting-place for young tourists and travellers from all over the world, who were drawn by the magic name of the centre.

After the advent of punk and the politically active squatters' movement of the 1970s the Melkweg threatened to become an anachronism. However, in subsequent years the centre underwent a facelift and cultivated a contemporary and progressive image. Only the pleasantly relaxed atmosphere recalls the early years.

Besides a café and an exhibition space, the Melkweg has a theatre, a cinema and a concert hall. On four or five evenings a week there is a varied programme of both reggae and African and other roots music, and a large number of pop concerts. In addition there are weekly dance evenings (on Saturdays, for example, after the live acts), which attract a large and colourful public. The atmosphere is informal: no one is turned away at the door because of the way they are dressed.

Other pop venues

On Mondays and Tuesdays things are pretty quiet: the city is getting its breath back after the weekend's exertions, but for the rest of the week the pop fan need never have a dull moment. Only the months of July and August are rather slack – bands seldom tour in the summer.

Information on concerts and other pop events can be found in the Wednesday edition of the daily paper *Het Parool* or in the music paper *OOR*, the most important Dutch pop magazine. Not specifically geared to pop is the **Uitkrant**, a free publication obtainable from, for example, the Amsterdam Uit Buro (Leidseplein 26, District 4, tel. 21 12 11). **Get Records** (Utrechtsestraat 105, District 4, tel. 22 34 41), besides being an excellent record shop, is one of the places for buying pop-concert tickets in advance, as is the **Nieuwe Muziekhandel** (Leidsestraat 50, District 4, tel. 23 14 00), which has a special information phone line (23 72 21) on ticket sales for all big pop events in the country.

The largest venue for the biggest pop events, the **Ahoy** Sports Palace, is not in Amsterdam but in Rotterdam. Big pop concerts in Amsterdam are rare, though there is occasionally something on in the **Jaap Edenhal**, an ice rink with a stuffy, sweaty atmosphere not really suited to pop events. **Theatre Carré** (Amstel 115–125, District 3, tel. 22 52 25) has a lot more class, but has little pop on offer, the more so because it is not really suitable for rock 'n' roll: it has fixed seats, which makes the theatre ideal for listening to concerts.

The most important venue for African and other world music is the Melkweg. However, in adition, on a smaller scale, there are concerts in venues like the **Soeterijn** (Linnaeusstraat 2, tel. 56 88 00), the **Tropeninstituut** (Mauritskade 63, tel. 568 87 11) and **Buurttheater De Klus** (Van Musschenbroekstraat 106, tel. 93 33 80), the last of these offering live music by African and Latin American groups. These intimate venues are important less as concert halls than as meeting-places. The same applies to the **Centre for Chilean Culture in the Netherlands** (Herengracht 259, tel. 26 52 58), which besides a bookshop and a café also has a stage, featuring mostly South American and Caribbean music.

JAZZ

Partly because of the system of subsidies, which in comparison with other countries operates reasonably well (the Ministry of Welfare, Health and Culture set aside more than two million guilders for jazz and improvised music in 1987), the Netherlands has a broad spectrum of concert activity. The range of approaches extends from the composition/improvisation of Guus Janssen and Maarten Altena, which interfaces with jazz only indirectly, to the 'neo-classical' bop of young virtuosos like Jarmo Hoogendijk and Rob van Bavel, who have jazz diplomas from the conservatory. A number of American (and South American) performers have found a permanent place on the Amsterdam music scene. They include Sean Bergin, Michael Moore, Michael Vatcher, Tristan Honsinger and Curtis Clark. A particularly colourful additon were musicians from the former colonies of Surinam and the Netherlands Antilles, who introduced Caribbean music in new hybrid forms such as 'Paramaribop' (Fra Fra Sound, Surinam Music Ensemble, Franky Douglas' Sunchild).

The BIM-huis

Every metropolis has jazz in all shapes and sizes, and it is scarcely a secret that for *real* jazz you do not generally go to the lounges of five-star hotels, but to grubby back streets and clubs that at first sight may not look particularly reputable. Amsterdam is no exception. The most important jazz venue in the country is not in one of the night-life centres around the Leidseplein or the Rembrandtplein, but on a quiet, out-of-the-way canal next to a municipal rubbish dump. Very picturesque, but in the summer the atmosphere can get pretty funky.

Apart from its not particularly smart location, the **BIM-huis** (Oude Schans 73–77, District 1, tel. 23 33 73) is a well-nigh ideal venue: for fifteen years, week in week out, it has offered well-balanced programmes featuring top-flight international and local musicians in every conceivable style: Charles Mingus, Cecil Taylor, Sun Ra and Dexter Gordon have played there, but so have Derek Bailey, John Scofield, Hermeto Pascoal and John Zorn.

The continuous programme of three concerts per week (Thursday–Saturday, starting at 9 p.m.) has gained the venue a very diverse audience: on some nights there seem to be nothing but rusty old bikes parked outside and you know that most probably some highly thought-of avant-garde act has been booked. On other days, the taxis come and go, evening dresses rustle and the applause rings out for veterans like the singer Betty Carter or the pianist Tommy Flanagan.

But what makes the BIM-huis special is not so much this catholic programming and the consequent catholic public (from well-to-do folk in their fifties in Lacoste and Armani suits to militant post-punks in their squatter's outfits). The BIM-huis differs from a number of similar European jazz venues in that commercial interests play a very minor role. It is an internationally orientated jazz club without any of the unpleasant, 'inevitable' features one often encounters in such places: there is no compulsory consumption, there are no rules on dress or inflated prices for food and drink, the bartenders do not go into a flap if someone turns out to be smoking marijuana or hash, and there is no question of a new admission charge at the start of each set. The other side of the informal atmosphere is that there is only very exceptionally an attended cloakroom; the BIM-huis is far from being a *dangerous* place, but keeping a watchful eye on your things can do no harm.

The BIM-huis is there first and foremost for the music. A large number of Dutch jazz musicians are regular visitors, which means that the place is usually full of attentive listeners. Perhaps it would be even more correct to say that the BIM-huis is the brainchild and the property of Dutch jazz musicians. The venue owes its existence to the initiative of a number of politically active musicians (including Willem Breuker, Willem van Manen and Hans Dulfer) who at the beginning of the 1970s were able to secure a government subsidy for jazz, and founded a national union of improvisational musicians (the BIM, which now has more than 250 members), and at the same time got a permanent jazz centre off the ground: in 1974 the BIM-huis, run by the musicians themselves, opened its doors for the first time.

In 1984, after the first Spartan years on bare concrete, an ambitious conversion was carried out with the help of a subsidy from the city council, creating an auditorium (with a café that can if necessary be closed off from the concert area) that can comfortably accommodate an audience of 600. Admission prices vary from 7.50 to (in the case of outstanding acts) 17.50 guilders. It is not usually necessary to book, but if Archie Shepp or local hero J.C. Tans is playing, the place is usually sold out, so ...

The BIM café is open daily from 8 p.m. In the winter season, every Sunday, Monday and Tuesday from 10.30 p.m., the café holds jam sessions, led by top local musicians. Before that there are workshops for musicians just starting out, some of which are open to the public.

Other jazz venues

Theater Tuschinski, Reguliersbreestraat 26 (District 4), tel. 26 26 33. The relatively low admission prices charged by the BIM-huis have at least one drawback: some big American names, because of the fees they command, are beyond the reach of the BIM-huis. The record-shop chain Jazz Inn saw a gap in the market and since 1988, with some help from sponsors, has organized monthly concerts on Saturday nights in the architecturally spectacular Tuschinski cinema. In the seventy-year-old auditorium, where Judy Garland, Edith Piaf and Marlene Dietrich once performed, Jazz Inn presents such jazz greats as Dizzy Gillespie, the Modern Jazz Quartet and J.J. Johnson. The atmosphere oscillates between exclusive and nouveau riche, and the prices are correspondingly steep: from 35 to 80 guilders.

Koepelzaal, Sonesta Hotel, Kattengat 1 (District 6), tel. 21 22 23. Just as stylish and moderately conservative is the monthly programme organized here by the Swing Society. On Sunday afternoons during the winter months, mainly Dutch practitioners of swing and mainstream play here. They are led by such studio veterans as Herman Schoonderwalt.

Those less concerned with the guarantee of big names in up-market surroundings can take their pick of a number of **music cafés**. They usually charge no admission: this is taken care of by increased charges for drinks (a beer can easily cost 4 or 5 guilders in such places).

Café Alto, Korte Leidsedwarsstraat 115 (District 4), tel. 26 32 49. In the vicinity of the Leidseplein, amply provided with café terraces and restaurants, Café Alto offers live jazz seven days a week. The narrow building jammed between pizzerias can get pretty crowded, but it has an atmosphere that with a little good will could pass as that of a New York jazz club. The attractions vary from music students to second-rank Dutch and American performers, but Archie Shepp has also been known to drop in for a jam.

Bamboo-Bar, Lange Leidsedwarsstraat 66 (District 4), tel. 24 39 93. The Bamboo-Bar, one street further on in hamburger and pizza country, also has a daily programme. At the weekends Bamboo-Bar is inclined to book pop and funky-style groups; the rest of the week it is pure jazz.

De Engelbewaarder, Kloveniersburgwal 59 (District 1), tel. 25 37 72. The literary café De Engelbewaarder also has a long jazz tradition. Unfortunately, like many other cafés, it was forced to discontinue its sessions because of complaints about the noise. At the end of 1989 the café began a new series of Sunday afternoon concerts. Hopefully the same top-class Dutch musicians will again appear in this dark brown café, mostly frequented by journalists and 'artists'.

Brazilian music is a new trend in Amsterdam. The hot places for sambas, coconut cocktails and other tropical treats are **Rum Runners**, Prinsengracht 277 (District 6), tel. 27 40 79, which hosts concerts every Sunday from 4 p.m. on, and **Brazilian Bar Canecao**, Lange Leidsedwarsstraat 68–70 (District 4), tel. 38 06 11. Canecao has live music every evening. **Kapitein Zeppos**, Gebed Zonder End 5 (District 1), tel. 24 20 57, offers combinations of jazz and Brazilian music on Sunday afternoons. The location of this club, in an ancient alleyway near a former convent, is worth mentioning for its own sake.

There is real intercultural fare at **Spinoza** (tel. 86 14 30), which is a little way outside the centre at De Wittenstraat 25. Spinoza accommodates jazz, Latin, African, reggae and so on.

Maloe Melo, Lijnbaansgracht 160 (District 7), tel. 25 33 30. Anyone not put off by honest, thumping rhythm 'n' blues can give Maloe Melo a try. This blues club occasionally presents jazz and jump music with 'heavy' tenor-saxophonists like J.C. Tans, Hans Dulfer and Rinus Groeneveld. The adjacent jazz venue **De Kroeg**, the regular spot of the late trumpeter Chet Baker, closed down in 1988. This joint full of dope dealers had not been much fun fore quite a while.

Under a new management the **Nieuwe Kroeg** made a promising start by the end of 1989.

De String, Nes 98 (District 1), tel. 25 90 15, is an unpretentious venue for acoustic (guitar) blues, soft jazz and folk.

Cristofori, Prinsengracht 579 (District 5), tel. 26 84 85, is a large repair workshop and showroom for historic grand pianos. The foundation based here (see also p. 143) presents, along with classical piano concerts, jazz piano events. No more than two or three a year, but invariably of international quality.

Joseph Lam Jazzclub, Van Diemenstraat 8, tel. 22 80 86. Of course fans of dixieland and traditional jazz also have their own spot in Amsterdam. They do have to venture out of the centre; the Joseph Lam jazzclub is on the edge of the docklands, in an old warehouse. The tubas and banjos are unpacked every night, and on Sundays there are jam sessions from 10 p.m. onwards. Anyone wanting to have a go at the Charleston can use the dance-floor.

With the exception of the BIM-huis and a number of jazz cafés, many jazz venues wind down their activities in the summer months. This is compensated for to some extent by the annual **NOS Jazz Festival**, which for four successive days in mid-August presents top international stars in **De Meervaart** (Osdorpplein 67, tel. 10 74 98), a cultural centre in the suburb of Osdorp (easily reachable on tram 1).

Café Para, Martelaarsgracht 7 (District 6), is a place which jazz fans with a sense of history cannot forget. Though it is true that in this smoke-filled joint full of pool sharks there are more likely to be Surinamese – Antillan soul hits blaring out of the loudspeakers, this is still hallowed ground: it is where the tenor giant Ben Webster used to come in his Amsterdam days (the end of the 1960s) for his weekly game of billiards.

11 · Organized Tourism

You can have a wonderful time in Amsterdam without any help from a travel agency or a guide, but this book would not be complete without a brief survey of the possible ways of letting other people take care of your holiday, if only for a short time.

In Amsterdam, as in every self-respecting tourist town, there are hosts of tour operators dying to acquaint you with the clichés created by the brochures, the principal theme being 'typically Dutch'. Those wanting help to penetrate this touristic façade and to hear more than the obvious stories will find they have less choice. There are only a few organizations that go into things in more depth, and they are usually non-commercial outfits run by idealists prepared to pass on their knowledge of a particular subject for a song. In this chapter we shall deal with some of the more interesting tours available.

BOAT TOURS

One typically tourist activity is taking a canal boat trip. Like all businesses eager to move with the times, the boat tour operators have done their best to diversify their product as far as possible. Where once the visitor had the choice only of a straightforward, no-nonsense boat tour of the city, there is now a whole gamut of possibilities. There is, for example, the 'Old Amsterdam by Candlelight' tour, a two-hour evening trip, garnished with cheese and wine. Or a 'Surprising Luncheon Cruise', with traditional 'Dutch Morning Coffee' – I doubt if there are many Dutch people who know what that means – and a three-course lunch. Or the 'Surprising Dinner Cruise', featuring a four-course meal. The prices of these tours with meals included are extremely steep, which might raise a few eyebrows, as the boats used are actually not much more than modern, glass-covered versions of rubbish barges and seem scarcely equipped to serve haute cuisine meals. A tour round the canals is certainly very pleasant, but its charm resides in the fact that you can *see* Amsterdam for yourself from the water, which will be difficult if you need to concentrate on your knife and fork.

One tour worth a separate mention is the *Museum Boat*, which is really more of a cross between a tour and public transport. The Museum Boat leaves every half hour from the Central Station and stops off at ten important museums. You can alight at whatever museum you like and later take the boat to the next. There are day tickets, and you can get a reduction on admission prices for the museums. Information is available from the VVV.

To take a boat trip one can usually simply buy a ticket on the spot at the boat company's office. As far as travel agencies are concerned, they all offer more or less the same tours for the same prices, so that tips are unnecessary: you will find brochures with full information at the VVV.

GUIDED TOURS OF THE CITY

The established travel agencies of course offer an extensive range of tours round the city. The 'Nightwatch', the diamond works, the Anne Frank House, the Royal Palace on the Dam, the Narrow Bridge, the Albert Cuyp market, are all sights that you can see equally well under your own steam. If you prefer a guided tour the same applies: the prices and activities of the travel agencies are interchangeable.

There are, however, a few organizations with something special to offer. For example, there is a foundation which organizes tours of the red-light district, **Stichting FIS**. In contrast to a German outfit, since forced to close down, which ran a 'Kriminal Safari', FIS is not concerned with the sensational aspects of the internationally notorious quarter, but tries to give a realistic picture of the Wallen. Because of this serious approach a good understanding has developed in the course of time between the locals and the foundation's staff, based on mutual respect.

The tour deals with both the history and the present state of the quarter. Central themes are the social side of life in an area of prostitution, and the most beautiful examples of architecture. The guides draw for their information on their personal links with the district and from the archive that they have gradually built up and which is constantly brought up to date.

The tours last about two hours and cost 9.50 guilders. The maximum number per group is about twenty. It usually caters for complete groups; if you are alone you can in principle join in with a group. Depending on people's interests certain subjects are dealt with in greater depth than others.

Up to now there has been little interest from foreigners; FIS is not very well known and those wishing to go on a tour must plan ahead; when you ring up there may be no room until a few days later.

For information and bookings: Stichting FIS, P.O. Box 15666, tel. (020) 27 39 78.

If you want something a bit different from the standard tour of the city, you can try the Stichting Gilde-Amsterdam, which organizes walks through the old city centre and the Jordaan under the name **Mee in Mokum**. Your guide will be a man or woman of fifty-five or over, either a native of Amsterdam or a long-time resident. These volunteers show those in their group things that they themselves find interesting and plan their own favourite routes through the city. Their comments and explanations may not always be equally well informed, but they will certainly be very individual and often typically Amsterdam. This means that no two tours are the same and the atmosphere is much more informal and personal.

The walks take between two and two-and-a-half hours and cost 3.50 guilders per person. There is no problem for English- or German-speakers: it will be arranged for you to be accompanied by someone who knows the language.

For information and bookings: Mee in Mokum, Hartenstraat 18, 1016 CB Amsteram, tel. (020) 25 13 90/25 36 85.

Another foundation worth mentioning is **Archivisie**. This organization provides architectural tours in and outside Amsterdam from roughly mid-March to 1 October. Each year a new standard package of excursions on a particular theme is put together, featuring subjects like social housing, town planning and urban renewal. You can also submit a request for a particular sort of tour all year round.

Archivisie is approached by the most diverse categories of interested parties: the government refers groups of foreign visitors to them, and groups professionally concerned with architecture register for tours. However, individual visitors are also catered for. The excursions are led by expert guides speaking English, French and German, and if necessary Spanish or Italian-speaking guides can be provided. The special interests and degree of knowledge of the participants are taken into account as far as possible.

The standard tours from mid-March to 1 October take place on Saturdays. They last from two to two-and-a-half hours and cost 12.50 guilders each. The maximum number of participants is between fifteen and twenty. Depending on the subject and the size of the group, you travel on foot, by bike or by bus. If you want a tailor-made tour, you should arrange this with the foundation in advance. The price is determined by the size of the group and the nature of the tour.

Information and bookings: Stichting Archivisie, P.O. Box 14603, 1001 LC Amsterdam, tel. (020) 25 89 08.

Since February 1989 a bureau has been operating which arranges walks round art galleries, the **Amsterdam Gallery Guide**. The founder and up to now the sole guide is Marina Veronica, an American graduate of

Boston University. The tours focus on Dutch and foreign art produced in the last ten years.

From September to June you can walk round a total of eight galleries which at that moment have the most interesting shows of painting, sculpture, jewellery and photography. In July and August most galleries exhibiting painting and sculpture are closed, and tours then concentrate on photography, jewellery and interior design.

There is no minimum number of participants for these tours, but since Marina Veronica likes the personal approach there is a maximum of ten people. You can, however, ask for a special tour of a particular kind of gallery, for example, photographers' or interior design galleries. In that case there must be at least four in the group. Because of the extra preparation required for such a tour it may be a day or two before you can be accommodated.

The tours last about four-and-a-half hours and cost 35 guilders per person. For parties of four or more there is a small reduction.

Information and bookings: Amsterdam Gallery Guide, Kromme Englaan 31, 1404 B W Bussum, tel. 02159-33933.

You can tour the city on dry land on the **Tourist Tram**. For 7.50 guilders the Amsterdam Municipal Transport Company (GVB) will take you through the centre of town and the interesting outlying districts in a 1920s tram. The tour lasts about an hour. You are accompanied by a guide who tells you something about the districts, buildings and other sights, and the GVB gives you some incidental information on the way public transport functions in the city. You board and leave the tram on the Dam Square and cannot get off *en route*. Information from the VVV.

TOURS OUTSIDE AMSTERDAM

If you want to see more of the country than just Amsterdam, it is very questionable whether you should put your fate in the hands of a travel organization. They will show you mainly the things which are wrongly regarded as typically Dutch: folk costumes and clogs that are worn mostly for the benefit of tourists, windmills that no longer turn, dairies which still make cheese according to the traditional method, for which there is no real Dutch market, the pantomime known as the 'Alkmaar Cheese Market' and of course, in season, the 'Fabulous Flower Fields'. And you are given ample opportunity to stretch your legs for the benefit of the souvenir shops selling Delft blue or Makkum china.

Naturally there are also interesting trips to be made – for example, to the Delta works in Zeeland. Zeeland is quite a long way by public transport and an expert guide is needed. But as a general rule it is better to go on excursions under one's own steam. The Netherlands has an excellent public transport system and most places are easily reachable by train.

If you wish to visit the villages along the IJsselmeer, which are highly recommended, the best thing to do is to hire a car or go by bike. For a description of this area and an attractive cycle route, see pp. 232.

Quite touristy, but not a bad idea, is **Ena's Bike Tours**. This commercial bureau organizes half-day and whole-day bicycle trips through the surroundings of Amsterdam. You can benefit from the guides' knowledge of the area, and so will at least take a pleasant route. It is a shame that besides a rowing trip, a picnic and a swim the agenda also includes the old chestnuts: windmills, cheese dairies and suchlike.

Information: Ena's Bike Tours, P.O, Box 2807, 2601 CV Delft, tel. 015-14 37 97.

12 · Holidays and Special Events

JANUARY

On 1 January, **New Year's Day**, all businesses, government offices, banks and shops are closed, while the country sleeps off its hangover.

FEBRUARY

Either during February or at the beginning of March it is **Carnival** time, when the two southern provinces of Noord-Brabant and Limburg celebrate for three days on end. Nowadays Amsterdam also has a shot at creating a carnival, but without great success. The 'real' carnival towns include 's Hertogenbosch, Venlo and Maastricht.

On 25 February the 1941 **February Strike** is commemorated on the Jonas Daniël Meijerplein (see p. 25).

MARCH

Ice and weather permitting, the **Keukenhof** opens its gates at the beginning of March.

The Sunday closest to 15 March is the date of the **Stille Omgang** (Silent Procession), in which pilgrims commemorate the Miracle of Amsterdam (see p. 16) by walking in silence along a fixed route through the city.

On **Good Friday**, which falls around the end of March or the beginning of April, all banks and official agencies are closed. The first great tourist wave hits Amsterdam and it is usually *very* busy.

The same applies to **Easter**. Easter Monday is a national holiday, and shops, businesses, banks and government offices are closed.

APRIL

30 April is **Koninginnedag** (Queen's Day). The whole country takes a day off in order to celebrate the birthday of the former queen, Juliana.

Hundreds of thousands of people descend on Amsterdam to celebrate in the city's streets. Food and drink and all kinds of merchandise are on sale everywhere. There is lots of music and young and old try to earn money in the most varied ways. Many Amsterdammers complain that nowadays it is a little *too* busy in the city. Perhaps that is why since 1988 celebrations have got under way the night before, when stalls are put up to be sure of a prime spot. In this way a slightly smaller group of people have a foretaste of Koninginnedag.

Halfway through the month the **World Press Photo** exhibition reaches Amsterdam, and the photos can be seen in the Nieuwe Kerk.

MAY

1 May is **Labour Day**, but this is scarcely celebrated in the Netherlands any longer, and goverment agencies and banks, etc. are open all day.

4 May is the **Dodenherdenking** (National Remembrance Day). At 8 p.m. two minutes' silence is observed throughout the country to commemorate those killed in the Second World War, and there is a remembrance ceremony at the National Monument on the Dam.

The following day is **Bevrijdingsdag** (Liberation Day). There are various activities scattered throughout the city, but especially in the Vondelpark, where there is food, drink, music and stands with representatives of political and ideological organizations. There is also a free-for-all market, making it a repetition of Koninginnedag on a small scale. This is a little less crowded and perhaps because of that a little more enjoyable.

In mid-May Scheveningen celebrates **Vlaggetjesdag** (Flag Day), when the herring fleet is welcomed into port with the first catch of the season.

At the end of the month the **Kunst-Rai** art fair takes place and national and international art galleries display their collections (see p. 105).

Hemelvaartsdag (Ascension Day) falls in this month, and all shops, businesses, goverment offices and banks are closed. The city is extremely busy.

Whitsun, which also falls around this time or at the beginning of June, is also a national holiday.

JUNE

During June the **Holland Festival** takes place. This is a renowned international festival of theatre, music, opera and dance, with performances at various venues in the Netherlands (see p. 145).

This month also marks the opening of the **Vondelpark Festival**. Several times a week there are theatrical productions on the open-air stage in the Vondelpark and performances of modern and classical music. The Festival continues till the end of August.

In the last week in June you can attend the **Festival of Seduction**. The homosexual community celebrates Gay Pride Week and there are various exhibitions and theatrical performances.

JULY

In July the **Summer Festival** (Zomerfestijn) is organized in Amsterdam. This is an international festival of alternative theatre (see p. 145).

Around the end of July the **North Sea Jazz Festival**, one of the world's most important jazz festivals, takes place in The Hague. All kinds of jazz from scores of countries are represented, along with Latin, African and Arab music.

AUGUST

Sail Amsterdam takes place every five years; 1990 will be the next occasion. Sail Amsterdam is a regatta of sailing ships, with a special emphasis on tall ships (two, three and four-masters). Vessels from all over the world come to Amsterdam to parade on the IJ. In addition there is a water-borne flower pageant, a show of Dutch fishing-smacks and a fair. Everything is free apart from the fair. Sail Amsterdam sees Amsterdam at its busiest.

Halfway through August there is a four-day **jazz festival** in the Meervaart (see p. 156).

A week before the opening of the Dutch football league season, the pride of Amsterdam, Ajax, competes in the annual **Amsterdam-700** tournament. Competition is always top-class and the fans get their first view of the season of their club.

At the end of August Hotel Pulitzer and the piano manufacturers Cristofori organize an open-air concert on the Prinsengracht (see p. 156).

In the first weekend in August you can visit the **Uitmarkt**, the gala opening of the new Dutch artistic season. Huge numbers of visitors from all over the country flock to the Nes and the surrounding area to look at the stands of theatrical companies and publishers. There are previews of theatrical and musical productions.

At the end of August or the beginning of September the **Festival of Early Music** is held in Utrecht. This festival, which has now gained international stature, features music from the period of the earliest notation down to 1850. The musicians endeavour to perform the music as authentically as possible, and the concerts are given at various historical locations in Utrecht.

SEPTEMBER

In the first week of September the **Flower Parade**, with its procession of floral floats, winds its way through the city.

The **Jordaan Festival**, a street festival with music and market stalls held in the Jordaan district, occupies the third week of September.

NOVEMBER

Some time during November the **Stagedoor Festival**, an international festival of dance, music and theatre, is held (see p. 145).

On the second or fourth Saturday in November St Nicholas (the Dutch equivalent of Santa Claus) arrives in Holland. The Good Saint arrives by boat on the quayside in front of the Central Station. 'Sinterklaas' is largely a festival for children and the middle classes.

DECEMBER

5 December is known as **Pakjesavond** (gift evening). In honour of St Nicholas's birthday on 6 December, the Dutch exchange presents, often ingeniously wrapped and accompanied by anonymous poems. On 5 December shops shut approximately one hour early and at the start of the evening in particular it is very quiet in town.

25 and 26 December are the **Christmas** national holiday. On Christmas Eve banks usually close one hour earlier. In the evening families go out

in droves for a Christmas meal. If you wish to join in, you should book a table well in advance, especially if you want to eat in a good restaurant. On Christmas Day most restaurants and cafés are closed; the city is virtually deserted. The following day, however, when family duties have been fulfilled, night-life gets into full swing again.

On 31 December, **New Year's Eve**, shops, banks, businesses and government offices close their doors at 4 p.m. In the evening people celebrate at home. At twelve o'clock the New Year is heralded with vast amounts of fireworks, particularly in the centre of town, on the Dam. Afterwards most cafés and discos throw open their doors and gradually fill up. Celebrations continue until the last revellers have been bundled out of the door.

13 · Eight Districts of Amsterdam

1: THE 'WALLEN', THE NIEUWMARKT AND THE WATER-LOOPLEIN

In this part of town, the Nieuwmarkt and the 'Wallen', one sometimes has to walk no further than thirty or forty metres to step from one social world into another. A description of the area can only be a sketch, because everything and everyone is continually on the move. The décor is altering – things are continually being built, renovated or demolished – and the cafés and restaurants are constantly changing character as they pass into new hands or attract different kinds of customer. Of course there are a few more or less permanent elements: the whores on the Wallen (Amsterdam's red-light district), the junkies around the Nieuwmarkt, the police, the ethnic minorities (especially Chinese and Surinamers), the residents and the local shopkeepers, and some of the hoteliers and restaurateurs.

Much of the housing in the Nieuwmarkt area is new and designed for low-income groups from other parts of the city allocated flats here by the council. There are other newcomers, yuppies and intellectuals with a weakness for the strange hotch-potch found here and with enough money to buy up old properties and carry out elegant conversions. There is no shortage of contrasts in the area. Some houses are like fortresses, with security gates across the doorway to protect the video recorder from the light-fingered junkies who troop past the window, while the occupants sip glasses of wine in their Italian-designed interiors and hold forth to their guests (not without a degree of coquetry) on how colourful their everyday environment is. A few doors further the council may just have boarded up a property where a recently discovered gambling-den has been raided. The same applies to the shopkeepers, etc., as they too have to deal with very different sorts of customer. The Albert Heijn supermarket on the Nieuwmarkt is frequented by junkies dropping in for a lemon, alcoholics hoping to get through the day with the help of the cheapest fruit *jenever*, but also by well-dressed housewives with children and single people with good jobs planning on an avocado mousse or maybe a biscuit or two with smoked salmon for supper.

One cannot really talk about the Nieuwmarkt and the Wallen as though they are 'neighbourhoods': they are a conglomeration of sub-neighbourhoods, an archipelago of networks and sub-cultures, a riot of incongruities, a collection of urban villages which, all things considered, actually co-exist in admirable harmony in the square kilometre where it all 'happens'.

This is of course an Eldorado for village idiots, as it is for criminals, tramps, eccentrics, nosy provincials and, last but not least, tourists, who must sometimes wonder what kind of a loony bin they have wound up in. For them I have mapped out a short walk that will take no more than about twenty minutes at the most – not counting stops at cafés *en route*.

We shall begin at the Central Station (where on platform 2 there is a chic restaurant in the marvellously restored Art Deco waiting room), and turn left on to the Prins Hendrikkade. At the rear of the station, by the way, there is another very nice restaurant built on a pier – Pier 10. It looks as though a post-modernist designer has been let loose on the deckhouse of an old-fashioned freighter, and when you dine at the big windows it is as though you are sailing between the lights on the water.

Behind the Barbizon Hotel is the Zeedijk, the most notorious street in the country, which the Amsterdam council is hastily renovating in order to turn it into a safe and attractive pedestrian route between the station and the Nieuwmarkt (and from there to the Waterlooplein and the Opera). There is already something to show for their efforts: Hotel Barbizon, at the start of the Zeedijk, stands there as proud proof of the co-operation between local government and business interests, and is intended as an 'entrée for tourists'. Older residents, who have already seen much dirty water flow under the bridge, take a sceptical attitude and mutter to each other that they'll believe it when they see it, but it is an unmistakable fact that the drug-dealers no longer have the 'Dijk' all to themselves, since there are ordinary shops there again: a baker's and an excellent fishmonger's.

The landlord of a café on the Nieuwmarkt is among those who are doubtful about the outcome. 'Very soon it'll be like living in a zoo here,' he says gloomily. 'They'll put up posh hotels on the edge of the Nieuwmarkt and the Wallen, as all the tourists like to come and take a peek at the red-light district, and we'll be caught in the middle like some sort of peepshow. We could levy an entertainment tax. Not so long ago a copper from the Warmoesstraat station said I should put a security gate over the door if I didn't want junkies on my doorstep. That's what everyone was doing , he said. Well, I'm not going to start living behind a security gate! Try complaining at the station about the din they make at night, and they tell you cool as can be, "Call the mayor about it." So I said, "Could I have the mayor's number then?" And they hung up on me.'

The regulars in the café start laughing and an older man tells us with great relish how the other day he saw two policemen on horseback charging across the market at full gallop after a Moroccan lad, while the market traders fell about laughing and shouted encouragement: 'Go on, McCloud, get him!'

But we shan't stop off at that café, and we shan't go along the Dijk. We'll take the third side-street off the Prins Hendrikkade, the Kromme Waal, past the Seoul restaurant where there has been yet another shoot-out between two rival Chinese gangs in which the owner (a mafia chief) has been gunned down.

An old man comes dancing along the pavement. His pleated skirt whirls round his bare knees and a baby-blue sock hangs straight down in front of him. He has tied a bright ribbon round his grey ponytail. A little further on a junkie stands with his hands above his head against the wall while the police go through his pockets and unbutton his trousers. They've obviously found something, because they're taking him away to the station in handcuffs.

The customers at the tall windows of Café Miller on the corner are quite unperturbed and go on with their muted conversations or games of chess. And the landlady, who is clearing the café tables on the pavement, shrugs her shoulders. 'I know that lad. He used to come round cadging lemons or spoons, but I don't want to know. I don't let any junkies in here.'

At the café we turn right into the Binnen Bantammerstraat. This used to be the heart of Chinatown, where the restaurants belonged to those poor peanut-sellers who were trying to work their way up the social ladder by running their own business. Many of them succeeded, and their sons and grandsons now run expensive Far Eastern speciality restaurants serving authentic Chinese cuisine. The last Chinese has gone from the Binnen Bantammerstraat; the Lotus restaurant is run by Ari, a Dutchman.

There are still a few old-fashioned Chinese restaurants where the food is good and cheap and where the famous blackened 'thousand-year-old eggs' and the won ton soup are still served on paper tablecloths, surrounded by lampions and gilt dragons, but for that you need to go the 'bottom end' of the Zeedijk to Moy–Kong, for example, or Hoy Tin. Or to the even smaller, rather scruffy little joints where you can get Peking duck and a bowl of rice for 10 guilders. This last category of eating-houses is frequented mainly by the Chinese residents of the area, as they look about as inviting as the average launderette, and tourists turn up their noses at them.

The Binnen Bantammerstraat leads into the Geldersekade – the dividing line between the Nieuwmarkt and the whores' quarter, the Wallen and on the bridge over the water there is usually a group of dealers carrying on their noisy trade – unless there's a police 'clean-up' operation on, of course. Today they're up to their usual tricks. Five Surinamese lads are thumping each other and yelling insults in Surinam creole, which sounds to Dutch ears as though there could be bloodshed at any moment, but it usually blows over – like now. After a few minutes the argument gets bogged down in business matters and their attention once again turns to potential customers.

'Hey man! Wanna buy? White or brown?'

The Wallen are intimate. In no other European city is the whores' quarter so cosy, so chock-full of traditional pubs, old bridges, quaint little shops and ethnic restaurants. In the Warmoesstraat, for example, you can choose between Mexican, Spanish, Argentine and other exotic fare. The nicest Spanish restaurant, however, is in the Lange Niezel (just north of the Oude Kerk), at least if you like it simple: bare tables, tapas in the front part, no unnecessary frills, and generous glasses of rioja.

We won't join the hordes of tourists and punters shuffling along the Oudezijds Achterburgwal and the Oudezijds Voorburgwal, but will head for the terrace of Tisfris. There we find a man who has lived in the red-light district for twenty years and can tell us what it used to be like.

'It's still great here,' he says. 'But twenty years ago it was better, when everyone knew everyone else. They were all real characters, the pimps and whores, and there was a real feeling of solidarity. We hadn't heard about junkies then, we didn't even know the word. The tarts were prettier in those days, lovely blondes. They didn't sit at the windows in some skimpy swimsuit, they worked in long, elegant fur coats. The customers were different too. Today the men come mostly to ogle the girls – they don't dare go in. But in those days they used to drive up in great limousines. Of course there were the locals like the shopkeepers, but there were lots of intellectuals and artists as well, they felt at home, at least if they'd taken the trouble to fit in. Outsiders weren't accepted just like that in the whores' world – you had to make an effort. Now it's all changed. Now there are lots of coloured girls at the windows – foreign imports – and they don't bother about anyone. And since the police have started clearing the drugs and the junkies off the Zeedijk, they've headed in this direction. The worst places at the moment are the Oude Hoogstraat and the Damstraat – that's where the "bridge of pills" is, the packaging crunches under your feet when you walk across. That's where most thieving goes on too. But the situation changes day by day around here. The concentration may have shifted and gone somewhere else by tomorrow.'

On hot days it is nice and cool on the terrace at Tisfris, as there's always a breeze from the Amstel. Besides lousy service, Tisfris has quite a choice of trendy snacks, at least if you can get someone to bring you any. From here you can see the back of the new Town Hall – an ugly red-brick wall – in the same building as the Muziektheater, which stages opera and ballet. There are some steps leading down to the canal and at the bottom you find yourself on the Zwanenburgwal, where the junk market is now held on standard council-issue stalls. Before the war those stalls used to be on the Waterlooplein, a little further on, and they were run by Jewish market traders. This part of the area was the old Jewish quarter, but after 1945 there was almost nothing left of it: what you see here are the sorry remnants of what used to be the heart of the district.

In the St Antoniesbreestraat fashionable boutiques have sprung up where you can buy black-and-white punk trousers, or a theatrical terracotta column to put a vase of flowers on, and there are various secondhand clothes shops with 1920s hats at reduced prices or a beautifully pressed antique wedding-dress. The whole area has profited to some degree from the building of the opera house, and cafés and coffee shops have suddenly started calling themselves 'Puccini' or some such name. Often real-live designers are called in to fit them out with an appropriate interior, as in the orange-striped grand-café Waterloo. Those pre-war Jewish traders wouldn't have believed their eyes.

Finally we'll stroll through the Kalkmarkt and along the Binnenkant. In the early evening the Wallen are swarming with people and the terraces on the Nieuwmarkt are still in full swing, but here all is quiet. These streets (and the Krom Boomssloot and Recht Boomssloot) are a kind of golden fringe around the area, with homes for the more affluent. The ships of the Dutch East India Company once sailed past the majestic buildings along the the wide expanse of the Binnenkant, and one could see the dolphins leap, as there was still open access to the North Sea. There were shipowners' houses and wharves, and the houses still bear witness to this vanished glory with their imposing front doors and stylish windows.

One can see that this part of the area is becoming fashionable, because everywhere there have been plasterers at work stopping further deterioration, and the fortunate occupants of these monuments have taken up the occasional paving slab and trailed plants up the walls. On warm summer evenings there are quite a few people sitting out on the pavement reading their papers in the fading light, or else they have brought out the barbecue and are preparing complete meals in the street, with tables covered in damask and sparkling glasses of champagne. Yet these houses are less than a hundred metres from the MDHG, a council centre for addicts where the junkies' association is also located.

Such contrasts as these are less strange than they might appear at first sight, because the 'Lastage', as the area outside the city walls was traditionally known, was always a turbulent place, a haven for those who could not come to terms with the established order.

At the end of the 1960s, for example, there were squatters here who actively resisted the city council and unleashed a veritable civil war to prevent the building of the metro. In those days the area looked like a set of badly maintained teeth: full of cavities, gaps and decay. The decline dated from the war years when the Jewish occupants were deported to German camps and those who were left started breaking up the abandoned houses for firewood. Those that remained standing fell into ruin. This meant that by no means all the locals were opposed to the council's reconstruction plans in the 1960s: some of them were quite willing to be temporarily housed while the council got on with renovation, and in many cases demolition. Others were totally sceptical and became suspicious. What was going to happen to the area? The place was a-buzz with rumours and many properties stood empty.

Into this power vacuum stepped students and Marxist activists. In a certain sense they were continuing an old tradition, since back in the fifteenth century the Lastage had been outside the city gates and an odd collection of flotsam and jetsam was washed up there: seamen, cheapjacks, whores. It was no coincidence that this became the Jewish quarter, as even poor immigrants could find a niche. Whenever Amsterdam was besieged, the Lastage was invariably burned to the ground.

Later, long after the area had been enclosed by the city walls, it continued to serve the same function. From 1900 on Chinese settled in the Binnen Bantammerstraat, subsequently it was occupied by the squatters, and they were succeeded by the junkies. It was and is an area with a good character and a bad reputation, a whore with a heart of gold.

A woman who has lived here for more than fifteen years says: 'Tolerance is something this area has learned, and that didn't happen overnight. I came here as a squatter, when there were all kinds of action committees fighting council policy. There's a demolition ball hanging in the Nieuwmarkt metro station as a monument to the struggle. You can see exactly where the squatters defeated the council: it's the point where the narrow Antoniesbreestraat meets the widened section of the Jodenbreestraat. The council wanted to build a motorway there, and they didn't get their way! In those days people were more tolerant to those who departed from the norm. We read Marx and the classic anarchists. Squatting was a full-time job, a way of life. Everyone who lived here had their own "adopted junky" – we believed the junkies were part of it all too. We even hired a boat as a crisis centre for them, but of course it turned into a meeting-place for dealers, a complete shambles. But still it's good that we tried. There's still something of that big-hearted feeling about. That's why all sorts of people are so keen to live here, because something special is going on.'

That is both true and untrue. Perhaps it would be better to say that it is an area for devotees, you've got to love it. You've got to be able to put up with the diversity of the big city, have a stomach strong enough to contemplate the seediness one cannot escape in this place, and above all you must not be afraid. This is not an area that leaves those who live in it indifferent. Outsiders reading in the papers about a stabbing on the Zeedijk shudder and wonder who on earth would settle here of their own free will.

But the true devotees know better and dismiss such sanctimonious twitterings with scorn. 'Of course you've got to be a bit street-wise to be able to get on easily around here, but that's precisely what makes dealing with people here so exciting and surprising!' they exclaim enthusiastically, and proceed to deluge the critics with a torrent of anecdotes designed to show how unique the place is, how admirably tolerant, how truly urban and at the same time how much of a village, how manageable and at the same time how enchantingly unpredictable and adventurous. The true devotee lives here out of conviction and is proud of his inside knowledge of this mini-jungle – a Tarzan who knows every creeper like the back of his hand. Those who don't understand that will never learn, but then they won't live here, or at least not for long. That kind sooner or later move to Amsterdam-South – which is better for all concerned.

District 1: The 'Wallen', the Nieuwmarkt and the Waterlooplein

CAFÉS

1 Café Bern – Nieuwmarkt 9
2 Blincker – St. Barberenstraat 7-9
3 The Bulldog – Oudezijds Voorburgwal 132
4 Crea Café – Grimburgwal 10
5 De Engelbewaarder – Kloveniersburgwal 59
6 'Frascati – Nes 59
7 Kapitein Zeppos – Gebed Zonder End 5
8 Lokaal 't Loosje – Nieuwmarkt 32
9 Miller – Binnen Bantammerstraat 27
10 De Pieter – St Pieterspoortsteeg 29
11 Tisfris – St Anthoniesbreestraat 142
12 Waterloo – Zwanenburgwal 15

RESTAURANTS

13 Tango – Warmoesstraat 49
14 Moy-Kong – Zeedijk 87
15 Excelsior – Nieuwe Doelenstraat 2-8
16 Sukasari – Damstraat 26
17 Da Canova – Warmoesstraat 9
18 Pacifico – Warmoesstraat 31
19 De Roode Leeuw – Damrak 93-94
20 Centra – Lange Niezel 29
21 De Kooning van Siam – Oudezijds Voorburgwal 42
22 Lana Thai – Warmoesstraat 10
23 Tom Yam – Staalstraat 22
24 Alberto's Carreta – Spui 8

MUSEUMS

25 Allard Pierson Museum – Oude Turfmarkt 127
26 Rembrandthuis – Jodenbreestraat 4-6

OTHER

27 Stopera – Amstel 1

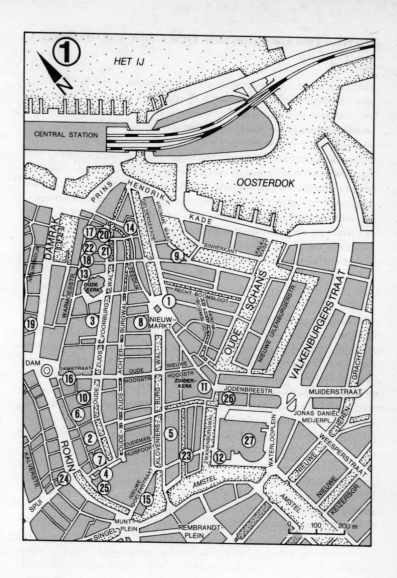

2: THE CONCERTGEBOUW QUARTER AND THE VON-DELPARK

You have to be blind not to see the enchantment of the early morning light playing over the canals. And only if you are particularly obtuse will the attractive, unconventional atmosphere of the Jordaan, for instance, be lost on you. However, it is not advisable to pay the Concertgebouw quarter a visit unless your senses are fully alert: it will shut up like a clam and reveal nothing of the uniqueness lurking behind all that brick.

The gateway to the section of Amsterdam-South known as the Concertgebouw quarter is a glorious one. From the Rijksmuseum you cross the Museumplein, known in Amsterdam circles as 'the shortest motorway in the country', and head straight for the golden harp on top of the Concertgebouw. And there lies the quarter spread out like a fan before you, with at its centre what on old maps may still be called the J.W. Brouwersplein, but which on the occasion of the centenary of the Concertgebouw in 1988 was rechristened the Concertgebouwplein.

The Museumplein causes the city council and those who live around it quite a few headaches and much annoyance. Even though the name might suggest it, Museum Square can scarcely be called the cultural heart of Amsterdam, because most of the museums on it turn only their inaccessible backs to face the square. In the spring a sea of blooming crocuses may give the square a certain charm, but apart from that the spacious but characterless expanse serves mainly as a temporary location for the tents of a touring theatre company, an assembly point for large-scale demonstrations or hordes of football supporters after their team has won a cup final or, especially in summer, as a parking space for huge columns of coaches. However, an exhibition at the Stedelijk Museum in 1988 of the designs entered for a competition organized by a daily newspaper showed that the square can set the blood of many a professional and amateur architect racing.

On either side of and behind the Concertgebouw – with its controversial glass extension added during a radical restoration in 1988 – is the Concertgebouw quarter. Though it does not swing ostentatiously, there is no denying that it is a musical area. Nowhere in town does one see so many violin cases strapped to backs. Small stickers in windows announce the concerts of the countless orchestras and occasional ensembles of which the neighbourhood boasts. At the beginning of the Willemsparkweg notice the exquisite shop of the late violin-maker Max Möller.

The look of the streets is anything but monotonous: there is a constant alternation of ponderous grandeur and light, leafy elegance, and at weekends the workaday bustle of a residential area with a proliferation of small businesses gives way to a charming, peaceful atmosphere. Children still play in the street, and it would not be at all surprising if a survey showed Amsterdam-South to have the largest concentration of cats in the whole city.

In the last decades of the nineteenth century a few splendid villas sprang up on the edge of the Vondelpark (see below), and on the Willemspark-weg, running parallel to it, a number of houses were put up which proved sufficiently grand to lure occupants of canal-side houses to this part of town. Apart from that, however, there was still no question of a residential area south of the city centre before the turn of the century. On its completion in 1888 the Concertgebouw stood in all its neo-classical Viennese splendour on the edge of Amsterdam as it then was, with open polderland behind it. It was only shortly after 1900 that the Amsterdam agglomeration really ventured south beyond the canal ring and a new, attractive residential area emerged behind the Concert-gebouw. The great diversity in size, style and materials used are an indication that the district was not built according to any precise plan, but by groups of houses and sections of streets. The spacious homes, with their servants' quarters, attracted residents of relatively high income and status to this part of town. Naturally, because of the proximity of the Concert-gebouw, famous conductors like Mengelberg and later Van Beinum settled in Amsterdam-South. The families had lots of children and the area became very dynamic. In the street there was a constant coming and going of parlour-maids, servants and coachmen. Quite soon a small publishing company saw a potential profit in specializing solely in postcards of streets in the area. These were avidly bought by domestic staff from the provinces. They marked the houses where they were in service with a cross and sent them to their families back home. Reprints of these cards can be still be seen at Fransen the chemist at Van Breestraat 100.

The Van Breestraat runs at right-angles to the back of the Concertge-bouw and is one of those streets with that airy, flamboyant character that is a constant surprise in Amsterdam-South. Fransen's dates from 1902 and is run by two nephews of the original shopkeeper. The interior of the shop, apart from the goods on display, has scarcely changed in the intervening eighty years and for that reason is one of the area's treasured relics of its kind. The same applies to the traditional little stationer's run by the Van der Schots round the corner from Fransen's, at Jacob Obrechtstraat 14. And at P.C. Hooftstraat 62 the dusty shop window of the haberdasher's belonging to the elderly Mrs Schade van Westrum immediately stands out among the trendy shop-fronts. To the great delight of her faithful customers in the area she has firmly rejected all the seductive offers made by developers to get hold of her property.

In the Banstraat, which runs at right-angles to the Van Breestraat near Fransen's, at No. 22, is another small shopkeeeper, Ko van Leest, whose bookshop carries nothing but literature on its shelves. Behind the large shop window framed with dark woodwork is his still rather dimly lit bookshop, which has the venerable air of a carefully tended private library. People don't go there to pick up a book in a hurry, but to browse around and review the state of world literature with Van Leest as one's guide. He is renowned for his collection of books by and on Rilke and his stock of Dutch, English, French and German poetry.

Back to the Concertgebouw quarter during the first heady decades of this century. Around the Jacob Obrechtkerk (1908) in the street of the same name, a flourishing centre of Roman Catholicism sprang up, and the convent school attached to the church attracted well-brought-up girls from all over Amsterdam. Owing to the pulling-power of the Concertgebouw and the Municipal Theatre, which was actually only a stone's throw away, the number of artistically inclined residents also increased. It is this combination of bourgeois and artistic Amsterdammers which is characteristic of the area, and that character has persisted over the years.

In the 1920s the Concertgebouw quarter expanded southwards. Blocks of houses appeared in the then very avant-garde style of the Amsterdam School, with its combination of straight and curved forms and daring detail. At the end of the 1930s Amsterdam-South was rounded off with the construction of an area of detached houses around the Apollolaan.

The economic crisis shortly before the Second World War passed by largely unnoticed in the prosperous district. Only in the 1950s were there transitional problems, when there was a growing discrepancy between the amount of living space available and the drastic reduction in family size. Empty houses were exploited by sharp operators as inadequately equipped old people's homes and boarding-houses for immigrant workers. Though the district as a whole did not decline it did suffer a loss of status for a short while. When the council began issuing ordinances requiring minimum standards to be met in the old people's homes and boarding-houses, they rapidly disappeared. Many large houses were divided up into flats, families with children returned and there was a revival of the district's original character, with its mixture of modern affluence and artistic flair.

That there are nevertheless differences between the various parts of Amsterdam-South, with its generally well-educated inhabitants, becomes apparent if you look at the three principal shopping streets.

The previously mentioned P.C. Hooftstraat (incidentally the oldest street in Amsterdam-South) and the nearby parts of the Van Baerlestraat have developed over the years into the most fashionable and also the priciest shopping area in Amsterdam. On Saturdays especially celebrities from the Dutch television and film world like to be seen nonchalantly shopping in the area.

In another corner of Amsterdam-South, not far from the Hilton Hotel with its legal casino, is the Beethovenstraat. This is the street where the more traditionally minded, chic inhabitants round the Apollolaan, including well-to-do Jewish families of Eastern European extraction, do their shopping, go to the hairdresser's, and in the afternoons take tea on one of the covered terraces.

In recent years, because of the explosive increase in the popularity of the Concertgebouw quarter, the Cornelis Schuytstraat has grown from a local shopping street into a classy thoroughfare. Two very exclusive and exuberant florists and a branch of Christie's auction house have raised this street above the suburban level. With any luck in the Cornelis Schuytstraat you will bump into Bobby, the stylish local drunk, about whose supposed wealth the wildest rumours are in circulation.

Like the shopping streets, the cafés too are an excellent barometer of the atmosphere of the district, the more so because this is never determined by tourists even in summer. They undoubtedly exist, but they never dominate. Renowned establishments in the Concertgebouw area are Bodega Keyzer, popular especially for dining after concerts, and the small Café Welling, where people conduct serious or not-so-serious culturally tinged conversations.

If you turn left into the Van Baerlestraat from the Museumplein and go as far as the Roelof Hartplein, you will find Café Wildschut. With its 1920s interior and roomy terrace it is a very popular meeting-place both for school pupils and students and for businessmen.

From Café Wildschut you can look down the J.M. Coenenstraat, with examples of Amsterdam School architecture on both sides. On the right an enormous block of houses strikes the eye and behind it is the synagogue, built in the same style and still in use as a place of worship. Tucked away on the left-hand side of the J.M. Coenenstraat is a more refined and moving example of the Amsterdam School's work, the Harmoniehof. Two rows of small houses covered with ivy, creepers and roses enclose an intimate little garden with a sweetly playing fountain.

At the end of a day spent exploring Amsterdam-South, don't head straight back to the centre of town. There are hosts of places to eat, varying from the very expensive and exclusive Kersentuin next to the Hilton Hotel and the more moderately priced brasseries in the Van Baerlestraat to the many more or less exotic restaurants and pubs serving food which are scattered throughout the area.

VONDELPARK

On the edge of Amsterdam-South lies the most popular and best-known municipal park in the Netherlands, the Vondelpark. Some six to eight million people visit it each year. Despite this enormous number, the park, thanks to its balanced design, often gives visitors the impression that they are in the country. In some spots you need to take a good deep breath to remind yourself that you are still in a landscape dominated by noxious fumes.

It was the landscape architect Zocher who in the middle of the last century was commissioned to transform the fallow fields – then still on the edge of Amsterdam – into a city park in the so-called 'landscape style'. This style aims at imitating an Arcadian landscape by means of a balanced interplay of groups of trees, rivulets with greenery along their banks, differences in levels and winding paths. Zocher's original conception has, however, been somewhat lost. The park is on peaty soil and ever since it has existed has been continuously sinking into the morass. Money had and still has to be pumped into it to replace the mildewed vegetation and to raise the level of the soil by a few centimetres.

Since the park became the property of the city in 1953, sufficient resources have been available to maintain it, to the delight of many people – it is not the largest park in the city, but it is the most popular. Not only the residents of the surrounding districts – prosperous Amsterdam-South on one side and the deteriorating early twentieth-century working-class areas on the other – visit it for recreation. From all over the city both tourists and Amsterdammers come there to do the things one does in a large city park: take the dog for a walk, jog, stroll, sit out on a terrace, sunbathe. The atmosphere is relaxed, the composition of the visitors varied.

In the winter the park can look gloomy and desolate. Spring and summer are the period for happenings. On Koninginnedag and Liberation Day (5 May) the whole population is allowed to trade in the street without a permit and the masses stroll shoulder to shoulder through the Vondelpark. From July to September there are weekly theatrical and musical performances.

Sundays are busiest. The three big café terraces, of which the Film Museum's is the nicest, are jam-packed. Illegal hawkers with all kinds of food, clothing and jewellery display their wares, much to the annoyance of their legal competitors in the area, palmists tell fortunes and musicians and entertainers from all over the world perform. Walkers wishing to avoid this hubbub will have to make for the western section of the park. Beyond the Rose Garden, where slightly more sedate Amsterdammers go and at weekends Muslim residents of the adjacent working-class area, it is a little quieter. During the week, and especially around dinner time (7 p.m.), there are many places where quiet reigns and the constant hum of the big city is heard only in the background.

The park has its regular visitors. These are made up in part of young unemployed people, for whom the park is a sort of substitute for a day in the country or even for a holiday. The park is sometimes mockingly called 'Costa del Vondelpark'. It was these people who felt most deprived when in 1989 the occupants of the big houses directly overlooking the park refused to have their quiet Sundays disturbed any longer and took out an injunction to put an end to the free pop concerts in the park. The resistance of those living in the area to excessive noise was not limited to organized activities: buskers who resort to the Vondelpark now run the risk of having their instruments confiscated by the police if they produce too many decibels.

For many people the Vondelpark is a relic of the end of the 1960s, when for a while Amsterdam was one of the magical centres of the world. In the space of three months a total of 100,000 people sleeping rough was counted. This group especially will regret that the park is losing some of its ebullience. But there is still enough going on there, and who knows what new attractions will replace those that have been lost.

District 2: The Concertgebouw Quarter and the Vondelpark

CAFÉS
1 Welling – Johannes Verhulststraat 2
2 Wildschut – Roelof Hartplein 1
3 Bodega Keyzer – Van Baerlestraat 96

RESTAURANTS
4 L'Entrecôte – P.C. Hooftstraat 70
5 Beddington's – Roelof Hartstraat 6–8
6 De Trechter – Hobbemakade 63
7 Mirafiori – Hobbemastraat 2
8 Kyo – Jan Luijkenstraat 2/a

MUSEUMS
9 Filmmuseum – Vondelpark 3
10 Museum Overholland – Museumplein 4
11 Museum Vincent van Gogh – Paulus Potterstraat 7
12 Rijksmuseum – Stadhouderskade 42
13 Stedelijk Museum – Paulus Potterstraat 13

OTHER
14 Concertgebouw [Concert hall] – van Baerlestraat 98

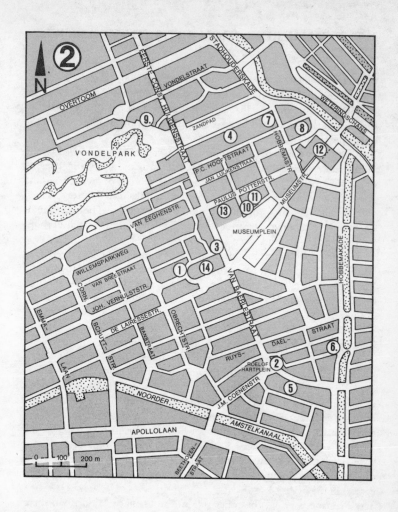

3: THE CANAL RING: FROM ARTIS TO THE AMSTEL

Close to the centre of town, between Artis and the Amstel, is the Plantage–Weesp quarter, which is actually made up of two districts. Between the Entrepotdok and the Plantage Muidergracht is the Plantage, and to the west of this, along the 'New' canals, the eastward continuation of the canal ring, is the Weesp quarter.

It is a district where not many tourists go, as it is not characterized by the immediately apparent intensity of the Wallen or the lively street scenes of the Jordaan. Its charm resides in the large amounts of greenery, in the grand houses with their white stucco-work and in its rich history, which will remain hidden from the uninformed passer-by. The Plantage is small: there is a butcher's, a greengrocer's, a dairy, a little bunch of shops that will probably shrink even further.

The Plantage is quiet. If the Plantage Middenlaan and the Plantage Kerklaan were not a through connection between the centre and Amsterdam-East, the Plantage would be a friendly village. But even with the through traffic it is quieter than one would imagine, being so close to the centre of town.

The Plantage, both the district and its residents, is old. The Inspector of Education refuses to give the local primary school permission to expand on the grounds that the average age in the district is rising steeply. Statistically speaking he is right, the Plantage is full of elderly people. However, he is neglecting the pull exerted by the (old, established) character of the district on its direct surroundings, where urban renewal and new building are attracting a whole new population. The Plantage will, as an older district, acquire a greater 'donor function' for its surroundings: the residents of the new estates will draw on the area for some of the urban style lacking in their own environment. Denying this developement, as the inspector is doing, is the same as nipping potential new life in the district in the bud.

The Plantage is posh. On either side of the Plantage Middenlaan there are a dozen or so elegant nineteenth-century villas, at Henri Polaklaan 9 a building by Berlage, at number 11 a villa by Van Gendt, the architect of the Concertgebouw, and so on. There are lots of white stucco housefronts, a light touch not found in Amsterdam till comparatively recently.

The Plantage, in short, is small, quiet, old and distinguished, and will probably remain so. New building and renovation in the immediate vicinity might prevent the area from withering into a static monument. The influx could make the Plantage into a lively backdrop for modern dynamism. The Plantage needs such fresh blood urgently.

THE ORIGIN OF THE PLANTAGE

Around 1600 Amsterdam had about 40,000 inhabitants, within an area not big enough to accommodate half that many. Sixty years later the number had increased fivefold. The Golden Age had arrived: from far and wide merchants and manual workers headed for the city which set a higher value on trade than anywhere else. Everyone willing to work was welcome, even dissidents and members of religious minorities persecuted elsewhere.

The 200,000 inhabitants living in the town in 1660 were given the room they needed. In the period of explosive growth the canal ring, which gives Amsterdam its crescent shape, was laid out, and with the inclusion of the Jordaan increased the town's area to three times the size.

The building of the canal ring proceeded from west to east and made good progress as far as the Amstel. However, it took some time before investment in the building of the 'new' canals was embarked upon. The expensive expansion of the town stagnated because the wealthy had been provided for and the rest of the population – the vast majority – could not afford a house on the canals.

When in the 1680s the growth in the population came to a quite abrupt halt, the council began looking for new uses for the building land between the Amstel and the Nieuwe Vaart. The elderly were a grateful target group, and have remained so to this day. In the Weesp quarter there are still two almshouses and four large old people's homes. But it was not possible to fill up the area with the elderly alone, and so someone hit upon the unusual idea of using the remaining land for laying out gardens. The town, which was earning nothing from the land at the time, could then rent out the garden plots to those same wealthy people who might have a canal house, but did not yet have country houses.

On 16 January 1682 the council decided to lay out the Plantage, a garden complex between the present Plantage Muidergracht, Nieuwe Herengracht and the Entrepotdok. Despite the eminently respectable intentions of the council some less wealthy people were also able to secure themselves a place amid the greenery. They began providing illicit forms of recreation, and soon cafés, gambling-dens and brothels were tucked away behind the (compulsory) high walls and fences. The gardens became an anarchic no-man's land. Of course the respectable residents who came there to relax protested, and the council issued a series of *Keuren* or prohibitions, and appointed a sheriff, but the Plantage never became as idyllic as had been intended.

ARTIS

The fact that half of the original Plantage is still green is due in part to the efforts of the Natura Artis Magistra society, founded in 1838. This society, which only the social élite could join, aimed to 'promote the knowledge of Natural History in a pleasant and graphic way', and in the course of the nineteenth century the membership decided to construct a zoological garden. To obtain the land necessary for this, the Artis committee set itself up as a guardian of morals: the 'gardens surrounded by funereal fences and walls and the low dens of vice and immorality' were to be transformed into a 'charming miniature landscape, a place of enchantment for every walker' (read 'for every *well-to-do* walker').

At the moment history seems to be repeating itself. In 1981 the land behind Artis was abandoned by the Netherlands Railways and since then has been occupied by urban nomads, a group of caravan-dwellers with an anarchic lifestyle. In 1989, on the occasion of the 150th anniversary of the founding of Artis, the council made over the land to it. Artis is again expanding at the cost of a 'lawless area' and is as little concerned now as it was last time about the fate of those who have to make way for it, or about the desirability of an expansion where local interests are concerned.

THE UNIVERSITY IN THE PLANTAGE

The Hortus Botanicus of the University of Amsterdam is the last portion of original Plantage remaining. As early as 1683 the marshy corner between the Nieuwe Herengracht and the Plantage Middenlaan was sown with the intention of making it into a 'Hortus Medicus' or 'Medicinal Garden'. The growing of medicinal herbs and the collecting of exotic plant varieties formed the basis on which Hugo de Vries developed his theory of heredity around 1900.

Over the centuries, but particularly from the end of the nineteenth century, the university, like Artis, gained more and more ground in the Plantage–Weesp quarter. After the Hortus the Zoological Institute and related institutes were established along the edge of Artis, and the Department of Natural History found a place along the Plantage Muidergracht. Because of this the Plantage can boast two Nobel-prizewinners (Van der Waals and Zeeman), and a study visit by Einstein to Zeeman, but with the large-scale expansion of the University on Roeters Island the less desirable side of these developments could be seen. The Plantage threatened to vanish as a residential area. Roeters Island was only a beginning: if it had been left to the University, twenty-five per cent of the houses would have given way to university buildings. This would not have been so bad if such buildings were not becoming increasingly large and self-contained. The district gains nothing from colossal structures that cannot support so much as a local coffee shop.

THE JEWS IN THE PLANTAGE

However important Artis and the University may be for the history of the area, their presence is a threat to the intimate life of the Plantage, and this is all the more vulnerable now that the Jewish community, once the hub of its vitality, has gone. The Jewish presence, which was so strong in the Plantage–Weesp quarter, bequeathed many Yiddish words to Amsterdam popular speech, words whose origin has long been forgotten.

The details of the manner in which Jewish life was destroyed are still unimaginably shocking. But the same is true of the broad development of Jewish history in Amsterdam. That history began in the course of the seventeenth century. There were Portuguese Jews, mostly rich merchants, and a much larger group of Central European Jews who had fled to Amsterdam in destitution. The original difference in wealth disappeared over the centuries. In the first instance the Portuguese had been to a limited extent co-beneficiaries of the Golden Age, but in the course of the eighteenth century, compared to their Christian colleagues, they were hit particularly hard by the stagnation of the economy. The Eastern European Jews had meanwhile managed to improve their position somewhat, but most still lived a marginal existence.

The explanation is a simple one: the Jews were excluded from all the guilds and hence could not exercise a trade. One exception was diamond-cutting, a trade that the Jews themselves had introduced. In 1749, however, the Christian diamond-cutters submitted a petition to the town council, in which, God help them, they requested permission to set up a guild to exclude Jews from the trade 'as it is impossible for us, of our very nature, to earn our livelihood as the Jews can, by cleaning, or selling combs or spectacles, or to exist like swine, ten or twelve to a sty, as can be seen in Marken and elsewhere, where five or six households with women and children live under one roof, for which reason they require less than Christians for their subsistence' (A.M. Van Diaz, *Het Amsterdamse Jodenkwartier* (The Jewish Quarter of Amsterdam, Amsterdam 1937).

When the economy recovered in the second half of the nineteenth century, many Jews became reasonably well-off for the first time, particularly as a result of the opening-up of the Netherlands Indies to private capital and the discovery of the Cape diamond mines. The Plantage benefited from these developments. The imposing villas were erected, and between 1875 and 1892 four important theatres were built alongside the pubs and music-halls of yore: the Plantage Theatre, Frascati, the Park Theatre and the Dutch Theatre.

For half a century the Plantage was the top entertainment area in the city, where popular theatre and operettas flourished and where the Nederlandse Opera was born. Between the First and Second World Wars, however, this entertainment centre shifted slowly but surely back to more centrally located areas such as the Leidseplein and the Rembrandtplein. The area became a little quieter, but the Jews were thriving: Van Diaz records that the last slums, the result of the restrictive working practices, were cleared in 1937. After they had finally got their heads above water, the deportations which followed soon after were a *coup de grâce* which shrouded the area in appalled silence. The Dutch Theatre, the assembly point for deportees, is a monument to this indescribable nadir in the nation's history.

Artis, the University, the villas and the theatres, these are just a small selection from the many traces left by the area's history. In the case of the Jews these are so poignant that it is difficult to contemplate them. The waters are too deep for our feet to be able to touch the bottom, we are still a little in limbo, the area does not belong to us. But the future advances inexorably.

On the edge of the area thousands of houses are to be built. The Entrepotdok, an exceptional warehouse-renovation project, opened the series. All these projects are concerned with social housing, and represent the tail-end of the period in which Amsterdam, just as it had been in the 1920s, was a Mecca of working-class housing. After the council has ensured, over a period of about twelve years, that there is sufficient housing available for the less well-off, it is now, at the end of the 1980s, the turn of the up-market house-buyer: the flats for sale in the Plantage Doklaan fetched high prices. Behind the Oranje Nassau barracks there are to be four high-rise blocks, a slightly fancier version of social housing, which henceforward will be available only to home-buyers.

Many of these thousands of new residents will find the district attractive in comparison with living in the nearby Dapperstraat area or moving to the centre. But what will they find to live up to their expectations? First of all Eik en Linde, the oldest café, named after the hospitable couple Philemon and Baucis, described by Ovid in his *Metamorphoses* as being immortalized as oak and lime trees. The café, from where the weekly broadcasts of the VPRO radio programme Plantage are put out, began in Artis and is now at its fourth location in the area.

Diagonally opposite is the colourful Moederhuis built by Aldo van Eyck and next door to it a school for Advanced Individual Artistic Instruction (IVKO), which brings a number of liberated teenagers into the area. There is the Bicycle Repair Shop in the Plantage Kerklaan, with the jeweller's La Finestra on its left and Loesje Hansen's secondhand bookshop on its right. In the direction of the Sarphatistraat you pass the late-night shop of Stien and Monnie, and in the Sarphatistraat itself, at 187, is the local brothel, where exotic, rather mature ladies specialize in massage. Almost next to it, at 213, lives the lone campaigner against this last piece of indecent entertainment left in the area.

And then there is the Hortus. Not Artis – Artis is trying to become a modern, well-organized theme park and consequently retains less and less of the former charm of the park. The Hortus is the oldest piece of the Plantage, but requires lots of money for its upkeep.

In the words of Richter Roegholt, the historian, the Plantage was once 'unused space' and became the spare room in the house, good enough for the old, the zoo, laboratories and for having a good time in. Much of what was there has gone – and the door is still open.

District 3: The Canal Ring: from Artis to the Amstel

CAFÉS
1 Eik en Linde – Plantage Middenlaan 22
2 't Entredok – Entrepotdok 64

MUSEUMS
3 Joods Historisch Museum [Jewish history] – J.D. Meijerplein 2-4

OTHER
4 Hortus Botanicus – Plantage Middenlaan 2

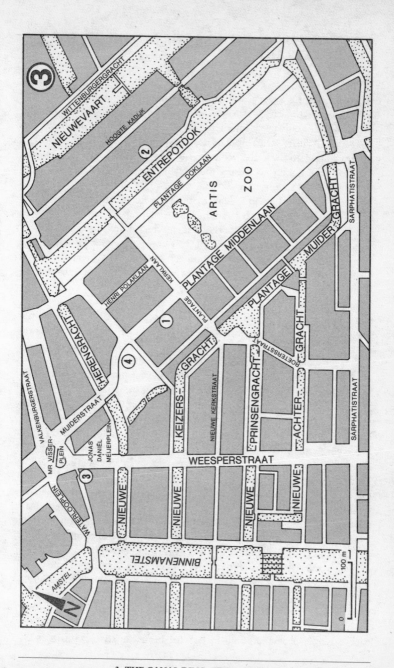

Map labels:
- WITTENBURGERGRACHT
- NIEUWEVAART
- HOOGTE KADIJK
- ENTREPOTDOK
- PLANTAGE DOKLAAN
- ARTIS ZOO
- SARPHATISTRAAT
- PLANTAGE MIDDENLAAN
- MUIDERGRACHT
- KERKLAAN
- HENRI POLAKLAAN
- PLANTAGE
- PLANTAGE
- ROETERSSTRAAT
- ACHTER- GRACHT
- HERENGRACHT
- KEIZERS- GRACHT
- PRINSENGRACHT
- SARPHATISTRAAT
- VALKENBURGERSTRAAT
- MUIDERSTRAAT
- NIEUWE KERKSTRAAT
- JONAS DANIËL MEIJERPLEIN
- MR VISSER- PLEIN
- WEESPERSTRAAT
- WATERLOOPLEIN
- NIEUWE
- NIEUWE
- NIEUWE
- NIEUWE
- AMSTEL
- BINNENAMSTEL
- 0 100 m
- N

4: THE CANAL RING: FROM THE AMSTEL TO THE LEIDSESTRAAT

Anyone planning a day's walk through Amsterdam should start out well fed: although the city is small in comparison with other metropolises, there are still quite a few kilometres to cover between the old houses on the canals. A hearty Dutch breakfast is recommended. Those who set out on an empty stomach are liable to fall prey to unhealthy temptations, such as fatty, sticky rolls passing themselves off as French delicacies – not the sort of food to finish a walk on.

We shall begin at the Muntplein, by the large flower market, floating on the Singel like a fragrant garland. This spot immediately confronts us with a historical problem: was the Singel, which flows under the Muntplein and which beyond the Hotel de l'Europe broadens out into the city's river, the Amstel, once, around the start of the Christian era, the Drusus Canal? This was an important two-way route for transporting Roman troops and their weapons, long before Amsterdam existed. The Muntplein is one of the oldest central landmarks in Amsterdam, and its name indicates that coins must have once been minted there. It was the first building to undergo thorough renovation after the Second World War in the kitschy style then in vogue, which is why the renovated part is a mess, while the old tower has come off unscathed.

At the foot of the tower there are some badly planned pedestrian crossings, which are potentially lethal even for the most agile. The people crossing the street, ignoring red lights, are the office workers who pour out of the banks in the lunch break, guests from the big hotels in the area and the staff of all the firms that manage to operate in the cramped inner city, which has its beauties but also its limitations: the difficulty of access and the impossibility of parking a car or even a bicycle safely.

From the Munt there is a tramline leading to the Rembrandtplein down the Reguliersbreestraat. This once chic shopping street is now a lively mixture of first-class patisseries, excellent greengrocers with fresh fruit from all over the world and immaculately kept flower stalls on the one hand, and badly ventilated porno dens and cheap chemists on the other. The people there, who often spill over on to the tramlines, are a motley crowd: young mothers with their children, old gentlemen and their smartly dressed wives, who have been eating cakes at one of the popular patisseries. In and out among them rush people who frequent the café terraces and restaurants of the Rembrandtplein during their lunch break. Two striking monuments in this short, busy shopping street are the big dark Tuschinski cinema, built in late Art Nouveau style, with its richly carpeted interior full of little Art Nouveau patterned lamps, and right opposite its antithesis, the Cineac, a small disused cinema fashionable in the 1930s. One could drop in there at any time to watch the newsreels and sometimes a good double bill of cartoons, one of which was always the adventures of Popeye the Sailorman. There was nothing so popular in those days as 'popping along to the Cineac' and afterwards eating Italian ices at the Gamba ice-cream parlour next door. The Cineac is one of the early monuments to the last Dutch architectural style to raise the Netherlands to international level, De Stijl, an expression of the New Functionalism which was opposed to the swirling ornamentation of Art Nouveau and produced the now world-famous paintings of Mondriaan, which fetch record prices at international auctions. The city council has not yet decided whether the cinema is to be preserved as a monument or demolished. How ideal this little place would be as an art house devoted solely to avant-garde work!

Alongside grill windows with chicken carcases turning on spits basted with curry and dripping with oil, there is now a fairly anonymous kiosk. Here in the 1960s there used to be a walk-in bookshop which by virtue of its fantastic stock of quality paperbacks (Harper Torch, Harper Colophon, Penguin and Pelican) became a meeting-place for intellectuals. It was a chance combination of the affluent society (reprints of all kinds of academic books which had long been unobtainable) and a legendary bookseller, who has now moved to the leafy south of the city. Ko van Leest now runs his small specialized shop at Banstraat 22, near the Vondelpark. Young people who used to be regular customers and met each other there are now the trend-setters in the Dutch media.

Before we reach the Rembrandtplein at the end of the Reguliersbreestraat, we pass a triangular building which has now been reduced to an amusement arcade, but which before the war was one of the first fast-food businesses. Even then it was possible to eat from vending-machines. The assortment at Heck's, as the shop was called, was notable for high quality and simplicity: croquettes, filled rolls, bowls of soup and slices of mocca cake. Almost every older Amsterdammer had his or her first outing at Heck's.

For the last few years the Rembrandtplein has been a pedestrian precinct and with its well-maintained flowerbed has brought life to the centre of town. A nice contrast: in the mornings, when the last inebriated customers leave their local cafés, the landlords throw open all the doors and windows and spread the smell of flat beer over the square. At the same time in the tourist season the fresh flowers that were closed during the night open up and the sprinklers send a spiral of water over the green grass. On the Rembrandtplein too there used to be a branch of Heck's, with live music on Sunday afternoons for the whole family, who with their twelve or so kids would occupy a table for two glasses of mineral water with six straws each and a carefully divided apple turnover, while the proud Mum and Dad enjoyed their glass of old *jenever* with a spoonful of sugar in it. The orchestra played the hits from before the German occupation and those who had been through the war and remembered the words sang along ...

Both branches of Heck have disappeared as a result of the rise of the first big property speculator in the Netherlands. Everything had to be bigger and more beautiful, and finally the whole house of cards, which had been held together by nothing but bluff, came tumbling down, bringing about the ignominious demise of Heck with it. Even now a large part of the square is in the hands of speculators and all round it empty spaces await whatever use they are destined for. A cinema complex that took the place of Heck's Live also went under.

Is there an explanation for this decline, when even last century the Rembrandtplein was an important entertainment centre with famous restaurants, cabarets and little theatres? Unfortunately there is. Around the turn of the century the Rembrandtplein was the leisure centre for Jewish Amsterdammers who had become prosperous and lived in the Plantage–Weesp quarter and on the canals across the Amstel. They were all deported and very few survived the holocaust. Besides, the managers of the cafés and restaurants had previously contributed to their own downfall by barring the diamond merchants, who were in the habit of concluding their business deals on their premises. The managements expected that after the departure of these generally rather noisy visitors they would be able to attract a better class of customer, but these were not forthcoming. The traders built their own centre, the Diamond Exchange, the first in the world, and did not return. The success of the Diamond Exchange became legendary, and the fate of the Rembrandtplein was sealed.

Walking across the rectangular square, which on the short side in front of us is bordered by a large bank building, we come on the opposite side to a famous café on the corner. A comedian once used to perform here with a big gloomy face, and night after night in a packed room he would pour a stream of humour over his audience, not the spiteful variety of his American contemporary Lenny Bruce, but an endless series of jokes about failures and misunderstandings. He was always prepared to give up part of his income, and was willing to put his repertoire at the disposal of deserving causes. A little further on we come face to face with Schiller, a hotel with various restaurants and bars, and one of the most popular meeting-places in Amsterdam. Schiller, the founder of this mini-empire, managed to become a famous (Sunday) painter in his free time. Once round the corner we are on the Thorbeckeplein, well restored and with a with a bandstand in the middle. The square is notable for its splendid view of the most beautiful cross-canal in Amsterdam, the Reguliersgracht, which runs at right-angles to it, and the intersection of bridges that reappears in every bit of footage of Amsterdam used in films, or misused in commercials. During the day the café terraces are filled with customers having coffee or fresh fruit juice.

At night the action shifts to the red-lit pubs around and the square is bathed in a Christmasy glow. In the windows of these establishments there are photos designed to entice passers-by in to see shows which remind one of the great cabarets from the most prudish period of the last century, when naughty night-life nevertheless had its heyday. Everything the little man dreamed of could come true after dark in the adventurous world of the night-clubs. This merry-go-round of carnival-style licence, coupled with the newest hit songs and risqué entertainment, was definitively celebrated by the German composer Kurt Weill and the dramatist Bertolt Brecht in their *Mahagonny*, an opera about a prairie town where the stranded prospectors and lumberjacks could enjoy illicit pleasures for as long as they went on paying. With the downfall of 1920s Berlin, the days of this world were numbered: the decline was rapid.

In Amsterdam cabaret also enjoyed a boom in those days, which culminated in a drama of passion involving the murder of the country's most popular cabaret performer. He was famous for his popular songs, and a ballad – which people would find just as compelling today – about a banquet of statesmen where Death gives the toast. Did the life go out of night-club entertainment with this man's murder? All that is left is a nocturnal scene of pimps, young tourists, idlers and men cruising for pick-ups. There is a pub whose window contains photographs of 'The World's Unique Woman Cigarette Manipulations Show'(sic): a helpless looking woman in an old silver swimsuit. A pianist smiles stiffly, as though realizing too late that he has left his false teeth in his pocket. Discoloured pin-ups of men and women who have lost all illusions, whose brothers and sisters are already grandparents, and whose customers know that they have nothing more to refuse. A cardboard inferno.

There is nothing to detain us here: there are enough theatres elsewhere, drinks are cheaper further on, and sex can be bought more safely in other areas. Anyone who is persuaded to step inside by the bulky doorman knows that once there he will long for fresh night air and will be homesick for his wife and family.

We retrace our footsteps and cross the Rembrandtplein. In the middle of the seedy Amstelstraat we suddenly stumble completely unexpectedly on

a well maintained eighteenth-century palace garden. Low bushes, everything immaculately pruned, and the beds symmmetrically laid out. A
small sign reveals that this is the back entrance to a museum.

Soon we are looking out over the Amstel. The beauty of this rather run-
down area has been completely revived by the building of the Stopera, a
combination of opera house and town hall. Young entrepreneurs have
eagerly bought and refurbished houses in the immediate vicinity. New
restaurants and bars have opened up, and on the site of the famous
Waterlooplein flea market the Stopera has risen, a building of red brick
and white marble.

The Amstel is at its widest here and nothing would have disturbed the
view had not the council in its democratic wisdom given permission for
the permanent mooring of hideous houseboats which during the construction were temporarily located elsewhere. A rubbish barge with an
old vagrant on board blocks the view of the nicest part of the Stopera.
Nevertheless the Amstel remains splendid. We can see the Groenburgwal, formerly obscured by a number of builders' huts 'temporarily'
placed there – in Amsterdam 'temporarily' means an eternity. Standing
in front of the Blauwbrug, linking the centre and the old part of Amsterdam-East, we can see on the other side the beginning of the former Amsterdam Jewish quarter – not a ghetto in the true sense of the word but a
conglomeration of streets with a majority of Jewish residents.

Turning right, we walk along the Amstel and have the marvellous view
of the three main canals of Amsterdam. These parallel canals curve round
the heart of the city, making the first much shorter than the third. They
link the Amstel with the waters round the Central Station and each has a
very distinct character of its own.

The Herengracht is characterized by imposing houses and distinguished
buildings, all possessing spacious back gardens one would not have
thought possible in the middle of a town. The trees on the Herengracht
are relatively old and as a result of the size of the houses, the quaysides
and the width of the water, the canal has, especially in the setting sun a
mysterious, enigmatic look. The light is restrained and there is an air of
solemnity about it. The Herengracht contains mainly banks and stock-
brokers' offices – there are few private residents.

The Keizersgracht, which can boast more well-preserved seventeenth-
century houses than the Herengracht, has younger trees, is a little wider
and is decidedly lighter in atmosphere. There is none of the restrained
grandeur of the Herengracht, which has given way to a joyful air wich is
unique to the Keizersgracht. The canal has a mixture of offices, houses
occupied by eccentrics and posh art dealers.

Before reaching the Prinsengracht, we pass the Kerkstraat, a street which originated from the mews serving the Prinsengracht and the Keizersgracht. It is linked with the Nieuwe Kerkstraat, still a run-down area of town, by the unique wooden drawbridge over the Amstel, the Magere Brug, or Skinny Bridge, one of the few wooden bridges still in use in Amsterdam, which can be raised to allow shipping on the Amstel through. For a long time the Kerkstraat was also in decline, but particularly successful renovations have restored the splendid house-fronts in all their former glory, making it a joy to walk down as far as the Leidsegracht.

The Prinsengracht offers a picturesque ensemble of small old canal houses. Perhaps the heritage of the seventeenth century is best preserved on this canal, with its again totally different light. When there is snow the Prinsengracht looks just like a row of houses out of Hansel and Gretel. The canal is full of countless little shops.

As well as by the main roads the canals are intersected by small cross-streets of great charm which sometimes contain wonderful old houses. The ancient canal houses themselves have, for those with an eye for such things, their own faces, which show their character as clearly as if they were human beings or animals. Some houses, for example on the Herengracht, are all in perfect proportion, distinguished and stiff. Each house ignores the next as far as it can, like weary businessmen in a packed first-class compartment of an aeroplane. Along the canals some houses mourn for their previous occupants, while alongside impertinently inclining façades try to look indifferent, hiding their true feelings. The still, confined water of the canals seems to give these houses a golden frame. The walker is constantly aware of the unreachable far bank marked by the water.

Alongside examples of progressive decay, dilapidated old houses where squatters have made a home, are houses of astonishing beauty, converted into priceless luxury dwellings. Scattered among them there are newly built flats that a few years ago were still pristine but whose concrete is already showing patches of decay. Here live the original local inhabitants, who were allowed to return after the renovations – not to their expensively converted old rented flats, but to new flats that are little better than the run-down mansions they were forced to leave ... Some of the imposing mansions have no nameplates: nothing tells you who lives, works or lodges there. The tall windows are rippled and have a light purple tinge produced by a long-forgotten glass-making formula.

Along the Achtergracht there are a dozen exemplary warehouses, a delight to the eye, with wooden shutters alongside the windows, placed in an irregular pattern on the façades. A little street full of palaces, each of them bearing the name of one of the months of the year. The passer-by asks himself what privileged folk live here, each in their own apartment. Are they top jurists, trendsetting couturiers, the élite of the universities? The answer is: no one! These houses, possibly the most beautiful in the country, have no residents, no bathrooms, no bedrooms. The twelve happy faces are a mask behind which lurks the Nederlandse Bank. In the evenings it is deserted here, there are no children playing in the doorways of the houses, there is no actor leaning out of the open window, glass of wine in hand. When the moon shines the switchboard is silent in this office building where during the day the lines are red-hot. Here we can begin to see a vision of a city taken over by the big banks. In some cases they have blessed the area with restorations in which money was no object, but they have often put a curse on it with their philistine arrogance. The passionate criticism of Prince Charles that one's own architects often do more damage with their rebuilding than the German Luftwaffe did with its bombs could be equally well applied here. Nice places to live, where children can play, are almost nowhere to be found.

As luck would have it there is one such hidden paradise just behind the twelve mask houses, in a street that goes nowhere, the Maarten Jansz. Kosterstraat. Three adjacent houses show that ordinary people live here, people who, as can be seen through the frequently open windows, do not always do their washing up and regard their part of the street as an extension of their home. On the pavement one father has made a little play garden for his children and put in flowerbeds. A sign asks the visitor who happens to find his way there not to pick the flowers. The children have long since left home, as can be seen from the wood of the slide and and the climbing frame: it is weathered and the damp corners are green with moss. This street has the intimacy and tranquillity of an almshouse courtyard. A little further on the houses have once again resumed their functional anonymity, and only an overhanging branch of rhododendron betrays the fact that there are sometimes gardens tucked away behind the houses. An Art Nouveau tile mosaic announces a long-vanished gymnastics association, which in other parts of town has found its trendy imitators in the sort of fitness clubs which can be found anywhere in the world.

Walking to the end of this street, we come back to the Amstel, with a view of the Hogesluis and obliquely opposite the Amstel Hotel, whose history goes back to the Napoleonic period. On this side of the Hogesluis is the beginning of the Sarphatistraat, one of the best-known streets in Amsterdam, named after the doctor who once gave the impetus to the building of the Paleis voor Volksvlijt (Palace of Popular Industry), a triumph of nineteenth-century architecture and technology. The panache and the materials used anticipated the Eiffel Tower.

Here the beautiful nineteenth-century houses have been ousted by colossal, unimaginative banks which are the grim reverse side of the canal-side warehouses. On the left the eye is immediately struck by a bank building of huge proportions, embellished with a square and a round office tower, a playful touch by the architects, which serves to underline its ugliness. This is where the Paleis voor Volksvlijt once was, and at the beginning of this century a Dutch writer called this spot the most beautiful in Europe. In 1929 the building burned down, leaving only one gallery, which was converted into a series of one-person dwellings. With the demolition of the gallery there disappeared one of the last monuments of early Dutch Art Nouveau. As a consolation the Frederiksplein has been given a park criss-crossed by tramlines together with flowerbeds and a fountain.

From the Frederiksplein runs the Weteringschans, originally a busy traffic artery, now reserved for trams, has become rather quiet and desolate. Only the imposing houses betray something of its pre-war elegance. From the Weteringschans we proceed to the Vijzelgracht: here there are new blocks of flats and a little way down it suddenly some marvellous old houses, preserved almost intact since they were built by members of the Vingboons family. These are the famous weavers' houses.

Returning along the Lijnbaansgracht, a stretch of water that is constantly interrupted by streets and partial damming, we reach the Reguliersgracht, one of the most beautiful cross-canals. It contains some of the oldest houses and warehouses in Amsterdam, largely privately occupied, mostly by well-paid intellectuals, and in the case of the slightly smaller properties, by doctors and performers from the arts world. Along the Prinsengracht we can see the Amstelveld, with a wooden church of a type unusual in the Netherlands, which is soon – but will this also mean waiting for an eternity? – to be restored.

The Utrechtsestraat runs parallel with the Reguliersgracht. Despite the rather obstructive tramline there is a great deal of traffic and a constant stream of cyclists. The Utrechtsestraat has gradually developed into a street for gourmets, with countless speciality restaurants interspersed with little shops selling a large assortment of meats and cheeses. In a wide area around this street bargain-hunters and small collectors will find an Eldorado in which everything conceivable is on sale, though it varies greatly in quality.

From the Utrechtsestraat it is only a short walk across the Rembrandtplein to the Reguliersdwarsstraat, which links the Amstel and Leidsestraat areas and is popular on account of its large number of pubs, bars and discos. There are always entrepreneurs willing to convert dilapidated buildings into ultra-trendy shops, often short-lived. At a cost of hundreds

District 4: From the Amstel to the Leidsestraat

CAFÉS
1 Americain – Leidseplein 28
2 Amstel Taveerne – Amstel 54
3 April – Reguliersdwarsstraat 37
4 De Balie –
  Kleine Gartmanplantsoen 10
5 Discothèque It – Amstelstraat 24
6 Discothèque Bios – Leidseplein 12
7 Café Cox – Marnixstraat 427
8 Discothèque Escape –
  Rembrandtplein 11-15
9 Discothèque Exit –
  Reguliersdwarsstraat 42
10 De Favoriet – Reguliersdwarsstraat 87
11 Gay Life – Amstelstraat 32
12 De Gieter –
  Korte Leidsedwarsstraat 174
13 Happy View –
  Lange Leidsedwarsstraat 66
14 Havana – Reguliersdwarsstraat 17-19
15 Het Hok –
  Lange Leidsedwarsstraat 134
16 Markx – Reguliersdwarsstraat 12
17 Oblomow – Reguliersdwarsstraat 40
18 Oosterling – Utrechtsestraat 140
19 Discothèque 36 op de schaal van
  Richter – Reguliersdwarsstraat 36
20 Discothèque Roxy – Singel 465
21 Schiller – Rembrandtplein 26
22 De Smoeshaan – Leidsekade 90
23 Traffic – Reguliersdwarsstraat 11
24 Vivelavie – Amstelstraat 7
25 Weber – Marnixstraat 397
26 Onni's Verjaardag – Marnixstraat 381
27 Bruin – Voetboogstraat 4
28 Dansen bij Jansen –
  Handboogstraat 11
29 Schutter – Voetboogstraat 13-15

RESTAURANTS
30 An American Place –
  Utrechtsedwarsstraat 141
31 Do Brasil –
  Lange Leidsedwarsstraat 84

32 Sichuan Food –
  Reguliersdwarsstraat 35
33 Brasserie Sjef Schets – Leidsestraat 20
34 Les Quatre Canetons –
  Prinsengracht 1111
35 The Tandoor – Leidseplein 19
36 Tempo Doeloe – Utrechtsestraat 75
37 La Torre di Pisa – Reguliersgracht 95
38 Yoichi – Weteringschans 128
39 Rose's Cantina –
  Reguliersdwarsstraat 38
40 La Cherna – Utrechtsestraat 124
41 Dynasty – Reguliersdwarsstraat 30
42 The Salad Garden –
  Weteringschans 75
43 Tartufo – Singel 449
44 Piet de Leeuw – Noorderstraat 11
45 Sousse – Lijnbaansgracht 274

MUSEUMS
46 Fodor – Keizersgracht 609
47 Museum van Loon –
  Keizersgracht 672
48 Museum Willet-Holthuysen –
  Herengracht 605

OTHER
49 Theater Tuschinski –
  Reguliersbreestraat 26–28
50 Stopera – Amstel 1

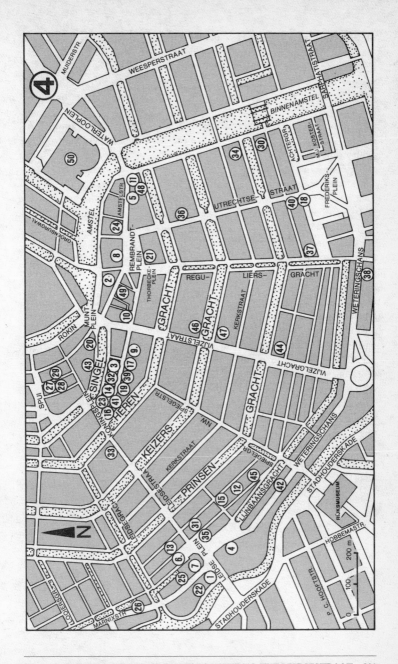

of thousands of guilders these people create glittering dreamworlds to entice a relatively small number of fashion-conscious and affluent customers. Business is lucrative but fickle, and there are always new investors waiting to take their place. The street runs into the Koningsplein, from where there is a splendid view of the Singel, one of the oldest canals.

The adjoining Leidsestraat is a street of travel agencies and airlines. As you get nearer the Leidseplein, one of the big entertainment centres, the dreary office buildings, interspersed it must be said with a few nice shops and a restaurant, give way to the marble of *bureaux de change* and the tattiness of mayonnaise culture. Money-changing establishments are fond of giving their businesses status by facing them with marble. Young tourists and inexperienced travellers occasionally change their currency here, sometimes at unfavourable rates. The signs warning one against pickpockets seem to be a dig at the staff behind the armoured glass ... The mayonnaise is bought with the chips in the many chip-shops, which with their high turnover are better able than anyone else to afford the high rents.

Is it the high rents that cause many entrepreneurs to slip into the least creative ways of making money? Or is this part of Amsterdam lacking in creative people, who might have continued the tradition of quality shops with a combination of expertise and service? Something must have happened, something inexplicable, just as no one knows how the sparrows, those once ubiquitous little grey thieves, were driven out by the pigeons, who live on rubbish and add to the pollution.

The Leidseplein, now ironically rechristened La Place de la Mayonnaise, with its café terraces in summer and ice rink in the winter, is the heart of this world. When Ajax win an important game, it is celebrated here by the team, together with anyone else who wants to come along. Although it is sometimes seems to be drifting out of control, Amsterdammers love this place.

5: THE CANAL RING: FROM THE LEIDSESTRAAT TO THE RAADHUISSTRAAT

If Amsterdam is a city with a village feeling, a cosmopolitan village whose intimacy contains the diversity of all the cultures of the world, where the visual arts, theatre, the world of books and of publishing go hand in hand with those of the international gourmet and the fashionable world traveller with an eye to his wallet, if Amsterdam can only be truly itself by a quiet canal, on a café terrace under the trees without the hectic comings and goings of coach-loads of day trippers, then this district is the essence of Amsterdam. It is wedged in between the Leidseplein, an entertainment centre and tourist magnet; the Spui, around which the city's bookshops are ranged and which for that reason could be called an intellectual centre; the Dam, the official heart of the city, with the former Town Hall (as the recalcitrant Amsterdammers still call the present Royal Palace) and the National Monument, which might be called the national centre; and the Westermarkt and the Westertoren, watching over the Jordaan, the proverbial Amsterdam working-class quarter, celebrated in Amsterdam popular song, which could be called the popular centre.

This district adjoins the Jordaan; only the Prinsengracht divides us; one might call the area 'cis-Jordaan'. Many people think this *is* the Jordaan. Here too there are a large number of little streets with particularly nice shops, but the streets – and the shops too – are just a fraction wider and more luxurious. And the canals are not the narrow ditches of the Jordaan but the broad, regal canals of the canal ring itself.

There has always been a great difference between the radial cross-streets and the canals. On the canals lived the patricians, the merchants, the true princes of Amsterdam, perhaps of the whole country. Not for nothing was the order of the names of the canals derived from the importance of those whose names they bore: first the Gentlemen, then the Emperors and finally the Princes. The gentlemen were the residents of the canals.

The side-streets were where the shopkeepers and tradesmen lived, and not much has changed. The gentlemen still live on the canals, and, just as they used to, have their offices there, though probably a portion of them live elsewhere, in more modern houses. The canals are for trading companies, lawyers, insurance companies and … gentlemen. In top rooms, attics and basements live the lesser gods, who also live in the side-streets.

There are still patricians who have occupied the same canal house for many generations – their princely dwellings are best compared to

Venetian palaces, because it is not only the canals that cause Amsterdam to be called the Venice of the North. In both places the merchants are gentlemen and the gentlemen merchants.

In the side-streets the turnover of residents is much more rapid. It as though real life goes on there, while those on the canals doze, keeping a firm hold of the purse-strings. With a few exceptions, the many shops, restaurants and cafés are all in the side-streets. During the day they are full of strollers and shoppers; in the evenings one finds diners and café customers, who in the summer months hang around the café terraces till deep into the night. While the canals are as quiet as a suburb, in the sides-streets it's party-time.

The names of the canals are not that difficult to remember. It is all the more difficult to keep the names of the side-streets apart. Even taxi-drivers sometimes can't manage it and have had a special map made showing nothing but the streets in this area. For there is no easy mnemonic to help one remember them and the residents themselves sometimes need a prop for the memory.

In the past the speciality of the area was the treating and marketing of leather, which is why so many names there are connected with it. Skins (*huiden*) were tanned (*gelooid*) with tan-bark (*run*), hence the Huiden-straat, Runstraat and Looiersgracht (the latter across the Prinsengracht). The bears of the Berenstraat, wolves of the Wolvenstraat, deer of the Hartenstraat and roes of the Reestraat were all leather suppliers.

The spirit of small craftsmen and shopkeepers still prevails in these streets. In the Wolvenstraat, for example, there is a shop selling nothing but buttons, and opposite it a shop specializing in ribbons, braid, tassels and lace-edging, in other words trimmings. You can buy the finest silk by the metre in the Hartenstraat, leather clothing in the Runstraat and hundreds of kinds of beer in the Huidenstraat. And everywhere there are shops with secondhand clothes or brocades, creative home designs, books, flowers, candles, exotic *objets d'art* and clocks and lamps.

Perhaps the whole area can be compared to a village, but each of the streets in the area is a district in turn, with a character of its own. More-over, the streets themselves, often no longer than eighty metres, can be subdivided into districts. In the Runstraat, for example, the residents fall into three groups: the Keizersgracht end, the middle and the Prinsen-gracht end. Those working or living at the Prinsengracht end have scarcely anything to do with the people from the other end. Those from the middle are the most sociable and consort with some of those at either end, but the further away people are the less contact there is.

When decisions have to be taken involving the street as a whole, it takes enormous effort to get everyone to pull together. Joint enterprises like putting up the Christmas illuminations cause great headaches, and if for example it involves co-operation with other streets, then the fat really is in the fire! In other words, the residents of the area are not docile sheep, but are all individuals with their own opinions, not only convinced that they are right, but wanting to have their own way. They are real Amsterdammers.

Along the canals are the larger buildings. There are Amsterdammers living there too, but you don't hear them. There are palaces among them that are recognizable as such from the outside. A former mayor's house, for example, where the art dealer once lived whom Rembrandt did business with. Rembrandt himself walked along the halls and up and down the staircases of the house, across the rosette inlaid with mother-of-pearl on the floor of the drawing room, whose ceiling was painted by Gerard de Lairesse. And what is even more difficult to surmise from the outside is the huge garden behind the house. Almost all the blocks in the quarter are built round gardens, which are unfortunately being gradually overrun with garages and other structures. Luckily a halt has been called to this trend. The occupants of this house, though, have never thought of such dastardly plans. The garden runs right through to the following canal, and is thus as long as a cross-street, minus the houses – over fifty metres. At its widest point the garden is even more than fifty metres, so that it cannot be much less than 2,000 square metres in area and there are many vestiges in it as old as the house itself, about three hundred years.

The owner can pick his own mulberries each year from his own ancient mulberry tree. His neighbour at the back, looking out over the garden from his tiny attic room in the cross-street, may be envious, but at the same time should be grateful. It is because of the fact that no uninterested company is located here that virtually the whole inner area is preserved as a splendid historic garden.

Patrician houses, commercial offices and cultural centres are clustered together. The district contains the Bible Museum, where you can go if you need the Bible in Urdu. And Felix Meritis, the former Communist bastion when the party was still popular after the war. Before that it was the entertainment centre for the local patricians, whose motto was 'Happy through Achievement'. Quite by chance it was discovered that the small concert hall there had perfect acoustic qualities, and the designer of the Concertgebouw made grateful use of it. The future of the building, which now houses the Shaffy Theatre, is uncertain. It puts on experimental theatre, but today's patricians, the ladies and gentlemen of the city council, are not too happy about it, and would prefer to see a music centre. Is theatre today perhaps a little too subversive for the ladies and gentlemen?

District 5: The Canal Ring from the Leidsestraat to the Raadhuisstraat

CAFÉS

1   De Doffer – Runstraat 12
2   Gollem – Raamsteeg 4
3   Hoppe – Spui 18-20
4   De Koningshut – Spuistraat 269
5   Het Land van Walem – Keizersgracht 449
6   Luxembourg – Spui 22
7   Harry's Cocktail Bar – Spuistraat 285
8   Morlang – Keizersgracht 451
9   Discothèque Odeon – Singel 460
10 Het Paleis – Paleisstraat 16
11 De Pels – Huidenstraat 25
12 Theatercafé Shaffy – Keizersgracht 324
13 De Zwart – Spuistraat 334
14 Van Puffelen – Prinsengracht 377
15 Aas van Bokalen – Keizersgracht 335

RESTAURANTS

16 Brasserie 404 – Singel 404
17 De Geparkeerde Mossel – Nieuwezijds Voorburgwal 306
18 Paris Brest – Prinsengracht 375
19 Tout Court – Runstraat 13
20 Kantjil en de Tijger – Spuistraat 291
21 d'Vijff Vlieghen – Spuistraat 294-302
22 Rias Altas – Westermarkt 25
23 De Bast – Huidenstraat 19
24 Lucius – Spuistraat 247
25 Koh-I-Noor – Westermarkt 29

MUSEUMS

26 Amsterdams Historisch Museum – Kalverstraat 92

OTHER

27 Openbare Bibliotheek [public library] – Prinsengracht 587

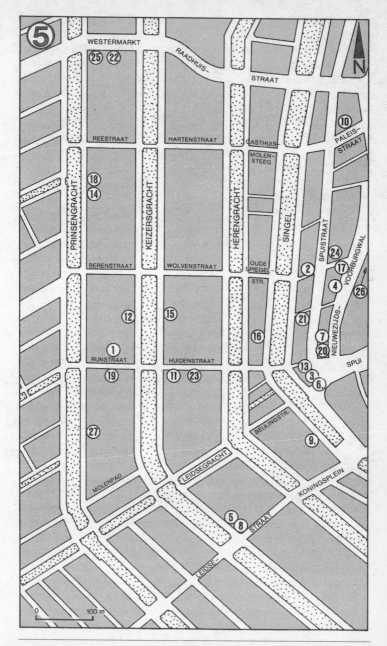

In this district of publishers, libraries, music lending libraries and concert halls, there is one company that occcupies a special place. The piano dealers Cristofori on the Prinsengracht, next to the large Public Library and Reading Room. Cristofori are not only sellers of musical instruments: in a former mattress store in a double warehouse, a cultural centre has been created which can boast a concert hall as big as the smaller auditorium of the Concertgebouw – and with excellent acoustics. A club-cum-restaurant for musicians is planned, and if everything goes accordingly there will be an international-class cultural centre here.

The owner of the complex proves his organizational talents each year, when in collaboration with the Pulitzer Hotel in the same quarter, he organizes an open-air piano concert on barges on the Prinsengracht at which great pianists perform. It is always televised, and so the world comes to a peaceful, but lively quarter of Amsterdam and that quarter goes out to the world.

6: THE CANAL RING: FROM THE WESTERMARKT TO THE HAARLEMMERSTRAAT

The stretch of the canals that extends from the Westermarkt to the Haarlem quarter is not the chiquest part. Chic enough of course, and certainly not intended to house the proletariat, which was the function assigned by the seventeenth-century town planners to the Jordaan, situated further westward.

But compared to the mansions in the curve of the Herengracht near the Leidsestraat, for example, one can see that the homes here were built by the rather less wealthy, up-and-coming merchants, whose fortunes, deriving from the seventeenth-century or eighteenth-century trade in pepper or coffee or from whaling, were still being made. A striking number of houses carry a picture of or reference to the source of income, such as the name of the town of Breslau, or a porpoise, or a ship.

This part of the canal ring is still a temporary haven, even now that the patricians of yesteryear have long given way to today's yuppies. Those who strike it really rich or are blessed with children will soon move to another part of town, as the houses are often small and hence also the flats into which they are divided up.

Private houses are what most properties here were built as, and that is what most of them have reverted to being. But anyone walking around the area twenty years ago would have seen a very different picture. After the Second World War the seventeenth- and eighteenth-century houses were regarded as old-fashioned and unattractive, and the few people still living there were mostly elderly. The imposing canal houses, often after an internal conversion, were fitted out for commercial use.

And whereas at the higher numbers along the canals it was mostly respectable office-workers who moved in, in this area industry was dominant, the garment trade in particular. In property after property, floor after floor, the busy fingers of seamstresses were at work and lorries loaded and unloaded, making driving along the canals a difficult business. No wonder therefore that in the 1960s serious proposals were put forward (and it must be said later rejected) simply to fill in the Herengracht, Keizersgracht and Prinsengracht, as had already been done in the nineteenth century with a number of canals in the Jordaan. True, it would have made the canals that much drearier, but it seemed the perfect answer for traffic and industry.

The canals have remained open, and on sunny days more boats than ever sail across the waters: tour boats, pleasure-craft bringing tourists from out of town, water bikes and even some of the owners of the houseboats, who get about the city in speedboats. The garment houses have departed to new headquarters outside the old centre. The area has regained its residential function – both on land and on the water, for this is the area for houseboats.

It is the district *par excellence* of Amsterdam's yuppies, with their coffee bars, bric-à-brac shops, designer furniture, ultra-modern hairdressing salons and the most expensive greengrocers in Amsterdam. The canal houses have been divided up into small flats and one can see lip-smacking estate agents walking about with potential clients in their wake, on whose troubled features one can read mental mortgage calculations. Living on the main canals is still just about affordable in this part of town, although that won't last much longer – the demand for apartments far outstrips the supply, and rumour has it that after the creation of the single European market in 1992 prices will shoot up even further. Residents meanwhile find odd covenants in their leases, an echo of the recent industrial past of their houses: on pain of fines of thousands of guilders they are forbidden to paint words such as 'Hollandia' or 'Spartak' on their windows, the names of companies who once moved from the premises and were afraid that someone might steal their customers behind their backs.

Only the cafés seemed to have escaped drastic remodelling and modernized interiors – the cafés have neither the planning permission nor the room to expand. The urge to sit out on a terrace to see and be seen, however, proves stronger than any city ordinance. Despite the wishes of the town council they expand from year to year: first a tentative row of chairs appears in front of the café, then chairs along the side of the canal on the other side of the roadway, and then the blow-heaters in winter and the sunshades in summer, and beneath them a hubbub of voices far into the night. The police mount a clean-up of unauthorized terraces from time to time, much to the delight of those who live next to them and much to the annoyance of the other local residents, who see their favourite terrace suddenly vanish. But it usually only lasts a week or so, and then the chairs are back again: the Amsterdam police have other things to do besides hounding good-humoured beer-drinkers.

The goings-on around these cafés are typical of Amsterdam, a city which some Dutch people have always regarded as the home of disorder. In some respects it certainly is: everywhere else in the country you are fined for riding a bike without lights at night, but in Amsterdam the police do not bother. And the tension between ordinary people and the authorities is also expressed in the houseboats, which many tourists find attractive, and which determine the look of the area, especially on the Prinsengracht and the Brouwersgracht. Concrete tubs equipped with a superstructure, real sea-going tugs adapted for living on, old ships and former flat-bottomed boats with living quarters – it was of course never the intention of the city council to fill the canals in this way, but they are.

With great ingenuity the occupants of the houseboats have connected themselves to mains electricity, the municipal water supply and cable television. The council, unwilling to use force, has begrudgingly begun levying charges for light, water and cable T.V. Because it is quite simply difficult to get rid of the boats, there are periodic 'legalization campaigns', demanding that those who have parked their boats in the canal without permission (and incidentally have to pay mooring costs for them anyway) are given permits. The result is that there are soon lots of new craft alongside the existing ones, bringing a new supply of law-breakers.

The houseboat occupants ensure that the social composition of the area stays more or less varied, according to income groups. On land those in lower-income groups are clearly losing ground. Only a few houses full of squatters are holding out. The black anarchist flags and exhortations to support the people of Tibet still adorn the gaudily painted house-fronts from which the squatters' colonies can be recognized. But the true ideological fervour of the 1970s is much more subdued now in the squatters' houses. The manifestos on the class struggle in the area, and on 'the expulsion of the poor from the centre of Amsterdam', are usually no match for the moving incentive payments offered by money-hungry developers.

This part of the canal ring does not constitute a district as such. The main road from the Westermarkt to the Royal Palace (formerly the Town Hall) on the Dam, the Raadhuisstraat, is the result of a nineteenth-century breach in the canal ring – as can be clearly seen from the the elegant curve and wrought-iron work of its arcade. There are no really important monuments, it is more an area for those wishing to sample the city.

The walker should be sure to glance across the Singel at the Torensteeg, where there is a typical bridge with an old lock-up built into its foundations and on top a bust of the great nineteenth-century Dutch writer Multatuli (1820–87). The same goes for the copper cupola of the former Lutheran church, with a miniature red-light district at its foot.

On the other side of the area the tower of the Westerkerk, which can be climbed, dominates the picture. The view from the top clearly shows the contrast between the narrow streets of the Jordaan and the sedate spaciousness of the canal ring. At the foot of the tower is the triangular Gay Monument, erected some years ago next to an old-fashioned urinal which in the 1950s served as a meeting-place for Amsterdam homosexuals. The urinal is the most famous one in Amsterdam, having been removed for the wedding of the present Queen Beatrix in the Wester-kerk. The smoke bombs thrown by members of the anarchist Provo movement on that occasion, at the top of the Raadhuisstraat, were in many ways the starting-signal for the mini-cultural revolution which made Amsterdam the capital of the 'permissive society'.

The Amsterdam tradition of tolerance is much older, as is apparent from the fact that the French philosopher Descartes lived here in the seventeenth century, as a Catholic thinker in a Protestant environment. And on the corner of the Prinsengracht is the Anne Frank House, a reminder of the persecution of the Jews in the Second World War, which still looms large in the Dutch national consciousness as a cruel interruption in a history characterized since 1813 by peaceloving and tolerant attitudes.

There are sometimes long queues of foreign tourists outside the house where some of the (few) Dutch people who dared actively to resist the Nazi authorities hid a group of Jews to save them from deportation to the extermination camps. The narrow staircases of the canal-side house can scarcely cope with the stream of tourists.

Plans to build a glass-covered staircase at the back of the house, so that tourists would no longer have to pass through the house and would be able to see the rear part of it through an opening in the back wall, met with fierce resistance from Amsterdam conservationists. The gardens behind the canal houses, with their often very old trees, are an important and beautiful feature of the city, if only for those who live in a house on a canal. For the town-planners who gave building permission imposed strict conditions: gates and passageways were not to be made, so that there was no chance for the casual passer-by to catch a glimpse of the gardens and interior courtyards.

Anyone walking along the canals in a northerly direction will notice a change in atmosphere. The Brouwersgracht, whose name recalls much older, medieval industrial activity in the area, was not designed as a canal for living on, but as a place to work. Yet its old warehouses have in many cases been converted into yuppie flats. Where once bales of goods were stored, winched up or lowered on the beams and hooks which are still there, there are now lamps and sofas, where the conversion has been successful, that is.

Not so long ago, in 1987, the purchasers of one such converted property found to their cost that a particular kind of beetle, which had been dormant since the seventeenth century, suddenly began flourishing in the warmth given off by the residential flats, and buzzing loudly began merrily gnawing away at the the age-old woodwork. The complex now stands empty – nature, even in such an urbanized environment, refuses to be trifled with.

Beyond the Brouwersgracht there is a district with a different character again, the Haarlem quarter, so called because this was the course of the dyke along which people had travelled to Haarlem since the Middle Ages. From time immemorial this has been an area of shabby houses and smallish shops, and it still is, although there are few of the original medieval buildings left. To this day the Haarlem quarter is a working-class area, but the time has long since gone when the local residents had a dialect distinct from that of the Jordaan, to say nothing of the respectable canals of course.

Still further north, under the railway line, are the Western Islands, again totally different, where there were once ships' wharves, and which despite their picturesqueness are scarcely visited by tourists. The municipal authorities have ambitious plans to build an area of high-rise buildings here on the banks of the IJ to house offices and industrial premises.

District 6: The Canal Ring: From the Westermarkt to the Haarlemmerstraat

CAFÉS

1   De Beiaard – Herengracht 90
2   De Drie Fleschjes – Gravenstraat 18
3   't Kalfje – Prinsenstraat 5
4   De Karpershoek – Martelaarsgracht 2
5   Discothèque 't Okshoofd – Herengracht 114
6   't Smakzeyl – Brouwersgracht 101
7   De Twee Prinsen – Prinsenstraat 27
8   De Vergulde Gaper – Prinsenstraat 30
9   Rum Runners – Prinsengracht 277

RESTAURANTS

10   Treasure – Nieuwezijds Voorburgwal 115
11   Christophe – Leliegracht 46
12   Annapurna Torensteeg 4–6
13   Marakech – Nieuwezijds Voorburgwal 134
14   Türkiye – Nieuwezijds Voorburgwal 169

MUSEUMS

15   Anne Frankhuis – Prinsengracht 263
16   Koninklijk Paleis [royal palace] – Dam

OTHER

17   Nieuwe Kerk – Dam/Mozes en Aäronstraat
18   Westerkerk – Westermarkt

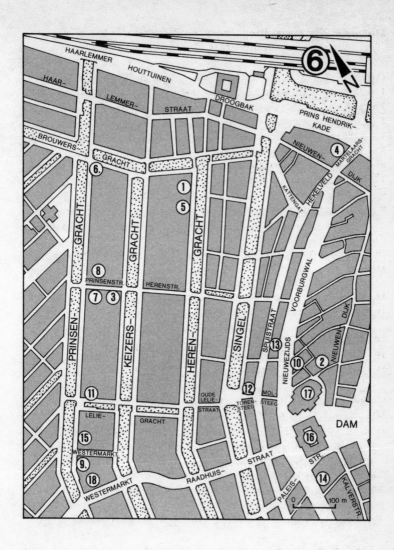

7: THE JORDAAN

Far into the twentieth century, the Jordaan, the area bounded by the Brouwersgracht, Passeerdersgracht, Lijnbaansgracht and Prinsengracht, had the reputation of being a slum, the home of the poorest of the poor, those who did not take moral standards too seriously and were a potential source of subversion. The area and its inhabitants were a thorn in the flesh of the representatives of law and order. During the Second World War a high-ranking policeman complained about the anti-social lifestyle of the Jordaaners. A number of families around the Anjeliersstraat particularly were, it was claimed, guilty of what in the eyes of thrifty Dutch citizens was a cardinal sin – living from hand to mouth. Deporting them to a work camp would teach them how to behave – but things did not go that far.

The people of the Jordaan defended themselves against the traditionally disapproving view of their area with a considerable dose of chauvinism, which saw the Jordaan as the most desirable place on earth, and those born and bred there as the warmest and liveliest people anywhere. The neighbourhood and its people are glorified in countless tear-jerking ditties, as is the beauty of the Westertoren, called in these popular songs 'Ouwe Wester'. For although the Westerkerk was built for the posher section of the population, those living on the canal ring, its lofty, crown-capped spire is the landmark *par excellence* of the district at its foot, as one can see on a short walk starting from the Westerstraat, through the Tweede Anjeliersdwarsstraat, Tweede Tuindwarsstraat, Tweede Egelantiersdwarsstraat and Eerste Leliedwarsstraat.

The Song of the Jordaan, that pearl of Amsterdam popular songs, is still a huge success. In typical Jordaan cafés like Rooie Nelis at Laurierstraat 101, and Café Nol, much visited by tourists, at Westerstraat 109, the tradition is kept up, preferably with live music. As it is in the Twee Zwaantjes at Prinsengracht 114, where the regulars sing along at the top of their voices to accordion accompaniment not only with the sentimental songs, but with the opera tunes popular with many Jordaaners.

The Jordaan came into being at the beginning of the seventeenth century, when because of massive immigration the pressure of population in Amsterdam increased so alarmingly that the council decided upon a new, large-scale expansion of the town. Four new districts were created: the Western Islands, north of the railway, the area around the Haarlemmerdijk, the canal ring for the rich, and the Jordaan, which accommodated all the dirty, hazardous and noisy industries in the town.

Even before that the area beyond the town moat had been used as a place of banishment for all those not welcome within its walls. Here were situated the Leper House and the Carthusian monastery in whose cemetery plague victims were buried. The rest of the area was taken up with vegetable gardens and meadows belonging to the townspeople.

Because the town authorities were able to use inside knowledge and canny speculation to push up the price of building plots, it was decided not to lay out the area in a pattern uniform with that of the canal ring. Instead the town surveyor was instructed to widen the existing tracks across the fields and ditches into streets, or deepen them to form canals.

This approach resulted in a district in the shape of an irregular hexagon, consisting of some eleven canals and fourteen streets running parallel to them. Dozens of narrow cross-streets linked these streets and canals. For the names of the district's network of streets, originally called the Nieuw Werck or New Project, the planners drew on the workshops based there and on the vegetable kingdom.

The plant names given to the streets and canals explain the later name given to the area as a whole: 'Jordaan' is a corruption of the French *jardin*, or garden. The French immigrants, refugees who fled their country before and after the revocation of the Edict of Nantes and settled in Amsterdam as tradesmen, spoke of their neighbourhood as 'Les Jardins'.

The stench and pollution produced by the industries caused the Jordaan to degenerate quickly and irrevocably. Despite the expansion the great shortage of housing for the poor continued throughout the seventeenth century, and to meet the demand for accommodation one-family houses were divided up into a number of dwellings, the so-called 'forts'. In addition an extensive building programme of courtyard housing was decided upon, only accessible through narrow passages and alleys. Because there was no room for wide houses, they were built higher, giving the streets an eerie, cave-like look. With the exception of one or two canals the Jordaan turned into a slum for the dregs of society. The rapid decline of the area was also accelerated by the fact that it was isolated, deprived of good connections with the town's road network and routes to other, surrounding towns.

Only in the second half of the nineteenth century did the liberal bourgeoisie begin to pay attention to the terrible poverty and intellectual starvation of the urban proletariat. Partly from fear of a violent revolution, partly from the desire to edify the masses, missionaries, both liberal and Socialist, entered the district to see the plight of the population with their own eyes and to try to alleviate it. Admiration for the work of Arnold Toynbee in the London slums led to the setting-up of 'Ons Huis' in the Rozenstraat. When the building opened its doors in 1892, it contained a reading room and a library and classrooms for teaching cooking, sewing, reading and writing. This institute, set up by Hélène Mercier, was the first district centre and club of its kind in Europe.

At the same time new workers' houses were built in the Rozenstraat, but the private building companies set up on English lines were able to help only a small portion of the population.

In the 1930s the city council decided to redevelop the southern part of the Jordaan: the passages were to go, and the streets were to be widened. Much earlier, at the end of the nineteenth century, a number of canals had been filled in to combat the frequently occurring outbreaks of cholera and typhoid fever. The draining of the canals produced new through roads linking the Jordaan both with the city centre and with the new Amsterdam-West district built at the end of the nineteenth century. The Jordaan was no longer a backwater.

After the Second World War the city council decided on a change of plan. The idea was to allow the Jordaan to decline and eventually to demolish the area completely. In the place of the old dilapidated dwellings, high-rise flats the whole length of streets, like those in Osdorp and the Bijlmer, were to be constructed. This plan, however, was not carried through. In the 1960s the Jordaan was suddenly 'discovered' by students and artists. There was a housing shortage everywhere in the Netherlands, but in the Jordaan there were flats and houses for sale or rent for next to nothing. Younger families were moving out of the area and leaving behind houses at which average, less adventurous house-hunters turned up their noses. For those undeterred by the lack of a shower or acceptable toilet or the effort of a drastic conversion, there were opportunities galore here to get hold of a room, studio or shop. This influx of new, young residents gave the area a much-needed boost, and the local shops, still run by older Jordaaners, acquired more custom.

The Jordaan might still be a slum, but the continued expansion of the city meant that it was now in the centre. Together with its central location and the chance of establishing an attractive business with very little initial capital, the area was eminently suitable for young entrepreneurs short of funds to set up a shop, café or eating-place in.

This may be why the atmosphere of the 1960s still clings to the Jordaan: not only in the pavement gardens found in almost every street, where a few paving slabs have been lifted to make room for a rose-bush, a creeper or a few humble violets blasted by street dirt and the weather, but also in the countless little second-hand shops. The wares on offer range from indeterminate junk and worn-out clothing to marvellous equipment and ornaments from the 1950s and chic-er secondhand clothing. Some shops have specialized to an almost insane degree in one item, like the spectacle shop in the Noorderkerkstraat, whose owner has dedicated his life to the service of this article in all its forms. On display in his rather grimy shop window there are dirt-cheap National Health specs, but also very expensive avant-garde sunglasses, as well as collectors' items, like glasses with luxaflex lenses.

Beyond the Lauriergracht, where the Jordaan changes its tone, becoming quieter and more sedate, and is getting increasingly like the Spiegelgracht with its concentration of pricey antique shops and galleries, one can find the more up-market secondhand shops, and on the Elandsgracht there are the auction houses. But even here the informal atmosphere that is so characteristic of the Jordaan has not been entirely lost. The art and antiques centre De Looier regularly holds junk markets for private buyers.

Because the still narrow streets of the Jordaan are nowadays more easily accessible by car, public transport and especially by bike, shops, workshops, small factories and galleries are thriving. Provided they specialize and produce quality work or craft work, they attract a circle of customers consisting not so much of locals or passers-by but more of rather snobbish 'connoisseurs' from all over Amsterdam, and indeed all over the country. Anyone needing leaded lights or glassware or a piece of hand-turned antique furniture repaired, anyone wanting to buy a post-modernist designer lamp or pigments to mix their own colours for their artistic creations, anyone looking for the latest in modern Dutch art or a particularly rare children's book, is bound to have to resort to the Jordaan, even though the area, apart from one or two fairly busy streets, does not have the look of a shopping centre.

Today's visitor to the Jordaan will notice the enormous amount of building going on. This boom has its origin in a decree issued by the city council on 22 June 1972. A new development plan for the area came into being and henceforward became the guideline for planners: the historic character of the neighbourhood must not be violated, offending businesses must be removed and priority given to residential building. In the years following the decree a start was made on the redevelopment. Historic properties were restored, houses renovated or replaced by new buildings. Meanwhile the Rozenhofje on the Rozenstraat was restored, and not long ago the extensively refurbished *hofjes* in the Westerstraat and the Anjeliersstraat and the Laurierhofje with its low-rise flats were completed. Only here and there can one find the passages leading to the walled-in buildings, mostly closed off with a door leading to small factories tucked away behind the houses, such as that belonging to a neon-light works in the Willemsstraat. In that part of the area elderly residents still tell the story of how in earlier, poorer days the courtyards behind the passages would sometimes be covered over with tarpaulins to give shelter to homeless families.

Because the redevelopment entailed not only the temporary removal of the occupants but also a rise in rents, many Jordaaners moved away permanently to the nineteenth-century working-class areas in Amsterdam-West, Amsterdam-South (the 'Pijp') and Amsterdam-East. Others settled in new estates built round towns in the vicinity of Amsterdam, like Purmerend, Hoorn and Almere, which were more expensive but were set in green suroundings.

In the northern part of the Jordaan bounded by the Rozengracht with its mosque and shoarma restaurants run by Arabs, the original population mix is best preserved. Locals often account for this by the rise in home-ownership. Many Jordaaners, if they were able to put a little money aside, bought one or more properties with the aim of using the rent from them to provide for their old age. The house-owners did not give a hoot for municipal re-accommodation policy and decided for themselves who they wanted as tenants. Often they chose nephews and nieces, or other members of their family. Or else young Dutch people or, if the worst came to the worst, an Englishman or an American. Nor were the land-lords averse to putting pressure on protesting council officers to accept their unilateral decisions.

This course of events helps explain why in the Jordaan, in contrast to other older districts with cheap rented accommodation, there are re-markably few Surinamers or foreigners from the Mediterranean area, much to the chagrin of the city council, which prefers there to be in every district a mixture of ethnic minorities and native Dutch residents, rich and poor, tenants and home-owners.

A superficial estimate, made during a walk criss-crossing the Jordaan, ob-serving the outward appearance of passers-by, the look of the living rooms seen through the windows and the sort of music issuing from the houses, confirms the impression that in the northern section of the area the original Jordaaners are still in a comfortable majority, some sixty per cent, most of whom are elderly, against something less than forty per cent of newcomers who have moved in during the last two decades. The latter, the artists, students and graduates who have since entered well-paid employment, are very different from the original inhabitants, not only because they are benevolently known as 'the ones who've studied', but also by virtue of their age and very different lifestyle.

They usually live alone or in couples, and have no strong ties either with their families or with the locals. Moreover, the fact is that their work and lives tend to be conducted indoors, while the careerists among them are almost never at home and devote little time to housekeeping. It is no accident that in the last years various meal delivery services and a well-stocked late-night shop should have opened up in the Jordaan.

Unlike the handful of squatters who, with their sloppy and aggressive appearance and strongholds daubed with slogans, and their pop music blaring out till all hours in summer, are a thorn in the flesh of the old-timers, the 'intellectuals' have been accepted by the Jordaaners, even if contact is usually limited to a chat in the street, often arising from the Jordaaner's proverbial nosiness or from a discussion on keeping the pavements and the common areas clean. Moreover, most Jordaaners feel slightly sorry for their new neighbours. In their eyes they lead pretty miserable lives: always alone, always with their noses stuck in books and swotting, and besides that in 'bare' and hence cheerless homes.

With increasing prosperity Jordaaners have not forgotten the old poverty, so that they are less concerned with managing their money than with spending it. Nothing is too luxurious for them: men and women like to adorn themselves with chunky gold jewellery, and at the first nip of winter get their sheepskins or fur-coats out of the wardrobe. A glance will tell that most of the women spend a lot of time and money at the hairdresser's; one favourite is having one's hair peroxided or tinted, while the older generation have a liking for piled-up hair-dos, created by the skilled hands of the stylist with the aid of perms and hairpieces.

Hidden away behind the narrow, unassuming house-fronts, usually no more than three windows wide, there are veritable palaces. See a neatly pleated net curtain at the window and you will be able to describe the décor of the front room with a predictability bordering on certainty. Crystal chandeliers, gleaming brass ornaments, sucrose paintings of shepherdesses, vases decorated with china roses, lots of burgundy plush and velvet, lots of pink tulle and lace. For while the aristocracy had its Baroque and the well-to-do bourgeoisie its Rococo, the Jordaan working class had its luxuriant hodge-podge of a-historical mock-antiques and pastoral motifs. Amid all this nostalgic ostentation, one usually finds the latest in audio-visual gadgetry. But the tiny living room is not full enough yet. Houseplants, caged songbirds and an aquarium brighten the house, which is insulated from the world by heavy dark-red curtains.

Jordaaners have the reputation of being monarchists, though they have never bothered themselves much about the forces of law and order. In the second half of the nineteenth century and at the beginning of the twentieth riots broke out in the district on several occasions. Because the Jordaaners belonged to the most socially vulnerable section of the population, every setback in the economy meant a worsening in living conditions. Hunger and deprivation were invariably the cause of the riots, even though they were sometimes ostensibly provoked by other things.

Like in 1886, when the Eel Riots broke out because of the ban on 'eel-heading'. This contest of agility, involving pulling a live, soap-covered eel from a rope strung across a canal, was regarded as an affront to public decency.

There was a clearly politically focused outburst in the Jordaan riots of 1934. The people of the Jordaan, employed as factory hands, casual labourers, small traders or prawn-peelers were suffering from the effects of the stockmarket crash. Whole streets were out of work and many families were living on the meagre dole. When news came that the prime minister Colijn was arguing for a reduction of the dole, the Socialists led by Domela Nieuwenhuis called a protest meeting at their headquarters on the Rozengracht. Afterwards there were disturbances and finally the police and army put down the rioting by force. Scores of people were killed or seriously injured, but the rebels achieved their aim – the dole was not reduced.

Because Jordaaners gradually began working for the council and wound up in jobs such as roadmender or bus or tram driver, trades from which the Dutch Communist Party (CPN) actively recruited members, the Communists gained much support in the Jordaan. This may have been why during the Second World War members of the CPN, which had been banned by the German occupiers, speaking in the Noordermarkt, called on the people of Amsterdam to strike in protest at the inhumane treatment of Jewish Amsterdammers. The following day, 25 February 1941, the February Strike took place. Although the strike did not change the Germans' attitude to the Jews, this unique gesture, in which a majority which had been largely left in peace by the occupying power showed its solidarity with an oppressed minority, is still commemorated annually.

On the Noordermarkt, opposite various monuments, not only the local riots and their victims are commemorated, but also national Remembrance Day and Liberation Day. Every year, at 8 p.m. on 4 May the last post is sounded. The buglers of the local Noorderspeeltuin drum band do their best, but usually only manage to get about one note in seven right. It is not only historical emotion which sends shivers down the spine of the assembled throng.

Dramatic events, shared poverty and the isolated position of the district turned the Jordaaners into a closely knit community. But much of the old life has of course disappeared. Very many of the former residents have moved away and their place has been taken by outsiders, often non-Amsterdammers. Changes such as the improvement of living conditions and the advent of the outsiders have brought about the disappearance of street life. Nevertheless Jordaaners do maintain a watered-down version of it – hanging out of the windows. As soon as the weather allows the sash windows are raised, a cushion is put out on the window ledge to protect their arms against the hard surface, and then all they do is look, waiting for something sensational to happen or the chance of a chat with a neighbour. Or else they take a bag of stale bread to the corner of the street to feed the pigeons and exchange a word or two with other locals.

But the golden age the people of the Jordaan are constantly singing the praises of will never return, and that gives them the chance to indulge to their heart's content in their favourite pastime: complaining. Nowhere is the phrase 'my life is not worth living' heard so often. A popular congregating time is the Jordaan festival, which is traditionally held in the third week of September. Like most popular festivals these days it is only a shadow of what it must once have been. The singers remain, but now they are amplified by technical wizardry, and often sing English-language hits. Only the beer-swilling has remained the same.

Although the Jordaan has never been an entertainment centre, there are lots of cafés — small working-class pubs that used to close early and where one could pop in for a crock of gin to take home. For as in all poor districts a lot of heavy drinking went on.

Many old cafés are still in use as cafés, but with the advent of the new residents numerous of them were converted into eateries and coffee shops, giving the Jordaan a wide spectrum of restaurants offering everything from exotic cuisine to simple Dutch fare at reasonable prices. Anyone preferring a taste of atmosphere rather than an extensive first-class meal can try JoMi at Westerstraat 76. The food is always good, though there is no choice beyond the day's menu. But the friendly atmosphere is unequalled: the family that runs the restaurant encourages a degree of familiarity between customers the windows quite often steam up with all the laughter. Some pleasant cafés are Chris, at Bloemstraat 42, founded in 1624, which makes it Amsterdam's oldest café; J. A. Hegeraad, at Noordermarkt 34, whose landlord has not yet succumbed to today's muzak disease; and 't Smalle, at Egelantiersgracht 12, which in the eighteenth century was a liqueur and gin distillery and public house belonging to the famous Pieter Hoppe, many glasses of whose young or old *jenever* are still poured in Dutch cafés.

From the terrace of the Kat in de Wijngaert, so called after the gable stone, at Lindengracht 160, the visitor has a good view of the former battlefield of the Eel Riots, as he does from the café opposite, De Bel, although this is totally different in atmosphere, being mainly frequented by the younger generations of Jordaaners. The men wear shiny tracksuits, the women tight-fitting, gaudy-coloured leotards, and both sexes have a

District 7: The Jordaan

CAFÉS

1 De Koophandel – Bloemgracht 49
2 Discothèque Mazzo – Rozengracht 114
3 Nol – Westerstraat 109
4 P'96 – Prinsengracht 96
5 De Prins – Prinsengracht 124
6 De Reiger – Nieuwe Leliestraat 34
7 Saarein – Elandsstraat 119
8 't Smalle – Egelantiersgracht 12
9 De Tuin – Tweede Tuindwarsstraat 13
10 De Twee Zwaantjes – Prinsengracht 114
11 Twiggy's – Marnixstraat 166
12 Vandenberg – Lindengracht 95
13 Rooie Nelis – Laurierstraat 101

RESTAURANTS

14 At Mango Bay – Westerstraat 91
15 Bordewijk – Noordermarkt 8
16 Dineau – Laurierstraat 63–65
17 Rhodos – Binnen Dommerstraat 13
18 Lonny's – Rozengracht 48
19 Claes Claesz. – Egelantiersstraat 24–26
20 De Gouden Leeuw – Prinsengracht 274

OTHER

21 Noordermarkt
22 Noorderkerk
23 Westerkerk

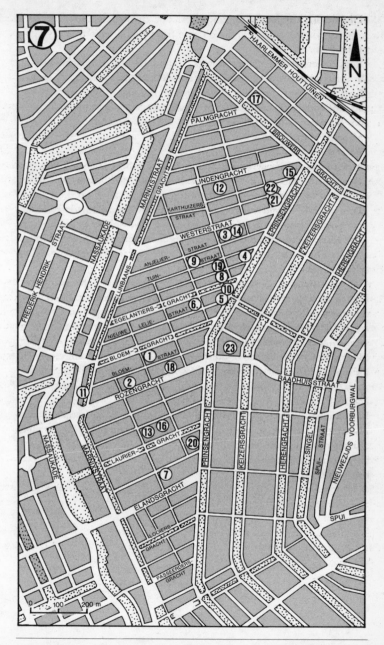

liking for big, aggressive-looking dogs. The clientele is noisy, and there is lots of coming and going by obscure figures who seem to be tying up shady deals.

During the day the coffee houses around the Lindengracht and the Westerstraat serve good coffee and excellent sandwiches. De Wester, at Westerstraat 30, is frequented early in the morning by shiftworkers, taxi and lorry-drivers, building labourers, and on market days by the market-traders. A few hours later, on Mondays and Saturdays, when the markets are held, if the weather is good the terraces are packed with market shoppers.

On Monday mornings an old clothes market is held in the Westerstraat and a flea market on the Noordermarkt (see also p.72). But the markets are busiest on Saturdays. Then there is a general market on the Linden-gracht and a bird and a farmers' market on the Noordermarkt. Old and new residents of the area mingle, and it is not only the 'intellectuals' who are interested in the wholefood produce on offer in the farmers' market. The Jordaaners too like to buy a nice piece of farmhouse cheese or lovely thick yoghurt straight from the farm.

Only the Bonders, a strict breakaway sect from the Calvinist church, keep aloof from all the worldly turmoil. The little group of zealots come from all over Amsterdam to the Noorderkerk to worship their Old Testament God of vengeance, the God who commands their women to wear frocks and cover their heads with hats.

On Sundays all the bustle of the week subsides. The Jordaaners have left for their caravans on the camping sites and many other residents are also away, the students visiting their parents, the artists and academics weekending in hotels on Texel or in Limburg.

It is so quiet in the streets that one can hear the cooing of the pigeons, usually only audible in the courtyards of the almshouses. The stranger can walk through the courtyard of the restored Huys-zittende-Weduwe-hofje in the Karthuizersstraat without running the gauntlet of the local residents' suspicious looks.

8: THE 'PIJP'

The Albert Cuypstraat is a strange street. Between about 9 in the evening and 6 in the morning only a few cars and bikes pass through this wide but very ordinary-looking street. However, during the day (except on Sundays) every inch of space is taken up by market-stalls, crates, traders and milling crowds of people. The biggest market in Europe, so they say, a spectacle that since the 1920s has been assembled and dismantled afresh every day.

In the early morning the stalls (on wheels) are brought by little electric trucks from their overnight storage depots in nearby streets. The traders arrive from the auctions and warehouses and start displaying their wares, and by 10 o'clock business is in full swing.

Tradition has it that the district with the Albert Cuyp market at its heart is an ugly area, hurriedly put up at the end of the last century, without much thought. For as long as anyone can remember it has been known as the 'Pijp' (Pipe), though precisely why is not clear. The name is most probably connected with the long, slightly curving streets and tall houses. A narrow, deep house is called in Dutch a *pijpenla* or pipe-drawer, after the drawers in which the long, white china Gouda pipes, also slightly curved, were kept.

The Pijp is no longer officially part of the centre, but is only a stone's throw away. Coming from the Rijksmuseum, the best thing is first to cross the bridge (on the east side) and then immediately turn right. You are now walking along the stretch of water called the Boerenwetering, which in 1850 was still an idyllic spot where Amsterdammers came for their days out, with all kinds of cafés and boats for hire.

The side-streets on the left all lead to the Frans Halsstraat, the oldest part of the Pijp. Building began in 1868, where there was nothing but fields, the odd factory and market gardens. Via these streets it is only a short walk to the corner of the Ferdinand Bolstraat and the Albert Cuypstraat. This is where the market begins. The reason why the Albert Cuypstraat is so wide in comparison with the other narrow streets is that it was once a waterway, the so-called 'Zaagmolensloot', where on either side windmills provided the energy for sawing timber. Because of the protests of the sawmill-owners and other small entrepreneurs, who relied on the waterway for transport, it took until 1889 before it could be filled in and built on.

The light here is at its most beautiful towards sunset. The low-lying sun shines straight down the long, quasi-uniform streets, and in the market they are clearing up. Prices are dropping. The really poor scavenge about among the seagulls for discarded vegetables. The municipal cleansing service arrives with its hose-carts, and the Albert Cuyp is prepared for the following day. The cafés fill up.

But earlier in the day there is more happening in the market. The crowds shuffle past the stalls. Besides being a market the Albert Cuypstraat is also a Dutch variant of the Italian *passeggiata*: many people go there to be seen, not to look, let alone buy anything.

The junction of the Albert Cuypstraat and the Eerste van der Helststraat could be regarded as the true centre of Amsterdam. Why? 'This is the place you find the prettiest girls in Europe,' as a fellow-writer recently obstinately maintained. And there is a lot in what he says. Chinese, Indian, black, white and every possible combination of these primary colours pass by, parade, stroll or hang around. On one corner the row of fish stalls begins, diagonally opposite you can buy all the vegetables and fruit the world has to offer, there are stalls where you can buy the cheapest jeans, and on the other side, behind the flowers, there is usually the pitch of 'Potato Piet'. The tobacconist sells Turkish, Portuguese, Italian, French, German, American, English and Surinamese papers.

Just round the corner on the left, on the Gerard Douplein, there is a terrace with even more international papers. The square is a nice place to get your breath back and look at the few low houses remaining from the time when there were still windmills here.

Returning through the Eerste van der Helststraat via the market, you walk in the direction of the Sarphatipark. On the corner of the Govert Flinckstraat, opposite each other, are the international bakery Runneboom (where a notice on the wall in at least ten languages requests one not to touch the bread) and Café Koekenbier, which is as old as the Pijp itself. Here they know how to serve draught beer as it should be served, in case you'd forgotten in Amsterdam.

It is only a short walk to the Sarphatipark, the Amsterdam counterpart of the Parc Monceau in Paris. It owes its name to the idealistic nineteenth-century town-planner Dr Samuel Sarphati, to whom a monument was erected here. It was unveiled on 11 July 1886, a year after the opening of the park. If Sarphati had had his way, incidentally, the park would have been many times larger. But then the first extension of the city since the seventeenth century might itself have looked very different. For a time there were serious plans to build the Central Station here and to run the railway-line along the southern edge of the town rather than along the harbour-front.

At any rate Sarphati does not have the Pijp in its present form on his conscience. The district is rather the arbitrary result of a series of compromises between the town council and property speculators. There are some nice examples of nineteenth-century architecture, with unique ornamentation in wood and stone, but there is also lots of cheap jerry-building. In recent years much of this has been demolished and replaced by attractive and varied new housing. The Pijp as it has developed over a century (and I am now talking about the old part, enclosed by the Stadhouderskade, the Ruysdaelkade, the Ceintuurbaan and the Amsteldijk) is inhabited by three classes of Amsterdammers: the descendants of the original residents, mostly workers; foreigners, the first of whom were the immigrant Turkish and Moroccan workers at the beginning of the 1960s; and the latest wave, the 'student types' and other younger people, who have introduced the yuppie lifestyle into the area.

On sunny days you can see them all in the Sarphatipark: around the playground veiled Moroccan mothers are taking a short break and can let their children run round the sand-pit for a bit. On the benches groups of older Turks are sitting. On the grass yuppies in expensive sports gear are doing their exercises, and round the monument you can see an Indian father teaching his son the rudiments of cricket. Further on, a pair of German junkies are scoring. A burly building worker is taking his bull-terrier out for a walk. A coach full of Czech tourists stops for a break on the Ceintuurbaan.

And everywhere in the area there are building works, conversions, improvements and repairs in progress. For the past few years the Pijp has been officially a city within a city, with its own council and elected representatives.

Finally it is an obvious thing to do to walk down to the Amstel. From the bridge at the end of the Ceintuurbaan (fully restored a short while ago) you first look towards town. On the right, on the far bank, is the historic café and centre for modern music the IJsbreker, with a pleasant café terrace under the trees. On the Pijp side long ago there was a beautiful hotel-restaurant called the Berebeit, located in the building with the turret. Now there is a garage in it. And over a hundred years ago there were lots of cafés down by the water. Don't forget to have a look at the 'House of the Gnomes' (Ceintuurbaan 251), an idiotic piece of neo-Gothic architecture, on top of which two gnomes are throwing a ball to each other – a joke whose meaning has been lost.

No, there are no real sights to see in the Pijp. What do you expect of a nineteenth-century working-class area? It was a mess from the very beginning and it still is. The only things really worth seeing in the Pijp are the people.

District 8: The Pijp

CAFÉS

1   Café de IJsbreker – Weesperzijde 23

RESTAURANTS

2   Café-Restaurant Witteveen – Ceintuurbaan 256–258
3   Cajun – Ceintuurbaan 260
4   Yamazato – Ferdinand Bolstraat 333 (Okura Hotel)

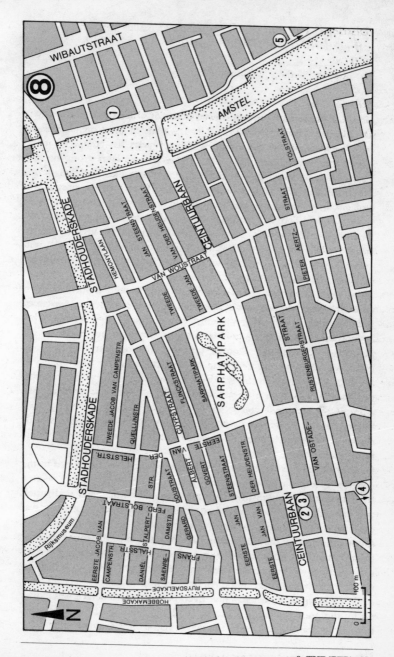

WIBAUTSTRAAT

AMSTEL

STADHOUDERSKADE

STADHOUDERSKADE

CEINTUURBAAN

VAN WOUSTRAAT

JAN STEENSTRAAT

VAN DER HEIJDENSTRAAT

HEMONYLAAN

TWEEDE JAN

TWEEDE

SARPHATIPARK

Sarphatipark

TOLSTRAAT

STRAAT

PIETER AERTZ-

STRAAT

RUSTENBURGERSTRAAT

TWEEDE JACOB VAN CAMPENSTR.

QUELLIJNSTR.

FLINCKSTRAAT

CUYPSTRAAT

EERSTE VAN DER

HELSTSTR.

STR.

ALBERT

GOVERT

STEENSTRAAT

DER HEIJDENSTR.

VAN OSTADE-

CEINTUURBAAN

Rijksmuseum

EERSTE JACOB VAN CAMPENSTR

DANIËL STALPERT-

SAENRE-

FERD. BOLSTRAAT

GERARD DAMSTR

FRANS HALSSTR.

JAN

EERSTE JAN VAN

EERSTE

CEINTUURBAAN

RUYSDAELKADE

HOBBEMAKADE

100 m

0

N

14 · The IJsselmeer Coast

North of Amsterdam tourism is even better organized than in the city it-self. North of Amsterdam all roads lead to Marken and Volendam. Espe-cially to **Volendam**, the village which for years has competed in the world tourist championship stakes and regularly comes out on top. Towns like Monnickendam and Edam, villages like Durgerdam and Broek in Waterland, tell us more about the history of the province of Holland, more about the area immediately north of Amsterdam, which is appropriately called Waterland, than Volendam does, and are in any case a hundred times prettier, but Volendam attracts all the visitors and the others are left out in the cold. Why is that? Not because of Volendam it-self, which is a fishing village without any important monuments, but because of its inhabitants, the Volendammers.

They bear the names Tol, Tuyp, Steur, Sier, Jonk, Zwarthoed, Veer-man, Schilder, Mooyer and Kwakman. There are few other surnames, and they all seem interrelated in some way or other. They live not *in* but *on* Volendam and amid the predominantly Protestant population of the area they are Catholic. Roman Catholic, that is, but they are also catholic in the wider sense: broad-minded and versatile. For when you live in a place which in the words of a recent chronicler 'God forgot to make', and belong to a 'a bunch of people that have washed up like scum on the coastline', you've got to look after yourself, write your own history, and in every age be a child of your time. And so the Volen-dammers are materialistic and carefree, Catholic and modern, oppor-tunistic and reliable.

Even in the past, when the village's fortunes were completely tied to the development of the fishing industry, you could get whatever you wanted from them. So people had a taste for those silly little smelt in Brussels and Paris, did they? Very well then. The tramline from Amsterdam was extended from Monnickendam so as to be able to transport the little fish south quickly. So the Amsterdammers wanted those vermin, prawns, fresh on their breakfast tables? Very well then. Every morning at 3 a.m. the fishermen of Volendam would be out on the IJ so as to be able to sell their catch, still alive, to the Amsterdam fish-buyers.

And that businesslike amenability. Even before the Zuiderzee was closed off by the great Enclosing Dyke in 1932 and the flag of the Volendam fish-market hung at half-mast, the village had its first souvenir shop. The local football club, one of the better teams in the country, was the first to sport advertising on its shirts, and the revival of pop music had no sooner begun with so-called 'beat' than the fishing village produced the Cats, for years the best-known group in Holland. It is this uninhibited quality, this childlike existentialism, that makes a visit to Volendam interesting, indeed pleasant.

Despite the promises of the travel agencies, we learn nothing there about the history of the Netherlands or of Waterland. But what we can savour is a unique form of historical consciousness, a consciousness that extends back only as far as the early morning of the same day. Living as they do in the present, the Volendammers are effortlessly up to date, modern to the point of absurdity. When hash was in fashion Volendammers in their twenties and thirties had the biggest lumps of the stuff in the country. When miniskirts were in vogue, the Volendam girls had the shortest ones. There is even a story that a lot of village couples started divorcing when news reached them through the popular press that divorce was the in thing. But even that was only a passing fad.

While the coach-loads of Japanese, Germans, Americans, Italians and Spaniards are dragged from their coaches to the shops and back again, laden with folk costumes, eels and Delft blue, we shall take a walk through old and new Volendam. Let's say it's Monday morning and there's a strong breeze blowing. The washing is hanging out to dry on high washing lines, held tightly between two ropes, as they don't use pegs here. Women, sometimes in costume, are doing the shopping. Men are sitting, in shirts and tight trousers, outside the cafés. It is tranquil and idyllic behind the dyke. One thing is very striking: nothing is old. While the inhabitants of, say, Edam, Monnickendam and Broek in Waterland take pains to keep their houses inside and out in harmony with their historic setting, the Volendammers are entirely unconcerned about such things. Nowhere is there a wainscoated wall, a wooden floor or an old piece of furniture to be seen. The authentic Volendam style is ostentation: lush flowered wallpaper, wall-to-wall carpeting, velvety three-piece suites and lampshades in the international catholic bourgeois style. Everything is brand new, pricey and pontifical.

The nicest features are the net curtains and the front doors. No two front doors are the same in Volendam, and no two sets of net curtains either. It is as though the windows are going to communion in virginal white, freshly starched lace veils. They hang in the windows in a myriad of folds and curves, always leaving the centre of the window-sill on view. This is the place for the museum piece, usually a multi-coloured china vase from some non-existent country. Next to them are the doors, in smooth, shiny-lacquered wood with raised panels in all shapes and sizes. In the middle is a framed window of coloured or stained glass, and hanging in it the *pièce de résistance*, a cast-iron or copper creation, a star, a boat, a bird or something abstract. This is surrounded by an odd array of knockers, bells, bell-pushes and nameplates. These nameplates are a special attraction, particularly for Dutch people. For because so many Volendammers have the same name, a whole range of nicknames has developed, and no one is shy about simply putting their nickname on the door.

Towards evening on this windy Monday, let's sit at the entrance to the harbour. With hands piously folded, the statue of the Virgin wishes all sailors a safe voyage. There are mostly pleasure craft, yachts and motorboats at anchor. We see Sunday sailors and their offspring buying chips and meatballs from the snackbar on the quay, the water laps against the dyke and it is just like the old chronicler once wrote: 'We see the women parading like elegant princesses, with their swaying hips, arm in arm in twos and threes, chattering and laughing, but all the while as they walk along they are glancing out over the endless expanse of water, where their brothers, young men and husbands spend their days, the menfolk, who may one day be snatched from them by that other mistress of their affections.'

The history of Volendam is still to a large extent the history of the sea. A book was once written about the history of the village, which for a long time languished as District 7 of Edam and during the Reformation was shunned by the Calvinist preachers, who saw no point in bothering with 'those few folk on that remote bend in the dyke' – the reason why Volendam has always remained Catholic. The book was written by a local amateur historian and the first sentence of the 288-page account reads: 'The history of Volendam will probably never be written.' As the book goes on to demonstrate.

As well as by coach, which stops off at the obligatory cheese-dairy selling mostly young, not particularly tasty Edam cheese, incongruously wrapped in red cellophane, you can get to Volendam by car (comfortable, but rather boring), by bus (rather complicated, but you meet some interesting people) or by bike (quite tiring, but by far the most spectacular way). The nicest route starts at the Schellingwoude Bridge in the east of Amsterdam and takes you through towns and villages which may not be as interesting sociologically as Volendam, but are certainly much prettier. The Schellingwouder Bridge – in fact two bridges, the first of which crosses the Amsterdam–Rhine Canal, and the second the IJ – is one of the links between Amsterdam and Amsterdam-North and has wonderful views, to the left across the IJ and to the right over the Outer IJ, the gateway to the IJsselmeer. Immediately across the bridges, and still part of Amsterdam, is the first beautiful village, **Schellingwoude**. Here you can already see what will strike you repeatedly along the whole route, that the people north of Amsterdam pay a lot of attention to their houses. There are a couple on the Noorder IJdijk like miniature castles, complete with moats and drawbridges. That dyke leads to the Oranje Sluices, from where there is a good view of the Amsterdam docks and the beginning of the IJsselmeer, and at the same time can observe the busy commercial and leisure traffic.

The next village is **Durgerdam**, rather busier, rather more touristy as well, as is clear from the many sailing boats moored along the dyke. Here we see those special dyke houses that have their extra storey not above the ground floor but below it.

Just outside Durgerdam, after the turn-off to Ransdorp, by a very modern windmill, is the beginning of one of the most beautiful routes in the country, the cycle path along the top of the dyke, which until just before Monnickendam has splendid views, to the right of the IJsselmeer and to the left of the inland lakes which make Waterland so watery. The path is well surfaced and every so often there are picnic tables and benches at the foot of the dyke, so that, provided there is not too much wind, this is the pleasantest cycle ride in the area around Amsterdam.

You can also turn left off the dyke and ride across Waterland through Ransdorp, with its oversized flat tower, and Holysloot. Or you can venture inland and experience the sensation of the high water level. The ditches seem so brim-full that riding along the narrow path you feel you are actually a little below the level of the water. The dyke route has other sensations to offer. For example the gradually changing view of the IJsselmeer, which a remarkable number of old sailing boats still use, and where the skies are constantly assuming new shapes, often so beautiful that you don't dare write home about them for fear of being taken for a raving Romantic.

To the left lies the Kinsel Meer, where you can see not only a great variety of wild birds, but also how the Dutch live in their summer cottages: immaculate, neatly fenced off, and with lots of statues, gates and other ornaments in the well-tended little gardens. At Uitdam, a quiet village with one café, you have to leave the dyke temporarily. Once past the village you can ride back on to it until the fork where the right-hand road leads to Marken and the left-hand one to Monnickendam.

Let's go to **Monnickendam**, an extraordinary little town. It strikes one as a miniature Amsterdam, which is not far off the mark, since Monnickendam has a history comparable to that of Amsterdam: rich merchants, worldwide trade links, great wealth and enough ideas, energy and good taste for the well-to-do classes to turn the place into a real gem.

If we walk into town from the Grote Kerk, also called the Sint Nico-laaskerk, one of the many Dutch churches that began as Catholic and became Calvinist, a fine, elegant church, we won't be able to believe our eyes. The amount of magnificent sixteenth, eighteenth, nineteenth, and above all seventeenth-century architecture preserved here is simply miraculous. It takes a little under an hour to walk through the town, along the Kerkstraat, the Burgwallen and the Noordeinde, savouring the beauty of the place, and finishing up in the harbour at the café-restaurant Stuttenbergh, which may be folkloristic, but is folkloristic in the best sense, full of wonderful old musical boxes and serving mouth-watering fish dishes.

And then on past Katwoude, along the foot of the dyke to Volendam, about which enough has already been said. In the harbour, amid the tourist bazaar selling simply everything that tourist bazaars ought to, there are boats to **Marken**, which in season leave every half hour. We take the boat to what used to be an island, but which for some time has been linked to the mainland by a causeway. Arriving in the harbour of Marken, we rub our eyes in disbelief. Is this a village or an open-air museum? It is both, and quite unique. All those wooden houses, painted green with dead-straight white stripes, all those women in colourful costumes, all those front lawns with the washing flapping as it dries, held between the twisted washing lines – isn't all this the ultimate self-caricature of Holland? It is, but it is also authentic, and quite pretty too. We walk through the harbour to the church quarter, buy some postcards and half an hour later take the boat back to Volendam.

From there we ride through the new estates to **Edam**. There are many expensive doors and jolly net curtains to be seen on the estates. In Edam we are back to the good old-fashioned style, even more beautiful than Monnickendam. In the sixteenth century Edam was a very prosperous town, richer and more powerful than Amsterdam. There are still many reminders of that opulence, for example in the Great Church or Sint Nicolaaskerk, which is indeed great, measuring no less than 80 by 50 metres, making it one of the largest churches in the Netherlands. And the buildings on the Lingerzijde and the Scheepmakersdijk, the property of an official body responsible for the water in Waterland. Or the merchants' houses in the Voorhaven and the Nieuwe Haven, the houses on the Kaasmarkt, on the Dam and in the Grote Kerkstraat. What affluence there must have once been here and what a strangely happy balance between ostentation and good taste the seventeenth-century Dutch were able to maintain.

From Edam we have a choice of different routes back to Amsterdam, but whichever one we take we must stop off at the village of **Broek in**

Waterland, which has the most, the largest and the finest wooden houses in the area. Rich merchants from Amsterdam once had their country houses there. They made them of wood, because wood, being lighter than stone, is less inclined to sink into the wet, marshy soil of Waterland. We shall walk along the Havenrak, the Leeteinde, the Roomeinde and De Erven. There must be wealthy people still living in Broek in Waterland: there is only one house that has not been newly restored, newly painted and put into perfect order. The rest are immaculate, and nothing more needs doing to them, it would seem. Yet everywhere we see ladders set against the fronts of houses and hear modern saws and drills whining away. The people north of Amsterdam simply can't leave their houses alone; they are always messing about with them, always putting the finishing touches to something or other. Tiring, but a treat for us travellers.

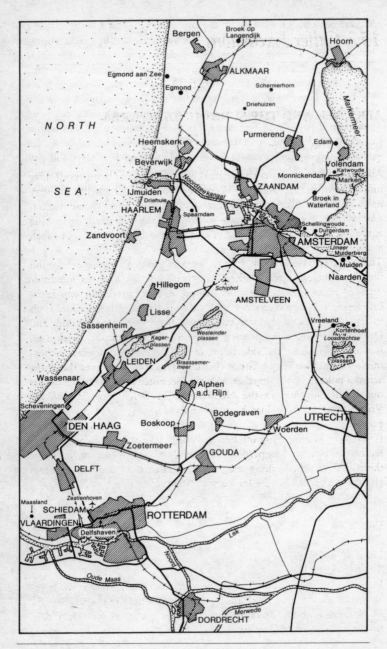

15 · Other Excursions

ALKMAAR AND THE SURROUNDING AREA

Local VVV: Waagplein 3
Tel. 072-11 42 84

Alkmaar is famous for its cheese market, which takes place every Friday morning in summer round the Weighing-House. It is a touristy and very noisy affair, and Alkmaar is much nicer when there is no cheese market. For example, for shopping on the Laat and in the Lagestraat, or looking at the splendid Weighing-House or one of the other beautiful spots, such as the Hof van Sonooy.

The area around Alkmaar is very well worth a visit. In a great arc around the town there are places like Broek op Langedijk with its hundred-year-old cattle auction, the artists' village of Bergen with its wonderful café terraces, Egmond aan Zee with its wide beach, Schermerhorn with its trio of mills and the scarcely known but lovely Mijzenpolder and Driehuizen, perhaps the prettiest village in Noord-Holland. Driehuizen is worth visiting for the ride alone, preferably via Stompetoren, Schermerhorn and picturesque Grootschermer. This road goes over the dykes across a polder, which together with the Beemster (a little further east) is one of the loveliest in the Netherlands. In Driehuizen, at café De Vriendschap, you can hire boats for a rowing trip round the Eilandspolder.

If you like walking along the beach you can take the bus from Alkmaar station to Hargen/Camperduin at the Hondsbossche sea wall. From there you can walk along the beach to Bergen (5 km) or Egmond (10 km), and then take the bus back to Alkmaar.

DELFT

Local VVV: Markt 85
Tel. 015-12 61 00

Delft is 55 minutes by train from Amsterdam. The ancient town is included in most tourist coach tours and is famous among other things for its blue china. But despite all the worn-out tourist clichés Delft does have real charm: the town has a rich history and a treasure-house of old architecture to admire. Delft is at its most beautiful on the canals, especially the Oude Delft.

Not far from Delft, slightly south, is Maasland, an old village with a marvellously preserved centre. Lopsided houses, trees, the 's Herenstraat and in the middle of it all the black waters of the canal.

DORDRECHT

Local VVV: Stationsweg 1
Tel. 078-13 28 00

Dordrecht is one of the oldest towns in the Netherlands, as can be seen, for example, on the Dolhuissteiger, behind the busy Voorstraat, or in the peace of the Arend Maartenshof, founded as 'a home for women in need and widows of soldiers who have died for their country'.

But Dordrecht is at its most beautiful on the Groothoofd, where the ancient link between the town and the water is clearly apparent. One of Holland's greatest poets, Hendrik Marsman, called this 'the Square of the Rivers', and Vincent van Gogh, who worked in Dordrecht as a bookseller, enthused to his brother Theo after returning from a walk along the Lower Merwede river: 'When the sun set this evening and was reflected in the water and in the windows and cast a fierce glow over everything, it was exactly like one of Cuyp's paintings.'

Dordrecht, with the striking leaning tower of its Grote Kerk, has inspired other great artists, including Marcel Proust, who wrote: 'One ought to stay in Dordrecht, whose ivy-clad church is reflected in the network of peaceful canals and in the golden waves of the Maas, where the ships gliding by in the evenings disturb the reflection of the dark lines of roofs and the blue sky ...'

The route of a walk round the most beautiful parts of the town is available from the VVV.

GOUDA

Local VVV: Markt 27
Tel. 01820-136 66

Gouda is known in the Netherlands not only as the town of cheese or candles, but also as the town of pipes, after the famous long-stemmed Gouda pipes manufactured here. Gouda too belongs on the list of tourist sights regarded as a must by every tour operator. Accordingly the local VVV puts on a craft fair on Thursday evening, featuring 'typically

Dutch crafts', and in the summer thousands of interested visitors shuffle through the streets.

Gouda's town hall is famous in Holland and together with the square on which it stands acted as a backdrop in the film *Nosferatu* by the German director Werner Herzog. Apart from the town hall the centre of Gouda has many more fine old buildings, and hence not a stone can be moved there without first seeking planning permission.

Less well known and precisely for that reason especially pleasant is the museum which has been housed in the Catharina Hospital in the Oosthaven. Anyone wondering what was worse in the seventeenth century, torture or being operated on, should go and take a look at this museum, which they may find alarming. There turns out to be little difference between the old surgeon's room and the contemporary seventeenth-century torture chamber.

HAARLEM

Local VVV: Stationsplein 1
Tel. 023-31 90 59

Haarlem is the provincial capital of Noord-Holland and is only a quarter of an hour from Amsterdam and from Zandvoort on the coast. On the outskirts of the city are a number of residential districts which are among the most beautiful and expensive in the country. The wealthy residents are one of the reasons that Haarlem has a certain stylishness and distinction.

The best-known crowd-pullers are the Grote or Sint Bavokerk and the Frans Hals Museum. But Haarlem is also nice just to walk around. There is one splendid shopping street, the Grote Houtstraat, many old almshouses and seventeenth-century quarters that have been preserved, and you can walk along the bank of the river Spaarne and the Mooie Nel to Spaarndam. This village has a pleasant little harbour and a tourist attraction in the shape of a statue of Hans Brinkers, a boy who is supposed to have saved Holland from yet another disastrous flood by sticking his finger in a hole in the dyke. But Hans Brinkers has never been much more than a symbol.

In the direction of Hoofddorp, on the ring canal, is Cruquius, a castle-like steam engine which helped drain the huge Haarlemmermeerpolder. With luck, you will be able to hear the warden, Mr Roe, tell the story of the pump.

THE HAGUE

Local VVV: Koningin Julianaplein
Tel. 070-364 62 00

The Hague is the seat of the Dutch government, and where foreign embassies are based. Consequently it is a rather stuffy, sedate city full of civil servants, which royal palaces, large amounts of greenery and wide avenues give a certain air of distinction. In recent years town planners have done their best to diminish the city's grandeur. The Hague is at its worst in the area round the Central Station: dirty grey concrete and flyovers full of roaring traffic.

Nevertheless, the rather fragmented city centre is still an agreeable place to shop. One of the main shopping areas is situated around a distinctive nineteenth-century arcade, the Passage. The Lange Voorhout is also worth a visit. This attractive square, which has a sedateness typical of The Hague, is close to the Binnenhof, the Dutch parliament building and government headquarters. In the square there is one of the many interesting art galleries the city possesses, Pulchri Studio. Leading into the Lange Voorhout is the Denneweg, a picturesque street containing antique shops, restaurants and another art gallery, the Haagse Kunstkring. Art dealers, galleries and good restaurants can be found in the Noordeinde, the street on which the Royal Palace is situated.

Since many inhabitants of the former Dutch colony of Indonesia settled in The Hague, the city has a large assortment of excellent Indonesian restaurants.

The Hague has three museums worth a special mention. Firstly the Mauritshuis, with its fine collection of seventeenth-century Dutch masters. Those interested in the Romantic Barbizon school can visit the National Hendrik Willem Mesdag Museum, which has the largest collection of the school's work outside France, with many Millets and Corots. Van Gogh is said to have drawn inspiration here. And finally the Gemeentemuseum (Municipal Museum), housed in a beautiful building, and with among other things a group of Mondriaan's works and an interesting collection of modern art.

The Hague also has Madurodam, a miniature town incorporating many Dutch architectural styles. Visitors will find, for example, models of a large number of important Dutch buildings, both modern and historical.

Adjoining The Hague, of which it is a part, is the seaside resort of Scheveningen. The modern, tiled promenade, the Boulevard, is fairly characterless: visitors will see that everything possible has been done to please the tourists.

LEIDEN

Local VVV: Stationsplein 210
Tel. 071-14 68 46

Leiden is an approximately thirty-minute train journey from Amsterdam. The old town has a rich history. As far back as the Middle Ages it was very prosperous on account of its cloth industry. A compulsory episode in all primary-school history books is the town's dogged resistance against the Spaniards in 1573–4. The town was relieved after William of Orange ordered the dykes to be breached to flood the surrounding countryside, after which the fleet was able to repel the Spaniards. As a reward for their endurance the people of Leiden were given a university, the first in the Northern Netherlands, by the Prince of Orange. The relief of Leiden is still enthusiastically celebrated each year on 3 October.

Though the centre of Leiden makes a rather cluttered impression, it is still one of the more attractive Dutch towns, and worth exploring on foot. There are many picturesque spots and narrow streets and there are often splendid courtyards tucked away behind the house-fronts, of which the Sint Annahofje is the best known and the Jean Pesijnhofje on the Kloksteeg the most picturesque.

Leiden also has a number of museums, most notable among them the National Museum of Antiquities, which contains archaeological finds from the Netherlands and objects from the Classical cultures around the Mediterranean. The high point is the temple of Taffah, which had to be dismantled because of the construction of the Aswan Dam in Egypt.

MUIDEN AND NAARDEN

Local VVV: Adriaan Dorstmanplein 1b
Tel. 02159-4 28 36

Naarden is a small fortified town east of Amsterdam. Its attraction lies in the charming walled centre. There is a foot and bicycle path along the top of the best preserved town ramparts in the country. The varied countryside around the town is well suited to bike trips. Bikes can be hired from the station in Naarden.

From Naarden you can make a bike excursion to Muiderberg and Muiden, taking you along the shore of the IJsselmeer past the magnificent country houses in Muiderberg. In Muiden, standing almost directly on the lakeshore, there is one of the few castles still to be found in the Netherlands, the Muiderslot.

You can then return via Weesp, along the Vecht, a romantic river where in the eighteenth and nineteenth centuries rich Amsterdam merchants took their ease, as can still be seen from the splendid villas. You make your way back to Naarden along a narrow shell path running from Nederhorst den Berg through the quiet Ankeveen ponds to Vreeland and Kortenhoef. Finally, after riding through Spaanderswoud, you arrive back in Naarden, having covered a distance of some 40 km.

ROTTERDAM

Local VVV: Coolsingel 67, and in the Central Station building
Tel. 010-402 32 00

In the Netherlands Rotterdam has the image of a city of hard workers. It is the arch-rival of Amsterdam, as emerges in the yearly fixtures of the cities' football clubs, Feijenoord and Ajax. The difference between the two teams is typical: through the years Rotterdam's Feijenoord has been a club of workmanlike persistence and Ajax of Amsterdam the team with the tactical brilliance and creativity.

Many people are under the impression that there is nothing much to do in Rotterdam. One explanation for this is undoubtedly the ravaging of the city in the Second World War: when the German armies invaded Holland, its bombers paved the way by pounding Rotterdam.

But years after the rebuilding of the city, during which it made a cold and characterless impression, the largest port in the world has managed to develop a style of its own, not least thanks to a number of splendid examples of modern architecture.

The heart of the city is the area around the old harbour, where when the weather is good it is extremely pleasant to sit out on the café terraces at the water's edge. And however difficult the window-cleaners may find the sloping windows of Piet Blom's tilting houses on stilts, his buildings, known to architects the world over, are certainly very exotic.

The obvious thing for many tourists to do in Rotterdam is to take a boat trip round the harbour and to visit the Euromast. At the foot of the Euromast is a park called simply 'Het Park'. It was laid out by Jan David Zocher, the man who was responsible for designing the Vondelpark in Amsterdam. Nothing very special, you might think, if the establishment of Zocher's were not tucked away in the park. It occupies a house of 1800, which has been transformed into a café-restaurant, wonderfully located and with splendid décor. There is a small, quite reasonable menu. On Sunday mornings from 10 a.m. one can breakfast there serenaded by a chamber-music ensemble.

Finally, mention should be made of the Museum Boymans-van Beuningen, which is known especially for its collection of older and modern art, its ceramics and industrial designs. The museum regularly organizes important exhibitions.

In the direction of Schiedam lies **Delfshaven**, which can be easily reached by public transport from Rotterdam. Delfshaven was an important whaling and herring port, and is also famous as the starting-point of the Pilgrim Fathers' voyage to America. Delfshaven has an interesting museum, De Dubbele Palmboom, where much can be learned about the town's earlier means of earning its livelihood.

A pleasant walk of about 2 km through Delfshaven would be as follows: from the Schiedamseweg turn right into the Aelbrechtskolk, take the first bridge on your left, turn right, walk as far as the 'Destilleerketel' mill (open to visitors), retrace your steps a little, turn right down a little alley and walk back to the Schiedamseweg via the Achterhaven and the Achterwater.

UTRECHT

Local VVV: Vredenburg 90
Tel. 030-31 41 32

Utrecht is 33 km from Amsterdam and is a major railway junction. The visitor alighting at the station finds himself immediately in the largest indoor shopping centre in the Netherlands, Hoog Catharijne, which is well worth visiting, though it now makes a rather run-down impression. A rival shopping centre, much more chic than Hoog Catharijne, called La Vie, recently opened opposite.

Utrecht is a real student town. Until a few years ago there was not much going on there, but thanks to some private initiatives the town now offers a much more varied range of things to do. Both during the day and in the evenings it is much livelier, though parts of it still have a calm provincial atmosphere.

The town's hallmark is the cathedral tower, the Domtoren, 110 metres high, from the top of which, in clear weather, one can see Amsterdam in the distance. There are a number of canals running through the centre of town, with a large number of café terraces down at the water's edge. The area around the Oudegracht is the busiest and has the most important shopping centre.

ZAANSE SCHANS

Very close to Amsterdam, a ten-minute train ride away, is one of the most important tourist attractions in the Netherlands, the Zaanse Schans. This open-air museum with its imitation sixteenth and seventeenth-century houses and windmills draws more than a million visitors each year. That might be a good reason for giving it a wide berth, but there is no getting away from the fact that the Zaanse Schans really is something special.

Its charm resides partly in the fact that the houses are occupied, so that it is not the kind of antiseptic open-air museum of which there are scores in Europe. There is washing billowing in the wind on the washing-lines, cocks crow in the backyards, there are flowers on the windowsills behind the sparklingly clean window panes.

The Zaanse Schans is more photogenic than most other places in the vicinity of Amsterdam, especially in the off season, or very early on a Sunday morning, when the coach-loads have not yet pulled into the car parks and the narrow streets have not yet filled with thousands of strolling visitors. And if it does get crowded, there is still a way out: on the other side of the road along which the Zaanse Schans is built there are some football pitches and a number of industrial estates. Walk down the unevenly surfaced road past the factories, and after about ten minutes you will find yourself in a neighbourhood scarcely known outside the Zaan area, called Haaldersbroek. It is very typical of the area, but not at all geared to tourism – the streets are too narrow and there are none of the facilities to be found in the Zaanse Schans.

16 · Practical Information

TRAVELLING TO AMSTERDAM

TRAVEL DOCUMENTS

Citizens of the United States and the United Kingdom require only a valid passport for entry into the Netherlands. There are sixty other countries – including most Western countries – whose citizens do not require a visa.

Those not requiring visas are usually allowed to stay in the country as tourists for a maximum of three months; for visitors from the United States the period is six months. If you wish to stay in the Netherlands for a longer period you require a residence permit, which can be obtained by contacting the Netherlands Embassy in your own country or, if you are in Amsterdam, the Bureau Vreemdelingenpolitie (tel. (020) 559 91 11). A longer stay is scarcely any problem for most EEC nationals.

Visas can if necessary be issued at the border, but if so you will be liable to a heavy penalty. Extension of the visa for three months is possible in principle on production of an outbound air ticket. For this one can also apply to the Bureau Vreemdelingenpolitie.

DUTY-FREE ALLOWANCES

In determining what goods may be imported duty-free, a distinction is made between goods bought in EEC countries and those bought elsewhere. As a rule you may import more when the goods originate from an EEC country; you must, however, be able to produce a receipt. The special EEC arrangements do not apply to goods bought duty-free in EEC countries.

Tobacco

From EEC countries: *either* 300 hundred cigarettes, *or* 75 cigars, *or* 150 cigarillos, *or* 400 grams of loose tobacco.

From other countries (or bought tax-free in an EEC country): *either* 200 cigarettes, *or* 50 cigars, *or* 100 cigarillos, *or* 250 grams of loose tobacco.

Alcohol

From EEC countries: *either* 1¹/₂ litres of strong drink (over 22%), *or* 3 litres of sparkling wine (champagne), port or sherry, etc. From other countries (or bought duty-free in another EEC country): *either* 1 litre of strong drink, *or* 2 litres of sparkling wine, port or sherry, etc.

In addition there are restrictions on amounts of coffee (1 kilo and 1/2 kilo respectively), tea (200 grams and 100 grams respectively) and perfume (75 grams and 50 grams respectively). Free import of goods such as cameras, watches and souvenirs is possible only up to a value of ƒ 890 (from EEC countries) or ƒ 125 (other countries).

CHOICE OF ROUTE

By train or bus

Almost all large European towns have connections to Amsterdam Central Station. Almost all international coach lines with services to Amsterdam also arrive here.

The Central Station lives up to its name: the nineteenth-century building, recently renovated, is the hub of the semi-circular inner city. It is only five minutes' walk from the Dam, at the heart of the city.

The station has an extensive range of facilities: there are two restaurants, a GWK *bureau de change* (open twenty-four hours), various shops, and bicycles can also be hired there. There are lockers where luggage can be left for up to twenty-four hours, and a left-luggage office which has the same opening times (approximately 5 a.m. to 1.30 a.m.).

As you come out of the station, you will find right opposite the main entrance the small concrete information office of the local public transport authority, the GVB. To the left of it, in the white wooden Amsterdam coffee house, is the local branch of the Dutch Tourist Information Service, the VVV.

By car

Cars are the least suitable means of transport in Amsterdam – driving can be hell during the day, certainly in the canal ring, with its narrow streets. There is no question of getting somewhere in a hurry: lorries loading or unloading, roadworks and long queues of cars at traffic-lights are typical sights. Parking places are as difficult to find as a needle in a haystack. For this reason it is a good idea to park your car somewhere outside the centre. The southern part of town, particularly south of the Museumplein, is ideally suited.

Unfortunately, cars with foreign number-plates – even empty ones – are a prime target for the local car thieves. If you wish to avoid that risk, the best thing to do would be to put your car in a covered car park.
The covered car parks in the centre of town are situated:
– on the Damrak, next to the Bijenkorf department store;
– in the Marnixstraat, at the intersection with the Elandsgracht;
– under the new Muziektheater on the Waterlooplein (expensive);
– in an annexe of the Krasnapolsky Hotel, near the Dam (expensive).

By air
General information number for Schiphol airport: (020) 601 09 66.
Amsterdam's airport, Schiphol, is often declared the world's best airport. The terminal is compact and it is easy to find one's way around it. The arrivals hall is on the ground floor and the departure hall on the first floor. Spread throughout the main departure hall and in the various piers, you will find a great many duty-free shops, selling a total of around 100,000 different (and cheaply priced!) items.
There are two banks in the arrivals hall, which are usually closed between about 12 a.m. (in winter) or 2 a.m. (in summer) and 6 a.m. The banks also have counters in the baggage reclaim area, so that you can change money while you are waiting for your suitcase. There is also a GWK *bureau de change* in the concourse of Schiphol railway station, opening hours: Monday–Saturday, 7 a.m.–9 p.m.; Sundays till 6 p.m.
The cheapest and usually the most convenient way to get from the airport to the centre of town is by train. There are trains every fifteen minutes throughout the day from Schiphol Station to Amsterdam Central Station. The 12 km journey takes twenty minutes. There are also rail connections to such cities as Utrecht, The Hague and Rotterdam, and even to Germany and Belgium. At night, between 1 a.m. and 5 a.m., trains leave every hour on the hour. You will find taxis in front of the terminal building; the fare to the city centre is between about ƒ 35 and ƒ 40.
There are no longer any regional bus services between Schiphol and Amsterdam. However, KLM buses run the so-called 'Hotel Shuttle': two different buses each follow a different route, stopping off at a number of the more expensive Amsterdam hotels. The 'Yellow Line' goes to the hotels in the southern part of town, while the 'Orange Line' links Schiphol with a number of hotels right in the centre. Anyone can make use of these buses both to and from Schiphol. They leave every half an hour. A single fare costs ƒ 15 (1989) and tickets are bought on the bus.

VVV

VVV Amsterdam
P.O. Box 3901
1001 AS Amsterdam
General information number: (020) 26 64 44 (from 9 a.m. to 5 p.m.)

The Amsterdam tourist information service, the VVV, has information
bureaux at two locations in the city:
– In the white Oud-Hollandse coffee house, directly opposite the main
entrance to the Central Station. April–September, open Monday–
Saturday, 9 a.m.–11.30 p.m., and Sundays till 9 p.m.; October–March,
open Monday–Saturday, 9 a.m.–6 p.m., and Sundays, 10 a.m.–5 p.m.
– Leidsestraat 106. Open: April–September, 9 a.m.–11.30 p.m. daily;
October–March, 9 a.m.–6 p.m. daily.
At the VVV bureaux you can obtain extensive information about Amsterdam and the rest of the Netherlands. Various brochures are available,
including one on cycle routes in and around Amsterdam, with theme
walking routes and with ideas for excursions, maps and the fortnightly
magazine *What's On*, containing information on exhibitions, theatre,
music and suchlike and also a public transport map.
From the VVV you can also obtain all the information you need on
trains, buses and trams in and outside Amsterdam. In addition the VVV
arranges reservations for hotels, excursions, car-hire, theatre performances and concerts. You can also book by telephone on: (020) 20 41
11, Monday–Saturday, 10 a.m.–6 p.m.
For information, advance tickets and bookings for cultural events, you
can also use the *Uit Buro*, Leidseplein 26, tel. (020) 21 12 11 (no phone
bookings). Open Monday–Saturday, 10 a.m.–6 p.m. The Uit Buro also
publishes the monthly *Uitkrant*, full of information on the arts and obtainable free in many theatres, libraries, hotels and restaurants. Because of
the clear presentation, the fact that the paper is in Dutch should not be
too much of a problem.

HOTELS

Prices
Travellers staying in Amsterdam can choose from about 270 hotels, with
a total of some 22,000 beds. All price categories are represented, from
basic sleep-inns to five-star hotels.

Up to a few years ago Amsterdam was very popular with low-budget visitors. Now that the market for the more affluent tourist has expanded, a considerable number of youth and low-budget hotels have been converted into middle-priced hotels. This has made it more difficult to spend the night in Amsterdam for next to nothing. Finding pleasant accommodation at a relatively reasonable price is, however, perfectly possible, although as in every city with a large number of visitors there are hotels charging exorbitant prices for poor accommodation. By walking into a hotel on the off chance you can eliminate this risk and get the feel of the place at your leisure. Another advantage is that, outside the high season at least, prices tend to be negotiable. As there are almost always plenty of hotels within walking distance of one another, one can see a reasonable number within a short space of time.

Reservations

In the tourist season, from the end of June to the end of August, booking hotel rooms in advance is recommended. The same applies to the periods around Easter, Christmas, New Year, Ascension Day, Whitsun and All Saints' Day. Because most hotels require a deposit, it is advisable to telephone or write well in advance.

Reservations can also be made through the:

Nationaal Reserverings Centrum
P.O. Box 404
2260 A K Leidschendam
Tel.: (070) 320 25 00
Fax: (070) 20 26 11
Telex: 33755

to which a large number of hotels belong.

Reserving a hotel on the spot

Reservations can be made at short notice by calling in person at the VVV Accommodation Service in the Leidsestraat (close to the Leidseplein) or opposite the Central Station. Here a list with an attached map including most Amsterdam hotels can also be obtained. In addition there is a special hotel counter in the arrivals hall at Schiphol airport.

So-called 'hotel runners' wait for newly arrived passengers in front of the Central Station and try to interest them in a particular hotel. Although there are undoubtedly hotel runners who do their work conscientiously, there are stories of tourists being badly misled by these practices.

Taxi-drivers may sometimes advise against a particular hotel in favour of another which pays them a commission on any new guests secured.

THE HOTELS SELECTED

For your benefit a large number of well-known Amsterdam hotels were subjected to a survey. Standard hotels like the Marriott or Holiday Inn were not included. Only those hotels that emerged as pleasant and reasonably priced are included in the following list, which makes no claims to exhaustive. All hotels listed are within walking distance of the centre.

Because prices can change very quickly, no precise amounts have been given; the hotels have been divided into price categories, taking the price of a double room as a standard. The hotels mentioned first in a price category are the cheapest, and the last mentioned the most expensive in the group. Where applicable, you will find after 'Location' a district number corresponding to the districts in Chapter 13 and the map at the end of the book.

Under ƒ 100
NJCH-City Hostel Vondelpark
Zandpad 5, 1054 GA Amsterdam
Tel.: (020) 83 17 44
Telex: 11031
Rooms: 26
Location: District 2

One of the cheapest places to spend the night in Amsterdam is the NJCH hostel. For individual travellers membership of the IWF is required. The sleeping accommodation is mostly in dormitories with bunk beds, with from four to twenty-two per dormitory. The hostel has a total of 315 beds. The dormitories are reasonably clean; the showers are badly ventilated and in most there is an unpleasant smell. The staff are reasonably friendly. Guests must be in by 2 a.m., when the door is locked. Pleasant location on the edge of the Vondelpark.

Facilities: common room, bar.

Young Budget Hotel Kabul
Warmoesstraat 38–42, 1012 JE Amsterdam
Tel.: (020) 23 71 58
Telex: 15443
Rooms: 53
Location: District 1

Situated in the heart of the red-light district this hotel is on a busy street full of bars and restaurants. Besides the usual one-, two- and three-person rooms (with or without their own shower), mostly dormitories with from four to ten beds. Both the rooms and the dormitories are basic and none too spacious. They are all equipped with lockable storage space. From the restaurant there is a view over the water of the Damrak. Breakfast extra.

Facilities: bar, restaurant, wheelchair access with help.

Hotel Pax

Raadhuisstraat 37, 1016 DC Amsterdam
Tel.: (020) 24 97 35
Rooms: 8
Location: District 5

There are a number of different hotels close to each other in the Raadhuisstraat, all offering more or less the same facilities at what are by Amsterdam standards low prices. Hotel Pax is one such. In the rooms at the front traffic noise can be a problem, but at the back it is quiet. The rooms are fairly spacious, simply, and considering the price, pleasantly furnished, though none has its own shower or toilet. If required, breakfast can be served in one's room. Breakfast is extra, but is very reasonably priced and the staff are friendly.

Facilities: none.

Casa Cara

Emmastraat 24, 1075 HV Amsterdam
Tel.: (020) 662 31 35
Rooms: 10
Location: District 2

A little further from the centre than most, but a reasonable hotel for its price category. It is in a very quiet location close to the Vondelpark. The two and three-person rooms are spacious and simply furnished. Some rooms have a little balcony, most have their own shower and toilet. The breakfast room is very small and stuffy. Pets not allowed.

Facilities: none.

De Leidsche Hof

Leidsegracht 14, 1016 CK Amsterdam
Tel.: (020) 23 21 48
Rooms: 10
Location: District 5

This quiet boarding-house is very centrally located. Some rooms have a lovely view of the canal. About half the rooms have their own bathroom. The hotel is clean and the atmosphere pleasant. Staff unenthusiastic, no breakfast served, no drinks available.

Hotel Weber
Marnixstraat 397, 1017 PJ Amsterdam
Tel.: (020) 27 05 74
Rooms: 10
Location: District 4
For travellers wishing to be within crawling distance of the Amsterdam night-life and not too fussy about room decoration, Hotel Weber is a possibility. The rooms are very basic but clean. No breakfast served, no drinks or snacks available. Most rooms have their own shower and toilet. In three rooms at the front there is considerable noise from the busy Marnixstraat.
Facilities: apartments.

Hotel Mikado
Amstel 107–111, 1018 EK Amsterdam
Tel.: (020) 23 70 68
Rooms: 26
Location: District 4
The many surrounding canals mean that almost all rooms have a splendid view. The hotel is in a quiet location. Rooms spacious and simply furnished. All rooms equipped with their own telephone. A surprising amount of attention paid to sleeping comfort: 75 per cent of the rooms contain excellent beds. A tiny bar, friendly staff. Good value for money.
Facilities: telephone in room, bar.

Hotel Adolesce
Nieuwe Keizersgracht 26, 1018 DS Amsterdam
Tel.: (020) 26 39 59
Rooms: 18
Location: District 3
A good, cheap hotel, situated on a quiet canal on the east bank of the Amstel. The simple rooms have been recently refitted and look clean and comfortable. Some two- and six-person rooms have their own bathrooms. There are three rooms in the hotel garden.
On the same canal there is an annexe to the hotel where young travellers can stay in four-person rooms. The owner puts his heart into his work. As he is in sole charge, he requires guests to be in by about 2 a.m. Pets are not welcome.
Facility: bar.

Hotel Fantasia

Nieuwe Keizersgracht 16, 1018 TR Amsterdam
Tel.: (020) 23 82 59
Fax: (020) 22 39 13
Rooms: 19
Location: District 3

Like the neighbouring Adolescence this hotel gives value for money. The size of the rooms varies; all rooms have their own bathroom. The interior has not been refurbished for years but is still in good condition. Breakfast is served in rooms. A good place for people who use hotels primarily for a good night's sleep. Closed every year from the beginning of November to mid-March. Pets not welcome.
Facilities: none.

Hotel Het Witte Huis

Marnixstraat 382, 1062 XX Amsterdam
Tel.: (020) 25 07 77
Rooms: 20
Location: District 4

The rooms in this hotel are light, small and basic. Both rooms and bathrooms are spotlessly clean. Rooms at the back are quiet. At the front traffic noise is a problem. Large breakfast, very friendly staff. Reasonable relation between price and quality.
Facilities: none.

Hotel Museumzicht

Jan Luijkenstraat 22, 1071 CN Amsterdam
Tel.: (020) 71 52 24
Rooms: 14
Location: District 2

Museumzicht is run by two friendly brothers and the wife of one of them. The atmosphere of the hotel shows their love of their work. All rooms are lovingly and tastefully decorated; in most there is a silk-screen print or an etching. Only three rooms are equipped with their own shower and toilet, though it is planned to extend this number. From the congenial breakfast room there is is a magnificent view of among other things the Rijksmuseum. Unfortunately the roads running past the hotel do produce a good deal of noise.
Facilities: none.

Hotel De Filosoof

Anna van den Vondelstraat 6, 1054 GZ Amsterdam
Tel.: (020) 83 30 13
Rooms: 17

This unusual little hotel is in very beautiful and quiet surroundings. From the conservatory guests have a view of the Vondelpark, and the garden is lovely in summer. The hotel is managed by three sisters and the husband of one of them. One of the ladies studied philosophy and her passion for the subject has been carried over into both the interior and the concept of the hotel. It is intended that in future all the rooms will have their own theme. A great number of rooms are already complete. For example, one can now stay in the Philosophers' Room, the Egyptian Room or the Degas Room. Several artists have done splendid work on the communal area. The theme evenings organized in Dutch every Wednesday give guests a chance of mixing with Amsterdammers.

Only double rooms with private shower and toilet are more than ƒ 100.
Facilities: bar, small restaurant for guests.

From ƒ 100 to ƒ 175

Hotel Seven Bridges

Reguliersgracht 31, 1017 LK Amsterdam
Tel.: (020) 23 13 29
Rooms: 11
Location: District 4

This small hotel is very close to the Rembrandtplein, a busy entertainment centre, but is not particularly noisy. The staff are hospitable. Room size is variable. They are all tastefully furnished, with framed posters, 1950s wicker chairs, or an antique mirrored wardrobe. The rooms at the front have a nice view of the canals. As there is no breakfast room, breakfast is served in individual rooms.

Facilities: T.V. in rooms.

Prinsen Hotel

Vondelstraat 36–38, 1054 GE Amsterdam
Tel.: (020) 16 23 23
Telex: 11336
Rooms: 39
Location: District 2

This hotel is in a pleasant, quiet area between the Vondelpark and the Leidseplein. The rooms are simply furnished and of reasonable size. Because they contain double beds, the single rooms are on the small side.

There are some fifteen hotels in the Vondelstraat and in the parallel Roemer Visscherstraat. Prices for a double room are between ƒ 100 and ƒ 200. A good area to look around at one's leisure for visitors wanting a hotel in this price category.

Facilities: telephone in room, bar.

Hotel Prinsenhof

Prinsengracht 810, 1017 JL Amsterdam
Tel.: (020) 23 17 72
Rooms: 10
Location: District 4

This quiet little hotel is between the Utrechtsestraat, a shopping street containing restaurants and cafés, and the river Amstel. There are small and spacious rooms, all cosily furnished. Half have their own bathroom. A striking feature, given the cheapness, is that each room has telephone and radio. The owners take the hotel business seriously. Closed for one month from the beginning of January. Pets are not welcome.

Facilities: telephone in room.

Hotel Acro

Jan Luijkenstraat 44, 1071 CN Amsterdam
Tel.: (020) 662 05 26
Telex: 10415
Rooms: 44
Location: District 2

All the rooms in this hotel are uniformly and rather impersonally furnished. Framed brightly coloured posters compensate somewhat for the grey, sterile décor. The rooms are spacious, very clean and reasonably priced. Only three single rooms are small and overpriced. The staff are efficient and reasonably friendly.

Facilities: bar, telephone and T.V. in room.

Singel Hotel

Singel 13–15, 1012 VC Amsterdam
Tel.: (020) 26 31 08
Fax: (020) 20 37 77
Rooms: 22
Location: District 6

The Singel Hotel is a modern hotel in a converted canal-side house. The rooms are spacious, comfortable and tasteful. The bar is open twenty-four hours a day and has a nice view of the canal. Friendly staff.

Facilities: bar, room service, telephone and T.V. in room.

Hotel Toro

Koningslaan 64, 1075 A G Amsterdam

Tel.: (020) 73 72 23

Rooms: 23

Hotel Toro is housed in two adjacent stylish houses. Guests looking outside from the lounge will scarcely be able imagine that they are in a city. The splendid view over the Vondelpark gives the hotel a rural quality. The breakfast room is furnished with tasteful antiques, and the lounge and the rooms are also classically and distinctively furnished. The hotel will be closed until March 1990 because of extension work. The hospitable couple who run the hotel go to great lengths to preserve the homely atmosphere. There are four rooms on the ground floor.

Facilities: fax, room service, telephone, T.V. and fridge in rooms, wheelchair access with help.

Hotel Cok (Tourist Class)

Koninginneweg 34–36, 1075 C Z Amsterdam

Tel.: (020) 664 61 11

Fax: (020) 664 53 04

Telex: 11679

Rooms: 120

Hotel Cok began as a student and young people's hotel. In 1989 the young people's and student portion was closed to make room for Superior Tourist Class rooms. It is intended to give these a comfortable and distinctive character. The remodelling is expected to be finished by April 1991; the price of these rooms is not yet known. The Superior Tourist Class and the Tourist Class rooms are in separate buildings. The Tourist Class rooms are practically and rather antiseptically furnished. Because the hotel also has First Class rooms, which will be described below, there are a large number of excellent hotel amenities. Situated a little way out of the centre, near the Vondelpark.

Facilities: bar, baby-sitting service, restaurant, secretarial service, meeting rooms, shop, room service, T.V. and telephone in room, wheelchair access with help.

From ƒ 175 to ƒ 300

Hotel Wiechmann
Prinsengracht 328, 1016 HX Amsterdam
Tel.: (020) 26 33 21
Rooms: 38
Location: District 5
The husband and wife who own the Hotel Wiechmann have been in the hotel business for forty years and still love their work. They do their best to accommodate their guests' wishes. The atmosphere in the hotel is pleasantly homely. The rooms are spacious, light and cosy. Each room is differently furnished, but all have the same degree of comfort. The rooms at the front of the hotel and the breakfast room have a beautiful view of the canal. The rooms at the back are very quiet.
Facilities: T.V. in room (on request), bar.

Hotel Damrak
Damrak 49, 1012 LL Amsterdam
Tel.: (020) 26 24 98
Fax: (020) 25 09 97
Telex: 15353
Location: District 1
This hotel is right on the busy Damrak, which links the Central Station with the Dam. The comfortable rooms were recently redecorated and equipped with all modern conveniences. The furniture is solid. In the rooms on the street side guests may have some trouble with the busy traffic. The staff are very friendly and helpful. The relation of price to quality is very good.
Facilities: T.V. and telephone in rooms, minibar, room service, restaurant, bars.

Hotel Estheréa
Singel 303–309, 1012 WJ Amsterdam
Tel.: (020) 24 51 46
Fax: (020) 23 90 01
Telex: 14019
Rooms: 75
Location: District 5
The hotel is centrally located and consists of eight adjoining houses. The four canal-side houses at the front are on one of the lovely main canals of Amsterdam. The other four buildings are on the Spuistraat; all are linked on every floor. Some rooms have recently been renovated. The rooms,

which are quite small, have been solidly furnished. The so-called Superiors are more spacious but also more expensive. The communal areas have a classical feel.
Facilities: bar, telephone and T.V. in room

Hotel Ambassade

Herengracht 335–353, 1016 A Z Amsterdam
Tel.: (020) 26 23 33
Fax: (020) 24 53 21
Telex: 10158
Rooms: 47
Location: District 5

The Hotel Ambassade is located in a row of seventeenth and eighteenth-century merchants' houses. It is a very pleasant and quiet hotel for business people and tourists alike. The friendly staff take great pains to ensure that guests enjoy their stay. All the rooms are individually and lovingly furnished in different styles. Some rooms have classical and antique furniture, others are more modern. All have the same degree of comfort. The rooms at the front have a fine view of the Herengracht, as does the spacious, pleasantly furnished lounge. There is a splendid collection of antique furniture scattered through the hotel.
Facilities: bar, room service, telephone and T.V. in room.

Hotel Cok (First Class)

Koninginneweg 34–36, 1075 C Z Amsterdam
Tel.: (020) 664 61 11
Fax: (020) 664 53 04
Rooms: 40
Location: District 2

The lobby of Hotel Cok is in the Tourist Class building. First Class guests stay in a separate building, where the luxury restaurant is located and where breakfast is also served. In the light corridors of the hotel there are temporary art exhibitions. The spacious rooms are modern, colourful and tastefullly furnished, and equipped with all modern conveniences. The hotel is situated a little way from the centre, near the Vondelpark.
Facilities: bar, baby-sitting service, meeting rooms, shop, room service, telephone and T.V. in room, wheelchair access with help.

Over _f_ 300

Hotel Pulitzer (Golden Tulip)

Prinsengracht 315–331, 1016 G Z Amsterdam
Tel.: (020) 22 83 33
Fax: (020) 27 67 53
Telex: 16508
Rooms: 241
Location: District 5

The Pulitzer Hotel occupies a total of twenty-four characteristic houses, completely joined together inside. There are a large number of excellent facilities, especially for business people. The Pulitzer Art Gallery has exhibitions all year round, and there are regular garden and chamber concerts. All this gives the hotel a unique atmosphere. Compared with the splendid gardens, the communal rooms, the art collection and the other communal areas, the guest rooms are something of a disappointment. They are equipped with every conceivable facility, but are by no means always spacious. The great majority are upholstered in brown and orange, a combination which in this day and age no longer fits such an artistic environment.

Facilities: bar, restaurant, coffee shop, business centre, secretarial service, fax, telex, meeting/conference areas, apartments, telephone and T.V. in room, minibar, room service.

Doelen Crest Hotel

Nieuwe Doelenstraat 24, 1012 C P Amsterdam
Tel.: (020) 22 07 22
Fax: (020) 22 10 84
Telex: 14399
Room: 86
Location: District 1

One of the oldest hotels in Amsterdam; in one of the houses now occupied by the hotel, Rembrandt painted the 'Nightwatch'. The monumental staircase, the galleries and the hotel lobby are well preserved and richly furnished with priceless antiques. The corridors and the guest rooms, however, make a rather cluttered impression. Many rooms are quite small in proportion to the price, dark and badly furnished. The approximately twenty renovated rooms, however, are pleasant, light and comfortable. All the rooms are gradually being refurbished.

Facilities: English pub, restaurant, conference/reception rooms, secretarial service, fax, telex, T.V. and telephone in rooms.

American Hotel

Leidsekade 97, 1017 PN Amsterdam
Tel.: (020) 24 53 22
Fax: (020) 25 32 36
Telex: 12545
Rooms: 188
Location: District 4

The distinctive American Hotel is in the Leidseplein, Amsterdam's liveliest square, next to the Municipal Theatre. Built between 1900 and 1902, it has been a listed building since 1972, rating as an important example of Art Nouveau. The hotel and café-restaurant have separate entrances, but the Art Nouveau café-restaurant serves as the breakfast room for guests. During the rest of the day it is much frequented by Amsterdammers. In the latest remodelling an attempt was made to restore the Art Nouveau feeling to the guest rooms. Both the rooms and the spacious lounge are tasteful, modern and comfortably furnished. The whole hotel has a very pleasant atmosphere.

Facilities: restaurant, bar, sauna, fitness centre, meeting/reception rooms, secretarial service, telex, fax, T.V. and telephone in rooms, room service, minibar.

Over ƒ 400

Amstel Hotel (Intercontinental)

Prof. Tulpplein 1, 1018 GX Amsterdam
Tel.: (020) 22 60 60
Fax: (020) 22 58 08
Telex: 11004
Rooms: 111

When the Amstel opened its doors to the public in 1867, it was the Netherlands' first Grand Hotel. It has a superb location directly on the River Amstel. Unfortunately much of the original interior has been sacrificed to the comfort of guests. The monumental lobby, however, can still bear comparison with the reception area of a good many palaces. The other communal areas also have an air of grandeur. At the beginning of the twentieth century private bathrooms were added to the rooms, at the cost of room space, which is accordingly somewhat small in relation to the price one pays.

Facilities: restaurant, brasserie, bar, conference/meeting rooms, fax, telex, secretarial service, private parking, T.V. and telephone in room, room service, minibar, wheelchair access with help.

Hotel de l'Europe
Nieuwe Doelenstraat 2–8, 1012 CP Amsterdam
Tel.: (020) 23 48 36
Fax: (020) 24 29 62
Telex: 12081
Rooms: 114
Location: District 1

In the heart of the city centre, with a splendid location on the Amstel, is the Hotel de l'Europe, opened in 1896. Despite the many necessary alterations over the years it has been able to preserve much of its nineteenth-century character. Both the hotel rooms and the communal areas are spacious, light and very distinctive. Everything the modern traveller or businessperson expects of a luxury metropolitan hotel is effortlessly provided. A nice touch is that the hotel has its own patisserie; the cakes and petit-fours made there are served in the lobby at tea-time. The Excelsior Restaurant has the reputation of being one of the better eating establishments in Amsterdam. The hotel has a pleasant terrace overlooking the Amstel.

Facilities: restaurant, coffee shop, bar, swimming pool, sauna, fitness centre, limousine service, business centre, meeting/conference rooms, secretarial service, T.V. and telephone in room, room service, minibar.

CAMPING

There are various places to camp in Amsterdam, some of which are listed below. Naturally all campsites have the usual amenities, such as shops, electricity, sanitation, washing facilities, etc. Some also rent out cabins for four people. The 'Gaasper' also has tents for hire.

The campsites in the city are close to the river IJ , that is, between the centre of town and the beautiful region of Waterland north of Amsterdam. They can be reached from the centre by bus in fifteen minutes.

Vliegenbos, Meeuwenlaan 138, 1022 AM Amsterdam, tel. (020) 36 88 55. Open: 1 April–30 September. Four-person huts with cooking facilities for hire (maximum three nights). Also a small restaurant, a covered terrace and a picnic area.

Zeeburg, Zuider IJdijk 44, 1095 KN Amsterdam, tel. (020) 94 44 30. Open: 1 April–30 September. Besides four-person cabins, tents and bikes for hire. Breakfast served, bar with terrace.

For those wanting to camp in beautiful green surroundings, there are the following two sites on the edge of the city:

Gaasper, Loosdrechtdreef 7, 1108 AZ Amsterdam, tel. (020) 96 73 26. Open all year round. This site is on the south-east edge of town, close to the A9 and 500 metres from the last station on the metro (twenty minutes to the centre). The wood and lakeland area, the 'Gaasperplas' adjoining the site, provides opportunities for walking, swimming, rowing and windsurfing. Restaurant, washing machines.

Het Amsterdamse Bos, Kleine Noorddijk 1, 1432 CC Aalsmeer, tel. (020) 41 68 68. Open: 1 April–30 September. This site is also close to the A9, but on the the south-west edge of town (about thirty minutes by bus to the centre), on the southern fringes of the Amsterdamse Bos, the huge municipal park which offers various sports and recreational facilities. Snackbar, fishing, no dogs allowed.

MONEY

The unit of currency
The Dutch unit of currency is the guilder (abbreviated as f, fl or Hfl). There are 5-cent, 10-cent, 25-cent, f 1, f 2.50 and f 5 coins. (Amounts in cents are rounded up or down: for example 97 cents becomes 95 cents and 98 cents becomes f 1.) Banknotes are issued in denominations of f 5, f 10, f 25, f 50, f 100, f 250 and f 1,000.

Changing money
You can change money at all banks in Amsterdam and at GWK *bureaux de change*. Most banks are open Monday–Friday, 9 a.m.–4 p.m.; some stay open till 5 p.m. and also on Thursday evenings, till 9 p.m. There are GWK branches at various points in the city:
– in the Central Station, open all week, 24 hours;
– in the metro station of the Central Station, Monday–Saturday, 7.30 a.m.–8 p.m. and Sundays, 9.30 a.m.–5 p.m.;
– at the Amstel Station, Monday–Saturday, 8 a.m.–8 p.m (Thursdays till 9 p.m.) and Sundays, 10 a.m.–6 p.m.;
– in the KLM office on the Leidseplein, Monday–Friday, 8.30 a.m.– 5.30 p.m. and Saturdays, 10 a.m.–2 p.m.

The banks and GWK branches give the best value for money. You will also find *bureaux de change* throughout the centre of town, but they are quite expensive. The exchange rates may sometimes look attractive, but the high commission charge is not indicated. Change Express, American Express and Thomas Cook are among the affordable exceptions.

Travellers cheques can be changed everywhere.

Credit cards
Although the use of credit cards is becoming more and more widespread in Amsterdam, you will still always need cash. Many shops, hotels, cafés, restaurants, etc. still do not accept them, or only do so if you spend a certain minimum amount. Places where you can use credit cards usually accept one or more of the major cards, such as American Express, Diners Club, Eurocard/Mastercard or Visa. If you want to draw cash on your credit card, you can do so at most *bureaux de change* (not at banks, except for the NMB Bank, which accepts Euro/Mastercard only). GWK branches charge no extra commission.

TRANSPORT IN AND AROUND AMSTERDAM

MUNICIPAL PUBLIC TRANSPORT

Information points for the Amsterdam Municipal Transport Authority (GVB):
- the GVB information kiosk, directly opposite the entrance to the Central Station (next to the VVV information office). Opening hours: Monday–Friday, 7 a.m.–11.30 p.m.;
- the GVB office in the Scheepvaarthuis, Prins Hendrikkade 108. Opening hours: Monday–Friday, 8.30 a.m.–4.30 p.m.;
- the GVB information window in the Amstel Station. Opening hours: Monday–Friday, 7 a.m.–8.30 p.m.; Saturday and Sunday, 10.15 a.m. –5 p.m.;
- telephone information: (020) 27 27 27, 8 a.m.–11 p.m. daily.

With its sixteen tram routes, thirty bus routes and two metro lines, the GVB covers the whole city. From approximately 6 a.m. until midnight most services run at between seven and fifteen-minute intervals.
The metro has only a few stations in the centre and after Amstel Station continues on into the suburbs. The buses (reddish-brown for local, yellow for regional) usually have final destinations in the suburbs or in the surrounding towns. A number of these buses will take you through the city centre, but usually follow the tram routes and use the same stops as the trams. If you are in Amsterdam as a tourist, you will probably be concentrating on the centre of town, and in that case the tram is the most suitable and the most typically Amsterdam means of transport.

How do you find the way?

On a good map of the city (available from the VVV) you will find all the routes and stops for public transport. At the GVB information points you can obtain a brochure on public transport in Amsterdam (in French, German and English). The brochure contains among other things a map giving not only all tram, bus and metro routes, but also the principal sights, such as museums, theatres, etc. In addition many bus and tram shelters have a map of the whole public transport system and a separate map showing the night routes. At every stop there is a yellow sign showing which numbers stop there and the routes they follow after that stop. In the trams, buses and in the metro trains there are also diagrams showing the stops and important destinations *en route*.

At the stop you can wave down trams and buses by raising your hand. Only on the buses do you have to get on at the front and show your ticket to the driver. On the trams you can if you wish stamp your ticket yourself in the yellow stamping machines which are always at the back of the tram and sometimes also halfway along.

Ticketing system

Throughout the Netherlands the same system is used, the so-called *strippenkaart*, an oblong ticket with numbered strips. You may have some trouble with this ticket at first, just as happened when it was introduced all over the country some years ago, so we shall give a brief explanation.

The distances you travel on the bus or the tram are divided into zones, and the number of zones you travel determines the number of strips you use. Now comes the illogical bit: for each journey you stamp one more strip than the number of zones you are travelling. So, if you are travelling one zone, you stamp two strips, two zones, three strips, and so on.

Stamping the strip is done as follows: you count the number of zones you want to travel from the top of the strip card downwards, fold it and put the next strip into the automatic ticket stamping machine. The preceding strips – those with the lower numbers – are then automatically valid. You can use one strip card for more than one person by counting off the same number of zones and stamping again. You can change buses or trams: the stamp remains valid until the time indicated.

If you stay in the centre of Amsterdam, you will not be travelling more than one zone. Outside things get more complicated, but don't hesitate to ask the driver for help: most Amsterdammers are also unsure how many zones they have to stamp in such cases.

Prices

Small strip cards for one-off use can be bought from the driver of a bus or tram, as well as cards with ten strips. However, this is almost twice as expensive as buying the strip card in advance. Cards can be bought in advance from the GVB information points (see p. 265), post offices, tobacconists and from railway ticket windows.

If you make a lot of use of public transport, a *dagkaart* (daily travel card) might work out cheaper. This gives you unlimited travel on the Amsterdam transport network for one day for *f* 8.85. Tickets for more than one day (*meerdagenkaarten*) are also available (two days cost *f* 11.50, three days *f* 14.50, and each additional day costs *f* 2.50). Do not forget to stamp your daily travel card on your first journey; otherwise it is not valid. Daily travel cards are available from bus- and tram-drivers and from advance sales points. Travel cards for more than one day are available only from advance sales points.

There is a reasonable chance that an inspector will check that you have a valid ticket: teams of uniformed inspectors will board the bus or tram. The fine for travellling without a ticket is *f* 26,50.

Night buses

After the 'ordinary' metro, tram and bus services have stopped running, it is possible to use one of the eight different night buses. All of these night buses leave from the Central Station, and each goes to a different suburb before returning to the station by the same route. Four of them (73, 74, 75 and 76) go right across the centre of town. At bus stops the numbers of night buses are indicated in a black square. The buses usually run every half hour, but note that only on Fridays and Saturdays does the service operate all night, and even then the drivers take half an hour's break, some time between 2 a.m. and 3 a.m. On other nights there is no service between approximately 2.15 a.m. and 4.15 a.m.

If you want to use the night bus, you can get a timetable in advance from one of the GVB information points or ring the GVB information line (till 11 p.m.).

The fares on the night buses are slightly higher than those during the day. Strip cards can also be used. Travel cards for one or more days are also valid for the following night.

TAXIS

The telephone number of the taxi switchboard is 77 77 77.

Besides this central number, you can also call one of a number of taxi ranks. These are given in the telephone directory, although you will need to know your way round Amsterdam, to know the best rank to call. The advantage of doing this, however, is that at busy times particularly you will get a taxi much more quickly; if you call the central switchboard you are often held in a long queue. The disadvantage is that it will be more difficult to trace the taxi if you leave something behind in it.

Late at night, between 4 a.m. and 6 a.m., when the discos close, it can be difficult to get hold of a taxi in the entertainment centres in the Leidseplein and the Rembrandtplein. There are sometimes queues a couple of hundred metres long.

Taxis are also quite expensive in Amsterdam. A tip is officially included in the fare, but an extra tip – approximately 10 per cent of the fare – is usually given.

Water taxis

A short while ago a water taxi service was introduced in Amsterdam. It is not yet an established means of transport, and is best regarded as an ideal combination of transport and sight-seeing.

The Amsterdam water taxis are spacious, well-constructed boats with room for a maximum of seven people, with seats inside and outside. The raised bows with a ladder on the deck make it easy to get on or off almost anywhere in Amsterdam. Beer, wine and soft drinks can be bought on board; catering and guides can be arranged.

If you see a water taxi with the sign *vrij* up, you can hail it, but because there are still only a small number and because they are becoming increasingly popular, it is advisable to book in advance. Tel. (020) 27 88 28. Water taxis operate from 9 a.m. to 1 a.m. daily.

Fares: There is an initial fare of *f* 4.50 and a fixed extra charge of *f* 1.50 per minute (50 per cent more out of town). The company has one large boat (maximum 20 people; *f* 10 plus *f* 2.50 per minute; out of town: plus 50 per cent).

WATER BIKES

Although water bikes suggest amusement parks, in Amsterdam they can serve as an alternative means of transport. Spread throughout the canal ring there are five jetties where you can hire two- or four-person water bikes:

– in front of the Central Station;
– Leidsebosje, off the Leidseplein next to Hotel American;
– diagonally opposite the Rijksmuseum;
– Prinsengracht, in front of the Westerkerk, near the Anne Frank House;
– Keizersgracht, on the corner of the Leidsestraat.

Water bikes hired from the jetty in front of the Central Station must be returned there. Bikes hired from one of the other jetties can be left at whatever jetty you like (except the Central Station jetty).

At the jetties you can obtain a folder with descriptions of routes and a map of the canal ring. A bit of rain need not be a problem: the bikes have rain-shields.

Canal Bike (tel. (020) 26 55 61) is open daily: in summer from 9 a.m. to 11 p.m. and before and after high season from 9 a.m. to 7 p.m. (it sometimes stays open during mild winters). Prices: two-person bikes ƒ 18.50 per hour; four-person bikes ƒ 27.50. Deposit: ƒ 50.

CARS

As we have seen, driving a car in Amsterdam traffic is no fun. It is difficult to get about fast; bikes are definitely a more agreeable and even faster means of transport. Be careful of the trams: they only have to give way when you are on a major road and they are not.

The greatest problem for car-owners is parking: it is always very difficult finding a parking spot in the centre and illegal parking can be very expensive (for the addresses of covered car parks, see p. 249). Day and night, tow trucks patrol the city to remove illegally parked cars. Cars towed away are taken to a supervised car pound in the eastern dock area. You can pick up your car from there twenty-four hours a day. The address is: Dienst Parkeerbeheer, Oostelijke Handelskade 2. Information on towed-away cars: (020) 25 57 06.

The high charge (over ƒ 200) must always be paid on the spot. Foreign money and credit cards are accepted. (Note that if you don't pick up your car within twelve hours, you pay a considerable amount extra for each succeeding twelve hours.) If you are parked too long on a parking meter or near an automatic parking-ticket dispenser, you run the risk of being wheel-clamped. The clamp will make it impossible for you to drive away, and only after you have paid the small fine at one of the offices of the Dienst Parkeerbeheer will the clamp be removed. The office where you have to pay will be given on the yellow sticker the traffic wardens fix to your windscreen. At the office you will have to tell them where your car is parked and give its registration number. Information on clamping: (020) 523 31 15.

The Dutch motorists' organization is the ANWB, Museumplein 5, 1071 DJ Amsterdam, tel. (020) 73 08 44. Open Monday–Friday, 8.45 a.m.–4.15 p.m.; Saturdays, 8.45 a.m.–12 p.m. They can also help you if you have a breakdown: call the Wegenwacht, tel. 26 82 51, twenty-four-hour service; membership of a foreign motoring organization also entitles you to free help.

Car hire

If you want to hire a car, you will find that a worldwide development has also affected Amsterdam: hiring a car without a credit card is virtually impossible. The number of stolen hire cars seems to have increased alarmingly in recent years, so that most hire-car companies are not all that keen on foreign customers; foreigners are difficult to trace.

In Amsterdam there are only a few companies one can use without a credit card. You have a reasonable chance at Kaspers and Lotte, Van Ostadestraat 232, 1073 TT Amsterdam (District 8), tel. (020) 71 07 33. Two other (cheaper) hire-companies require a person they can contact in the Netherlands: Adhé, Rijksstraatweg 40, 1115 AM Duivendrecht, tel. (020) 99 52 52 (the person must be a relative) and Ouke Baas, Van Ostadestraat 362–372, 1074 XA Amsterdam, tel. (020) 79 48 42 (even with a credit card you must have a person who can be contacted in the Netherlands).

Of course, the big international car-hire companies are also represented in Amsterdam: Avis (tel. (020) 564 16 33), Budget (tel. (020) 12 60 66), Europcar (tel. (020) 18 45 95), Hertz (tel. (020) 12 24 41) and Inter Rent (tel. (020) 662 66 14). These companies charge the so-called 'international rate', which is considerably higher than the local one.

A few other more reasonably priced care-hire firms are: Adam's Rent a Car, at various branches, including Nassaukade 344–347, 1053 LW Amsterdam, tel. (020) 85 01 11; Diks, whose branches include Van Ostadestraat 278–280, 1073 TW Amsterdam, tel. (020) 662 33 66; KAV, Johan Huizingalaan 91, 1065 HW Amsterdam, tel. (020) 14 14 35.

BICYCLES

As long as the weather is not too harsh, bikes are the ideal means of transport in Amsterdam. You can get anywhere in the centre within ten minutes, and bikes are also very suitable for making a tour of the surrounding area. Bike routes both in the city and outside are obtainable from the VVV.

For a reasonable sum (between ƒ 7 and ƒ 9 per day) bikes (usually with pedal-operated brakes) are available for hire, either for a few hours, by the day or longer. You should take your identification and enough money for the deposit (sometimes ƒ 100, sometimes ƒ 200).

Some addresses for bike-hire are:

Take a Bike, located beneath the Central Station, tel. (020) 24 83 91.

Koenders Rent Shop, Utrechtsedwarsstraat 105, 1017 VK, Amsterdam, tel. (020) 23 46 57

Rent-A-Bulldog Bike, Oudezijds Voorburgwal 126, 1012 GH Amsterdam, tel. (020) 24 82 48

Fiets-O-Fiets, Amstelveenseweg 880–900, 1081 JM Amsterdam, tel. (020) 44 54 73.

TRAINS

In the Netherlands
Information at railway stations and by telephone, tel. 06-899 11 31.
The Netherlands has a very extensive rail network. Trains are modern and comfortable, but not cheap; on most trains there is room to transport bikes.
The larger towns are linked by fast intercity services; booklets giving departure times are available free from stations.
At station ticket windows, apart from the usual single and return tickets, you can buy day and group tickets (two or more persons). If you have had no time to buy a ticket at one of the windows you can get one from the ticket-collector on the train (only singles and returns and you pay a little extra). A normal ticket is valid till 4 a.m. the following morning, so that you can also use it on the night services. You can interrupt your journey at any station, and continue on to your final destination later in the day.

Night trains
Between roughly 1 a.m. and 5 a.m. there are night trains, leaving every hour, between the larger towns in the western part of the Netherlands. They all follow the same route: Utrecht–Amsterdam–Schiphol–Leiden–The Hague–Delft–Rotterdam and back again. (Tickets from the previous day remain valid provided that you start your journey before 4 a.m.)

International
Information: International information counter at the Central Station. Open: Monday–Friday, 8 a.m.–10 p.m.; Saturdays and Sundays, 9 a.m.–8 p.m. It gets very busy in the summer!
Amsterdam Central Station has train connections with most large towns in Europe; on many routes there are night trains with sleeping facilities. On the routes to Central Europe (Austria, Switzerland) and Southern Europe (South of France, Italy and Yugoslavia) there are the so called 'car sleepers'.

REGIONAL BUSES

For information on regional bus transport to villages and towns in the vicinity of Amsterdam, telephone (020) 27 27 27 (7 a.m. to 11 p.m.).

International

Many travel agencies sell international bus tickets. There are two close together on the Dam and just round the corner, on the Rokin.

INTERNAL FLIGHTS

Information and reservations: (020) 74 77 47.

Though it is really a bit over the top to fly around a tiny country like the Netherlands (two-and-a-half hours on the train from Amsterdam takes you to the furthest corner of the country), it can be done, albeit on a limited scale. The only regular services are those operated by NLM and Netherlines between Amsterdam and Eindhoven (daily), Amsterdam and Maastricht (daily) and Eindhoven and Maastricht (weekdays only).

COMMUNICATIONS

POST
Letters and postcards

Most post offices in Amsterdam are open Monday–Friday, 9 a.m.–5 p.m. (closed Saturdays and Sundays). The address of the main PTT post office is: Nieuwezijds Voorburgwal 182, 1012 SJ Amsterdam. It is situated just behind the Palace on the Dam and its opening times are: Monday–Friday, 8.30 a.m.–6 p.m., Thursday evenings till 8 p.m. and Saturday mornings, 9 a.m.–12 p.m.

The post office at Oosterdokskade 3, close to the Central Station, is open daily till 8 p.m. On Saturday afternoons till 5 p.m. you can use the sub-post offices in the department stores De Bijenkorf (on the corner of the Dam and the Damrak) and Vroom en Dreesman (Kalverstraat, near the Munt).

Stamps for postcards (and sometimes also for letters) can often be bought from tobacconists.

Parcel post

The only two post offices that deal with parcel post are the main post office and the post office at Oosterdokskade 3, near the Central Station. At both one can buy sturdy boxes to send through the mail.

Poste restante

If not addressed to another post office in the Netherlands, all poste restante mail is sent to the main post office on the Nieuwezijds Voorburgwal. It is sufficient to address items: Poste Restante, Amsterdam, but it is safer and more correct to put:

Name of addressee
Poste-restante
Hoofdpostkantoor PTT
Nieuwezijds Voorburgwal 182
1012 SJ Amsterdam

Poste restante can be collected on production of suitable identification during normal post office opening hours.

Postal orders

Postal orders can be sent from any post office. If you yourself are waiting for a postal order, and are in a hurry, the best thing to do is to have it sent to you poste restante at the main post office. If you have the order sent to another address you will be notified by the PTT when it arrives, and will then have to let the PTT know which post office you wish to collect it from. All in all it takes about two days before you can get your money.

TELEPHONING

Information for the Netherlands: 008.
Information line for international calls (free): 06-04 18.
International operator: 06-04 10.
Telephone boxes take coins of f 0.25, f 1 and f 2.50; only unused whole units are returned. For calls within the Netherlands the procedure is as follows: wait for the dialling tone, insert the coins, dial the appropriate code, again wait for the dialling tone and then dial the subscriber's number. For local calls omit the STD code.

International calls

From all over the Netherlands, and hence also from Amsterdam, you can dial direct to more than 130 countries. Wait for the dialling tone, then dial 09 (the code for international calls), wait for the dialling code again, dial the country code, the area code (usually omitting the first digit, mostly an O) and finally the subscriber's number.

For some countries, including the USA, Australia, Canada and New Zealand, there is a so-called off-peak rate: calling those countries is cheaper at certain times than at others (mostly in the evenings, at night and early in the morning; for information ring 06-04 18).

If automatic dialling to a particular country is not possible, you can ask to be connected through Teleplus (06-04 10). You pay a higher rate if you use Teleplus for a call you could have made yourself automatically. In addition Teleplus deals with person-to-person, reverse charge and credit card calls.

Like almost everywhere in the world, calling from a hotel is quite expensive in Amsterdam. Telephone boxes are cheaper, but have the disadvantage of your needing the right change or having to wait in a queue. The cheapest and often the most convenient place for making international telephone calls is Telehouse, Raadhuisstraat 48, 1016 DG Amsterdam, tel. (020) 74 36 54. Open seven days a week, twenty-four hours a day. Telephone directories for the Netherlands and the whole of Western Europe can be consulted here.

TELEGRAMS, TELEX, FAX

For all these means of communication (as well as for memocom and viditel) one can use 'Telehouse' twenty-four hours a day seven days a week (see Telephones). You can also receive telex and fax messages through Telehouse without having a telex or fax machine of your own. To do so you can use the following numbers: for telex 11 101 TELEH NL or 15 470 TELEH NL; for fax (020) 26 38 71 or 26 53 26. The sender must supply, along with your name, the telephone number of the address you are staying at. You will be notified by telephone as soon as a message has arrived.

SPORTS, SAUNAS AND FITNESS CENTRES

For all inquiries connected with sport in the widest sense, you can approach the Amsterdamse Sportraad (Amsterdam Sports Council), P.O. Box 63150, 1005 LD Amsterdam, tel. (020) 83 07 91.

To make things easier for you there follows a fairly random selection of what is on offer in the sporting line, both for players and spectators.

PARTICIPATORY SPORTS

Billiards, pool and snooker

You will find billiard tables in many Amsterdam cafés, and coffee shops often have a pool table.

Biljartcentrum, Nieuwendijk 120–122, 1012 MS Amsterdam. tel. (020) 23 57 31. Open 11 a.m.–6 p.m. daily. Atmospheric hall with seven billiard tables and one snooker table.

Bavaria, Van Ostadestraat 97, 1071 ST Amsterdam, tel. (020) 76 40 59. Opening hours: for snooker and pool, 11 a.m.–1 p.m. daily; for billiards, Tuesday–Friday, 10 a.m.–1 p.m.; closed Saturdays, Sundays and Mondays after 6 p.m. Two separate floors, one with six snooker tables and a pool table, one with thirteen billiard tables.

De Keizers Snookerclub, Keizersgracht 256, 1016 EV Amsterdam. tel. (020) 23 15 86. Open 12 p.m.–1 a.m. daily, non-members allowed. Canal-side house with eight snooker tables in different rooms.

De Keu, Eerste Helmersstraat 5, 1054 CX Amsterdam, tel. (020) 16 61 56. Open 7 p.m.–1 a.m. daily (Fridays and Saturdays till 2 a.m.). Seven pool tables and a small billiard table with a bar in a fairly dark but friendly hall. Evocative 1970s and 1980s music.

Bowling
Knijn Bowlingcentrum, Scheldeplein 3, 1078 GR Amsterdam, tel. (020) 664 22 11. Open 10 a.m.–1 a.m. daily; Saturdays and Sundays till 2 a.m.

Golf
The city's three golf courses are all nine-hole:

Sportpark de Weeren, Volendammerweg 316, 1027 EA Amsterdam, tel. (020) 32 55 58 (no certificate of competence required).

Sportpark Overamstel, Ouderkerkerdijk 148, 1096 CR Amsterdam, tel. (020) 665 18 63.

Posher and more expensive: Amsterdamse Golf Club, Zwarte Laantje 4, 1099 CE Amterdam, tel. (020) 94 36 50.

Jogging
The favourite city park for jogging is the Vondelpark, in the centre of town (about 4 km per lap). On the southern outskirts of town is the much bigger Amsterdamse Bos, where it is much quieter; routes and various distances are marked.

Horseriding
Hollandse Manege, Vondelstraat 140, 1054 GT Amsterdam, tel. (020) 18 09 42. In the middle of town, with only indoor lessons. Individual and group rides.

Amstelland Manege, Jan Tooropplantsoen 17, 1182 AC Amstelveen, tel. (020) 43 24 68. Indoor and outdoor lessons, individual and group. Outdoor rides on Sundays.

De Amsterdamse Manege, Nieuwe Kalfjeslaan 25, 1182 AA Amstelveen, tel. (020) 43 13 42. Only group rides for between two and ten people through the Amsterdamse Bos.

Squash
There are two squash centres in the centre of town (both with saunas):

Squash City, Ketelmakerstraat 6, 1013 DE Amsterdam, tel. (020) 26 78 83. Open 9 a.m.–midnight daily; Tuesdays and Thursdays from 7 a.m.

Sporting Club Leidseplein, Korte Leidsedwarsstraat 18. 1017 RC Amsterdam, tel. (020) 20 66 31. Open 9 a.m.–midnight daily. (Also fitness centre and aerobics.)

Amsterdam Squash Rackets Club, Frans Ottenstadion, Stadionstraat 10, 1076 NL Amsterdam, tel. (020) 662 87 67. Open 9 a.m.–11 p.m. daily; Saturdays and Sundays till 6 p.m. (Also for tennis.)

Swimming
When the weather allows you can swim in a number of lakes and rivers. On the Kinselmeer (Amsterdam-North) and on the beautiful Gaasperplas there are facilities such as lawns, restaurants and toilets.
Close to the Amsterdamse Bos you can swim in the Bosbaan and in the Nieuwe Meer (no facilities).
The Amsterdam canals have not been a suitable place for a dip for a long time, but if you follow the river Amstel south till you get out of town, there is good swimming.
Just north of Amsterdam, between Oostzaan and Landsmeer, is the recreational area 'Het Twiske'. There you can also hire canoes, sailboards and sailing and rowing-boats. This area of greenery and water is easy to get to: by bus from the Central Station (twenty minutes; every half hour) or by bike (about forty minutes; via Landsmeer). Information: Beheersbureau 'Het Twiske', Noorderlaaikade, 1511 BX Oostzaan, tel. (02984) 43 38. Boat-hire: tel. (02984) 48 90.
The opening times of Amsterdam swimming pools vary throughout the year. This applies to both indoor and outdoor pools. Weather permitting, the latter are open from May till October. It is best to ring up before you go.
Except for the Mirandabad, outdoor pools are usually closed in the evenings.
Two indoor pools in the centre of town are:

Marnixbad, Marnixplein 9, 1015 ZM Amsterdam, tel. (020) 25 48 43. No-nonsense swimming pool for young and old on the edge of the Jordaan.

Zuiderbad, Hobbemastraat 26, 1071 ZC Amsterdam, tel. (020) 79 22 17. A very atmospheric old swimming pool, where many students and business people come to swim a few lengths. Close to the big museums.

For both indoor and outdoor swimming:

De Mirandabad, De Mirandalaan 9, 1079 PA Amsterdam, tel. (020) 42 80 80 (outdoor pool: 94 66 37). The indoor pool has a tropical feel with a wave pool, whirlpool, chute and a children's pool.

The Sloterparkbad, Slotermeerlaan 2, 1064 HB Amsterdam, tel. (020) 11 45 65 (outdoor pool: 13 37 00). 50-metre pools both indoors and outdoors, also suitable for small children.

Outdoor pool only:

Jan van Galenbad, Jan van Galenstraat 315, 1056 CB Amsterdam, tel. (020) 12 80 01. Simple outdoor pool with pleasant sun lawn; children's pool.

Table Tennis
Your can play table tennis at among other places the following addresses. Changing rooms, showers, bar, bats and balls available.

Het Tafeltennishuis, Overtoom 505, 1054 LH Amsterdam, tel. (020) 85 13 24. Open Friday–Monday, 2 p.m.–6 p.m., Tuesdays, Wednesdays and Thursdays until 1 a.m.

Leoos Tafeltenniscentrum, Eerste Marnixplantsoen 1, 1015 ZH Amsterdam, tel. (020) 24 22 87. Open Monday–Friday, 3 p.m.–1 a.m., Saturday till 7 p.m., closed Sundays.

Tafeltennis Centrum Amsterdam, Keizersgracht 209, 1016 DT Amsterdam, tel. (020) 24 57 80. Open 1 p.m.–1 a.m. (Mondays till 6 p.m.).

Tennis

Obviously, outdoor tennis in the Netherlands is heavily dependent on the weather. In the period November–March at any rate one has to use indoor courts. If you want to play tennis in Amsterdam, it is a good idea to ring or write to the 'Tennispool'. They can provide everything in the tennis line: courts, partners, coaching, rackets and tennis wear. De Tennispool, Kollenbergweg 2, 1101 AS Amsterdam, tel. (020) 91 16 07. Available on phone Monday–Friday, 8.30 a.m.–5 p.m.

If you want to book a court for yourself you can try one of the following centres:

Amstelpark, Karel Lotsylaan 8, 1082 LS Amsterdam, tel. (020) 44 54 36.

Goldstar, Karel Lotsylaan 20, 1081 HW Amsterdam, tel. (020) 44 56 65.

Frans Ottenstadion, see under Squash.

Watersports

There are numerous ponds and lakes in the vicinity of Amsterdam, as well as of course the IJsselmeer, the former Zuiderzee, with its historic harbours. Water enough then.

Addresses for boat-hire in Amsterdam:

Bosch Windsurfing, Jollenpad 10, 1081 KC Amsterdam, tel. (020) 44 96 96. On the Nieuwe Meer. Only sailboards.

Watersport Twellegea, Nieuwendammerdijk 284, 1023 BT Amsterdam, tel. (020) 32 48 77. In Amsterdam-North, close to the IJsselmeer. From small motorboats and sailing dinghies, up to large yachts, with or without a skipper.

In the Amsterdamse Bos, just outside town, you can hire canoes.

Outside Amsterdam:

Recreation area 'Het Twiske' (north of the town, see under Swimming), tel. (02984) 48 90. Hire of canoes, sailboards, sailing dinghies and rowing-boats.

On the Vinkeveen lakes (south of Amsterdam): Klinkhamer, Baamburgse Zuwe 202a, 3645 AM Vinkeveen, tel. (02949) 15 45. Hire of rowing-boats, motorboats and sailing boats.

WATCHING SPORT

The following list gives a selection of international-class sporting events:

Motor racing: Easter races on the Zandvoort track; March–April.

Motorcycling: Assen TT; end of June.

Showjumping: Jumping Amsterdam, held in November in the RAI complex.

Chess: Hoogovens Chess Tournament in Wijk aan Zee; January.

Tennis: ABN International Tournament in Rotterdam; February. Continental Grass Court Championship in Rosmalen; June. Netherlands International Tennis Championships in Hilversum; July/August.

Football: the Dutch professional football season runs from mid-August to mid-May (with a short break for Christmas and New Year). On average you can watch the Amsterdam team, Ajax, play at home once every two weeks. Amsterdam 700 is an annual international football tournament that takes place in August.

Cycling: Amstel Gold Race; ridden in Limburg (in the south of the Netherlands), usually in April.

SAUNAS AND FITNESS CLUBS

Amsterdam has dozens of sauna and fitness centres. Many centres have both facilities. A sample of what is available:

The Garden, Jodenbreestraat 158, 1011 NS Amsterdam, tel. (020) 26 87 72. A centre with an international clientele, with sauna, Turkish bath, whirlpool, sunroom, massage, weight-lifting equipment and aerobic and fitness training. Open Mondays, Wednesdays and Fridays, 9 a.m.–11 p.m., Tuesdays and Thursdays, from 12 p.m., and Saturdays and Sundays, 11 a.m.–7 p.m. (in summer closed on Saturdays).

Kime, Martelaarsgracht 18, 1012 TR Amsterdam, tel. (020) 22 59 10. A brand-new centre with sauna, Turkish bath, whirlpool, solarium, massage, weight training, aerobics and fitness training, beauty salon, etc. Open Mondays, 12–10 p.m., Tuesday–Friday, 10 a.m.–10 p.m. and Saturdays and Sundays, 12–6 p.m.

Splash, Kattengat 1, 1012 SZ Amsterdam, tel. (020) 27 10 44. Popular with Amsterdammers in their twenties and thirties. Sauna, Turkish bath, whirlpool, sunbed, massage, weight training, aerobics and fitness training. Open Mondays, Wednesdays and Fridays, 7.30 a.m.–10 p.m., Tuesdays and Thursdays, 10 a.m.–10 p.m. and Saturdays and Sundays, 12–6 p.m.

Sauna 74, Amstel 107, 1018 EM Amsterdam, tel. (020) 22 75 04. A cheap place with sauna, Turkish bath, whirlpool, sunbeds, massage, weight-lifting equipment, aerobics, fitness training. The saltwater relaxation tank is the only one in the city. Open Monday–Friday, 11 a.m.–11 p.m., Saturdays and Sundays from 2 p.m.

Sauna only:

Deco, Herengracht 115, 1015 DA Amsterdam, tel. (020) 23 82 15. Marvellous relaxation centre with 1920s Art Deco interior. Sauna, Turkish bath, plunge bath, sunbeds, massage. Open Monday–Saturday, 4–11 p.m. and Sundays, 1–6 p.m.

Damrak, Damrak 54, 1012 LL Amsterdam, tel. (020) 22 60 12. Men only. Sauna, Turkish bath, aqua-sauna, whirlpool, sunbed, rapid-tanner, massage. Open Monday–Friday, 10 a.m.–11 p.m., Saturday till 6 p.m.; closed Sundays.

Kylpy, Mercatorplein 25, 1057 BZ Amsterdam, tel. (020) 12 34 96. Women only. Sauna, Turkish bath, aqua-sauna, whirlpool, sunbed, rapid-tanner and massage. Open Monday–Saturday, 10 a.m.–11 p.m; closed Sundays (in the summer also closed on Saturdays).

USEFUL ADDRESSES

Police: (020) 22 22 22.
Ambulance: (020) 555 55 55.
Fire brigade: (020) 21 21 21.

First aid
Onze Lieve Vrouwe (OLV) Gasthuis (Amsterdam-East), 1e Oosterparkstraat 179, 1091 HA Amsterdam, tel. (020) 599 91 11.

St Lucas Ziekenhuis (Amsterdam-West), Jan Tooropstraat 164, 1061 AE Amsterdam, tel. (020) 510 89 11.

Doctors/dentists
Centrale Doktersdienst, twenty-four hours a day, tel. (020) 664 21 11 or 79 18 21. They will put you in touch with a duty doctor or dentist in your area (dentists from 8 a.m. till 10.30 p.m. only).

Dispensing chemists
Open Monday–Friday, 9 a.m.–5.30 p.m. Outside these times there is

one chemist open for prescriptions in each district of Amsterdam. For information ring the Centrale Doktersdienst, tel. (020) 664 21 11 or 79 18 21 (twenty-four hours a day).

Lost property
In the street: Police 'Lost Property', Waterlooplein 11, 1011 NV Amsterdam, tel. (020) 559 80 05, open Monday–Friday, 12–3.30 p.m. At weekends you can try the police station in the district where the item was lost.

Metro, trams and buses: Gemeentelijk Vervoer Bedrijf (GVB), Prins Hendrikkade 108, 1011 AK Amsterdam, tel. (020) 511 44 08, open Monday–Friday, 9 a.m.–4 p.m. If you lose something, it will only be possible to find out the following day between 2 p.m. and 4 p.m. whether it has been found.

Trains: Nederlandse Spoorwegen (NS), 'Lost Property' information, Amsterdam Central Station, Stationsplein 15, 1012 AB Amsterdam, tel. (020) 557 85 44, open twenty-four hours a day. After ten days all items are sent to a special department for the whole of the Netherlands. Address: Nederlandse Spoorwegen, Afdeling Verloren Voorwerpen, Concordiastraat 70, 3551 EM Utrecht.

CONSULATES AND EMBASSIES

Australia (Embassy): Koninginnegracht 23, 2514 AB The Hague, tel. (070) 363 09 83.
Canada (Embassy): Sophialaan 7, 2514 JP The Hague, tel. (070) 361 41 11.
Federal Republic of Germany (Consulate): de Lairessestraat 172, 1075 HN Amsterdam, tel. (020) 73 62 45.
France (Consulate): Vijzelgracht 2, 1017 HR Amsterdam, tel. (020) 24 83 46.
Italy (Consulate): Herengracht 609, 1017 CE Amsterdam, tel. (020) 24 00 43.
Japan (Consulate): Keizersgracht 634, 1017 ER Amsterdam, tel. (020) 24 35 81.
New Zealand (Embassy): Mauritskade 25, 2514 HD The Hague, tel. (070) 346 93 24.
United Kingdom (Consulate): Koningslaan 44, 1075 AE Amsterdam. tel. (020) 76 43 43.
United States of America (Consulate): Museumplein 19, 1017 DJ Amsterdam, tel. (020) 664 56 61.

OTHER ADDRESSES

Baby-sitting service

Babysit-centrale Kriterion, 2e Rozendwarsstraat 24 huis, 1016 PE Amsterdam, tel. (020) 24 58 48, reachable daily, 5.30–7.30 p.m.

Libraries

British Council Library: Keizersgracht 343, 1016 EH Amsterdam. tel. (020) 22 36 44. Open Monday–Friday, 11 a.m.–4.45 p.m.
Public Library: Prinsengracht 587, 1016 HT Amsterdam, tel. (020) 26 50 65. Open Monday–Friday, 10 a.m.–5 p.m. and 7–10 p.m. (Mondays from 1 p.m.); Saturdays, 10 a.m.–5 p.m.

University Library: Singel 425, 1012 WP Amsterdam, tel. (020) 525 23 26. Open Monday–Friday, 9.30 a.m.–12 a.m. (borrowing till 5.15 p.m.).

Select Bibliography on Amsterdam and the Netherlands

ARCHITECTURE

Amsterdam, an Architectural Lesson: edited by Maarten Kloos, photos by Jan Derwig; 118 pages. Amsterdam: Thoth Publishing House, 1988.
In the year when Amsterdam took its turn as the cultural capital of Europe, six prominent architects and town planners were invited to give their view of the development of the city. Beautifully illustrated.

Amsterdam Architecture: a Guide: edited by Guus Kemme, photos by Jan Derwig; 158 pages. Amsterdam: Thoth Publishing House, 1987.
A brief excursion through the capital's architectural history, from wooden dwellings to the most recent buildings.

Amsterdam Canal Guide: Hans Tulleners, Tim Killiam, Marieke van der Zeijden; 368 pages. Utrecht: Het Spectrum, 1978.
Contains about 300 drawings documenting the canal ring and its unique collection of houses. Concise information on period of construction, gable ornamentation and other relevant facts.

The Amsterdam School: Dutch Expressionist Architecture 1915-1930: Wim de Wit; 161 pages. New York: Cooper-Hewitt Museum/Cambridge, Massachusetts: The MIT Press, 1983.
A lavishly illustrated book on the exuberant early twentieth-century style, in which aesthetic concerns predominated.

Rietveld in Amsterdam: Dennis de Rond, Annemiek Terstal; 64 pages. Amsterdam: Uitgeverij Rietveld Academie/Rotterdam: Uitgeverij 010, 1988.
Chronological survey of all Rietveld's projects in Amsterdam and its immediate surroundings, providing a clear picture of his development.

PHOTOGRAPHY

Milky Way in Focus: Catrien Ariens; compiled by Cor Schlosser; 120 pages. Amsterdam: Bert Bakker, 1986.
An impression of performers and audiences in the famous 'Melkweg' cultural centre in Amsterdam, especially in the period 1980–85.

Paradiso Stills: Max Natkiel; text by Diana Ozon, edited by Stichting

Fragment Foto; 216 pages. Amsterdam, Fragment, 1986.
Photographic record of young visitors to the Paradiso pop temple in the years 1980–85.

24 hours Amsterdam: text by Rinus Ferdinandusse; 139 pages. London: Thames and Hudson, 1986.
Six of Holland's best photographers captured a day in Amsterdam on film; a chronological reportage.

HISTORY

Amsterdam: The Golden Age, 1275–1795: Renee Kistemaker and Roelof van Gelder; 280 pages. New York: Abbeville Press, 1983.
A wide-ranging, interesting book on the development of Amsterdam as a commercial centre.

The Embarrassment of Riches: an Interpretation of Dutch Culture in the Golden Age: Simon Schama; 698 pages. New York: Alfred A. Knopf, 1987.
Study of (mainly middle-class) thought and behaviour in the seventeenth-century Dutch Republic.

A Tour of the Anne Frank House in Amsterdam: A.C. Roodnat and M. de Klijn; 98 pages. Amsterdam: A. Frank Foundation, 1975.
A survey of the rise of fascism after the First World War and the course of the Second World War with the emphasis on the persecution of the Jewish population of the Netherlands.

ART AND CULTURE

Amsterdam Art Guide: Christian Reinewald; 119 pages. London: Art Guide, 1985.
A handy and original little guide containing the addresses of galleries, museums, cinemas, theatres, café's, art bookshops, etc. in Amsterdam.

Guide of the Jewish Historical Museum: edited by E. van Voolen, in collaboration with J. van Nes and P. Smeyer; 151 pages. The Hague: SDU Uitgeverij, 1988.
A guide to the history of the synagogue complex, summarizing the same story told at length in the museum itself.

A Guide to Jewish Amsterdam: Jan Stoutenbeek and Paul Vigeveno; 156 pages. Weesp: De Haan, 1985.
An introduction to the history of the Jewish community in Amsterdam is followed by a number of walks past buildings, objects and other interest-

ing spots (once) important in the daily life of that community.

Museum Guide for Amsterdam: Hans Vogel; 127 pages. Baarn: Bosch & Keuning, 1981.
Amsterdam may justly be called 'a city of museums', having more than forty. A book for enthusiasts.

Anne Frank Remembered: Miep Gies and Alison Leslie Gold; 254 pages. London: Corgi, 1988.
The story of Miep Gies, the woman who helped the Jewish Frank family during the German oocupation in the Second World War.

LITERATURE

The Assault: Harry Mulisch; 208 pages. Harmondsworth: Penguin, 1988.
A man who lost his family in the Second World War through a disastrous set of coincidences is confronted at various moments in his later life with the question of guilt. Amsterdam features prominently as the setting of much of the novel.

The Diary of Anne Frank: Anne Frank; 224 pages. London: Pan Books Ltd, 1954.
Diary in which a Jewish girl living in hiding in an Amsterdam canal house records her thoughts and emotions between the ages of thirteen and fifteen..

I'm Just Kidding: More of a Dutchman's Slight Adventures: Simon Carmiggelt; 94 pages. Amsterdam: De Arbeiderspers, 1972.
The author of this collection of stories was considered the chronicler *par excellence* of everyday life in Amsterdam. His short stories have an undertone of typically Dutch humour, are acutely observed and reveal a mild, melancholy outlook on life.

Last Call: Harry Mulisch; 288 pages. London: Collins Harvill, 1987.
An old man is cast in the leading role in a play about a dead actor. Modern Amsterdam gives him a fresh lease of life, but excessive identification with the main character proves his undoing.

Rituals: Cees Nooteboom; 145 pages. Baton Rouge, Harmondsworth: Viking, 1984.
A biting and moving portrait of a number of figures from the world of art dealing, share-trading, and the Dutch bourgeoisie of the 1950s and 1970s.

The Shame is Over: Anja Meulenbelt; 275 pages. London: The Women's Press, 1980.
A novel about the writer's personal history, designed to show that feminism is not just a theory but also a way of life.

MISCELLANEOUS

The Culinary Sleuth Amsterdam: Ben Ten Holter; 318 pages. Antwerpen-Utrecht: A.W. Bruna Uitgevers B.V., 1988.
Good restaurants, quality off-licences, choice greengrocers, the best patisseries, beer specialists, etc., arranged alphabetically and by type of establishment.

Hausboote = Houseboats = Woonboten: Franklin Hollander; 111 pages. Wiesbaden; Berlin: Bauverlag, 1983.
This photo book not only illustrates the many houseboats in Amsterdam, but also gives the reader a glimpse of the daily life of their occupants and provides concise information on the development of this stubbornly independent mode of living.

ISTA Guide to Amsterdam: Rafael Laudy, Lineke van Opzeeland, Anita van Schaick; 68 pages. Amsterdam: International Agency for Social Tourism Amsterdam, 1989.
A critical selection of café's, restaurants, discothèques and other reasonably priced establishments in the centre of town.

Living in Amsterdam: a City Protects its History Past: edited by Richter Roegholt. Amsterdam: J.C. Gieben/Stichting Amsterdam Monumentenstad 1987, 1987.
This book reveals Amsterdam's biggest secret: how it has been possible to preserve the old town centre.

Policing the Inner City; a Study of Amsterdam's Warmoesstraat: Maurice Punch; 231 pages. London: The Macmillan Press Ltd, 1979.
A study of the role, difficulties and mode of operation of the Amsterdam police in the city centre in the period 1974–6.

The Story of Amsterdam; an Explorer's Guide: Anthony van der Heyden; 126 pages. Amsterdam: Roodveldt Books, 1987.
This book, with more than three hundred colour photos, provides information on the history of important historical buildings in the capital. It focuses on details that most visitors are likely to miss on their sightseeing trips.

Notes on Contributors

Martin van Amerongen (1941) wrote Chapter 2, 'Amsterdam Today'. He is editor-in-chief of a quality weekly and contributes a regular column to a large Dutch evening paper. He has published twenty or so books, including a number of biographies and monographs.

Chapter 9 on 'The Performing Arts' was written by **Sue Baker**. She is a freelance journalist specializing in the field of film, theatre and art.

Erik van den Berg (1956) wrote the jazz section Chapter 10, 'Pop Music and Jazz'. He works as an art editor on one of the largest Dutch national dailies and contributes to various music magazines, specializing in jazz.

Raymond van den Boogaard (1951), who lives on the Keizersgracht and wrote 'The Canal Ring: From the Westermarkt to the Haarlemmerstraat' in Chapter 13, is a historian and at present works for a national evening paper. After a period as the paper's Moscow correspondent, he published a collection of articles on the Soviet Union.

Emma Brunt (1943) lives in the Nieuwmarkt quarter and contributed the section on 'The Wallen, the Nieuwmarkt and the Waterlooplein' to Chapter 13. Trained as a sociologist, she has published several books, including a collection of feminist articles and a survey of trends in the 1970s. She works as a journalist and publicist, writing for various magazines, but principally for the Netherlands' largest quality weekly.

Elena Manzano-Bunink (1939) wrote Chapter 5 on 'Shopping'. She worked for 15 years in the Netherlands as a freelance journalist for the *Holland Herald* and other publications. At present she is based in Paris.

Johannes van Dam (1946) wrote 'Eating Out' (Chapter 3) and 'The Canal Ring: From the Leidsestraat to the Westermarkt', in Chapter 13. For seven years he ran the Kookboekhandel in Amsterdam, a bookshop stocking virtually everything in the cookery field. He is a food writer and restaurant critic for various magazines and writes a daily column on Amsterdam in an Amsterdam paper.

Rob van den Dobbelsteen (1941) wrote 'Other Excursions', dealing with the principal towns around Amsterdam. A specialist in tourism, he writes for the Amsterdam daily *Het Parool* and other publications.

Dr Willem F. Heinemeijer (1922), the author of 'A History of Amsterdam' (Chapter 1), was born and bred in Amsterdam. He is an Emeritus Professor of the Amsterdam University, specializing in Urban Geography, and has published various books.

Guus Kemme (1958) wrote 'Architecture' (Chapter 7). Having studied art history, he graduated from a specialized publishing course, and went on to work in London for the art publishers Zwemmer Books. At present he is an editor with Gary Schwartz/SDU in the Netherlands.

Ghislain Kieft (1956), who wrote Chapter 6, 'Museums and Art', is an art historian. He teaches iconology at the University of Utrecht and works freelance for one of the largest national morning papers and for various (art) magazines.

Rob van Maanen (1950) lives on the edge of the area about which he wrote in 'The Canal Ring: From Artis to the Amstel' (Chapter 13). Since 1982 he has worked as a freelance photographer and since 1985 as a freelance publicist, in both cases mainly for specialist magazines serving the construction industry.

Alice Mielaert (1956) wrote the section 'The Jordaan' in Chapter 13. After graduating in Theatre Studies from the University of Amsterdam, she worked as a drama critic for various theatrical magazines. She is a playwright, and at present works as a freelance publicist.

'Hotels', in Chapter 16, was written jointly by **Pauline Oomen** (1960) and **Bart Sutorius** (1957), who also devised and conducted the hotel survey. Pauline Oomen is studying cultural anthropology, having previously worked for five years as an air hostess with the Netherlands' largest airline, getting to know hotels the world over. Bart Sutorius is a lawyer, at present completing a work placement with a London law firm, and as a seasoned globe-trotter has learned what makes a good hotel.

'The Canal Ring: From the Amstel to the Leidsestraat' in Chapter 13, was contributed by **Johan Polak** (1929) and **Frans Goddijn** (1956). Johan Polak is the Amsterdam-based ex-publisher of a renowned literary list, Frans Goddijn is a computer specialist and columnist. In 1988 they set up a writing partnership and since then have published reviews, columns and other material in newspapers and magazines on welfare work and information science.

The account of 'The 'Pijp' in Chapter 13 was written by **Monika Sauwer** (1946), who herself lives in the area. She has published three collections of stories and two novels, in which the Amsterdam setting plays an important part.

Gert van Veen wrote about 'Pop Music and Jazz'. He studied music in Utrecht and is a popular music correspondent of one of the largest national morning newspapers.

Petra Weeda (1948) lives in the Concertgebouw area and wrote about the Concertgebouw quarter (except for the section on the Vondelpark) in Chapter 13. She has worked for ten years on a fortnightly magazine inspired by anthroposophical thinking.

Vincent Westzaan, the editor of this guide, wrote the 'Introduction: Welcome to Amsterdam', 'Organised Tourism' (Chapter 11), 'Holidays and Special Events' (Chapter 12), and the section on the 'Vondelpark' in Chapter 13.

Bob Witman (1959), the author of 'Cafés and Night-Life' (Chapter 4), studied law and works as a journalist on one of the country's largest morning dailies.

Rik Zaal (1945) wrote Chapter 14, about 'The IJsselmeer Coast'. He is a journalist and radio broadcaster, with a weekly radio feature on the arts and a regular column in a broadcasting magazine. He also contributes weekly articles on travel and tourism to one of the largest national dailies.

Index

The eight districts of Amsterdam (see Chapter 13)

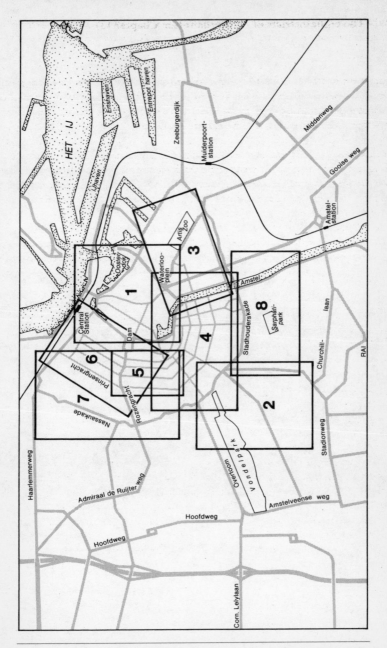